THE CONSERVATIVE PARTY IN OPPOSITION

1945–51

STUDIES IN SOCIETY

Edited by Ruth and David Glass

—

Already published

COLD REBELLION

The South's Oligarchy in Revolt

Lewis W. Jones

THE GOVERNOR EYRE CONTROVERSY

Bernard Semmel

THE BRITISH POLITICAL ELITE

1832–1935

W. L. Guttsman

THE RELIGIONS OF THE OPPRESSED

Vittorio Lanternari

THE HOME AND THE SCHOOL

J. W. B. Douglas

J. D. HOFFMAN

The Conservative Party in Opposition

1945–51

LONDON
MACGIBBON & KEE
MCMLXIV

FIRST PUBLISHED 1964 BY MACGIBBON & KEE LTD

PRINTED IN GREAT BRITAIN BY

COX AND WYMAN LTD

LONDON, READING AND FAKENHAM

FOR SYLVIA

CONTENTS

PREFACE

THE title of this book might well have a special poignancy for Conservatives before the year is out. The writing was begun, however, at a time when the return of the Conservative Party to opposition seemed remote indeed. The Labour Party, defeated in a general election for the third consecutive time, had entered a prolonged doldrum: intra-party conflict engendered by the brutal analysis – in public – of past failings and current performance had damaged the party's parliamentary effectiveness and its electoral prospects. Frequent references to 'the inefficiency of the Opposition' by speakers from both sides of the House and the debate centred around R. H. S. Crossman's criticism of the 'responsible opposition' approach of the Labour Party gave particular point to the suggestion that I look back on the record of the Conservative Party in opposition to see how it had fared. Begun with a focus on the parliamentary activities of the Conservative Party from 1945 to 1951, the study was soon expanded to take account of two equally important features of the Tory Opposition: the reconstruction of the party machine, and the reformulation of party policy.

The lessons to be learned from *this* retrospection, at least, cannot kindle high hopes for new (or old) leaders of the Opposition. The Conservative reformulation of party policy and the building up of the party organization – while not as important as some Conservative spokesmen prefer to believe – were consistent with the furtherance of the 'Tory Revival' in 1951; the activities of the parliamentary Opposition – neither as efficient nor effective as many now like to think – no doubt helped to weaken Labour's hold on the country in the early nineteen-fifties. But the great fact which seems to emerge, nevertheless, is the inability of the Opposition to shape the future by its own efforts alone. Oppositions may succeed in focusing criticism on government policies; they may develop significant alternatives to government actions; but four key advantages enjoyed by governments – secrecy, unity, initiative and dispatch – offer ruling parties considerable protection *so long as they are willing or able to utilize them.* When power changes hands, elections are not so much won by oppositions as lost by governments.

As a Canadian, aware of the difficulties of studying at close range the major parties in his own country, I wish to express my gratitude to the many Conservatives in Parliament and in the Party organization who so generously assisted my research through the provision of materials and the granting of interviews. I am especially indebted to the officers of the Conservative Research Department Library and the Cuttings Section of Conservative Central Office for their kindness and co-operation.

This book is a revised edition of a PhD thesis written for the London School of Economics and Political Science under the supervision of Mr R. H. Pear. For his encouragement, his helpful criticisms, and especially for his assistance in producing a final draft of the manuscript I am forever grateful. I wish to thank also Professor David Glass, Mr H. G. Nicholas and Mr R. G. Davis-Poynter for the many improvements they have suggested. For encouragement of the enterprise my thanks are due to Dr Bernard Crick and Professor David Raphael: to the former for suggesting the project, and to the latter for making it possible for me to complete it. I am also very grateful to Mrs Chris McCulloch for her efficient typing of several drafts of the manuscript. Finally, to my wife goes my deepest debt of gratitude. Typist, proof-reader, gad-fly and comforter, she helped me enormously throughout the writing of the book.

Assisted as I was by many kind friends, I remain responsible for all errors of fact and interpretation.

J.D.H.

McMaster University,
June 1964.

Every page a victory.
Who cooked the feast for the victors?
Every ten years a great man.
Who paid the bill?

So many reports
So many questions.

BRECHT: *Questions of a Literate Working Man*

THE CONSERVATIVE PARTY IN OPPOSITION

1945–51

CHAPTER I

The 1945 General Election and the Conservative Defeat

'BEFORE very long', said Sir Herbert Williams at the Conservative Party conference in March 1945, 'the Conservative Party, for the first time since 1931, will be free of its chains. That will make all the difference in the world. Then we will have a cause to fight for.'[1] Sir Herbert, of course, looked forward to the ending of the link with Labour; he could not know – indeed he, like most of his party, never dreamed – that within four months the Conservatives would let down the 'chains' of office, that the cause for which they would fight would be a more than six-year struggle to regain political power. For the first time in its history the Labour Party was returned in a general election with decisive control of the House. The Tories were back in opposition.

It is the purpose of this and the following chapter to consider reasons for the result as seen by Conservative and neutral observers, and to describe in some detail the condition of the Conservative Party as it entered opposition after its defeat in July 1945.

I

On 23 May, fifteen days after the ending of hostilities in Europe, Winston Churchill tendered his resignation thereby bringing the Coalition Government to an end. On the same day, after accepting the King's invitation to form a new government, he asked for the dissolution of Parliament on 15 June, 1945.

The considerations leading to the break-up of the Coalition, the decision to hold a July election, and Labour's reactions to the date have been developed at length elsewhere.[2] If 'the interests of Mr Churchill's party and those of the nation tended, on the whole, to converge rather than conflict',[3] it was nevertheless true that the timing of the election was intended to maximize the advantages – perhaps, more correctly, to minimize the disadvantages – that might accrue to the Conservative Party. Churchill's canvass of the opinion of leading Conservative ministers revealed majority support for the June polling date preferred by the 'Conservative managers'.[4] He himself did not like the idea of a June election; but he disliked the idea of an October poll even more.[5] In the event polling day for most of the country was 5 July. Tension mounted with the unprecedentedly long delay before the count; and when the results began to be announced on 26 July they came as a shock to many.[6]

The Conservative Party, which at dissolution had possessed 358 seats (with three Conservative seats vacant), had sustained its most decisive electoral defeat since 1906, and had been reduced to some 189 seats in the new House. Labour, with only 164 seats and two vacancies at dissolution, emerged with 393 places in the new Commons. The Liberals, with only 18 seats at dissolution, were reduced still further – to 12.

Such a brief description of the results, even in terms of seats won, is inadequate for all but the Liberal Party. Merely to note the number of seats won by candidates standing under the label of 'Conservative' or 'Labour' is to miss the complexity of the result in 1945. But it is not easy to know – especially in the case of the Labour Party – what additional groups ought to be placed along with it, and it is possible to arrive at different totals depending on whether one wishes to express pro-Labour, pro-socialist or even pro-government alliances. What I have selected as the most meaningful classification of results has been based on two main considerations. First it was thought desirable to find one set of figures which could reasonably be taken to represent Labour Government support *by both the electorate and the elected*, and thus avoid the difficulty encountered in using one set of figures to show one feature of the result and another set to illustrate another.[7] And secondly, groupings were sought which could usefully be compared with other elections, both before and after.

With this in mind, then, the arrangement of results followed by *The Times*,[8] according to which a division was made as between 'Government'–including not only I.L.P., Common Wealth, but also Liberals, Communists and Irish Nationalists – and 'Opposition', was rejected. More satisfactory is a modification of the results as arranged by McCallum and Readman.[9] Hindsight suggests, however, that there is no overwhelming reason for creating a category called 'Socialist' merely to accommodate – rather uneasily – the Communist Party candidates[10] in the 1945 general election. It is reasonable, from the point of view both of the supporting electorate and the behaviour of the M.P.s in the House of Commons, to include the I.L.P. and Common Wealth candidates in a category to be called 'Labour and allies'. By the same token it is realistic to include in a category which we have designated 'Conservatives and allies' the Ulster Unionists, Nationals and Liberal Nationals. There is something to be said for the idea of allotting independents to one or other of the main groups according to the general views expressed in the election campaign,[11] but since the main purpose of this analysis is to indicate the strength of Labour and Conservative *party* support (and since in any case most of the independents who were elected came from the universities, which did not enjoy a special franchise in later elections) there are good grounds for keeping the calculations as simple as possible and for considering independents as 'unaligned' – along with the Communists, Liberals, and Irish Nationalists. The result – in terms of seats won – according to this classification is set out in the following table.

TABLE I

Labour and Allies		*Conservatives and Allies*[12]		*Unaligned*	
Labour Party	393	Conservatives	189	Liberals	12
I.L.P.	3	Ulster Unionists	9	Independents	14
Common Wealth	1	National	2	Irish Nat.	2
		Liberal National	13	Communist	2
TOTAL	397	TOTAL	213	TOTAL	30

Grouping the 'allies' around the main parties in no way detracts from the extent of the Conservative defeat. 'Conservatives and allies' at dissolution possessed 392 seats including the vacant seats formerly held by Conservatives, one of which was a Liberal National's, and were cut to 213 seats; Labour and its allies with 172 seats at dissolution (including two vacant 'Labour seats') soared to 397 seats.[13] In amassing this total the Labour Party gained 201 seats from the Conservatives and their allies and recorded victories in 79 divisions which had never before returned a Labour candidate.[14]

More exactly, the Labour Party won 179 seats from the Conservatives, 16 from the Liberal Nationals and 6 from the Nationals. Eighteen per cent of the 79 Labour gains in constituencies which had never before voted Labour were in constituencies which had consistently voted Conservative. Two of them had been Liberal for at least 100 years. Although the Conservatives did make a few gains and the Labour Party suffered a few losses, the Conservative Party failed to gain any seats from Labour.

The most striking feature of the results was, of course, the emergence of the Labour Party with an absolute majority in the House for the first time. Although the Labour (and allies) majority of 154 over all other parties and groups in the House was smaller than the majorities of the Conservative Party and its allies in 1918, 1924, 1931, and 1935, and smaller also than the Liberal (and allies) majority in 1906, the position of the Labour Party alone – with a majority of 146 over all other parties and groups in a 640-seat House – was more impressive than the majority of 124 which the Liberal Party by itself possessed against all other parties in the 670-seat House in 1906.

But if the 1945 general election was a 'landslide' for Labour in terms of seats gained, it was not, after all, a wholesale rejection of the Conservative Party. Viewed today in the perspective of the last ten years of pessimism – with its emphasis on the 'deproletarianization' of the working-class basis of Labour's support – 1945 must certainly appear the 'high tide' of the party's potential in this century to date. Carried on by the democratic enthusiasm generated by the war, graced with leaders experienced and 'safe' enough to command the support of the most dubious radical, unhampered by the threat of a Liberal centre-left alternative, and facing a party stained by the (lately discovered) disgrace of appeasement, the Labour Party were indeed set fair for a triumph – if it were ever to come – of overwhelming proportions. How great was this victory in fact?

An average national 'swing' of votes[15] from Conservative to Labour of 12 per cent produced a net gain of seats for the Labour Party of 210 and a net loss of 173 seats for the Conservative Party. The tendency of the electoral system to exaggerate majorities of votes in terms of seats was in this case further distorted by the unequal size of constituencies,[16] but was minimized (to a lesser extent) by a 'bias of the electoral system' in favour of the Conservative Party (because of the Labour Party's tendency to concentrate huge majorities in safe seats).[17] The result of such a swing was to reduce the Conservative Party's parliamentary strength to its lowest point since 1906: only twice before in modern history – in 1832 and 1906 – had the party's parliamentary position been worse. But, as the figures in the following table indicate, the Conservative Party's support in the country was, if shaken, still impressively large.

TABLE II

Party Support in 1945 General Election

	Votes Received	*Percentage of Total Voters*
Labour and Allies		
Labour Party	11,992,292	
Common Wealth	101,634	
I.L.P.	46,679	
TOTAL.. ..	12,140,605	
Less deduction for two-member seats	397,288	
TOTAL SUPPORT	11,743,317	49·05
Conservative and Allies		
Conservative Party	8,665,566	
Ulster Unionists	392,454	
Nationals	142,906	
Liberal Nationals	749,883	
TOTAL.. ..	9,950,809	
Less deduction for two-member seats	552,572	
TOTAL SUPPORT	9,398,236	41·5

	Votes Received	*Percentage of Total Voters*
UNALIGNED		
Communist Party	102,780	
Scottish Nationalists	30,595	
Independents	179,471	
Irish Nationalists	148,078	
Liberal Party	2,239,668	
TOTAL.. ..	2,700,592	9·45

(*i*) In singling out 'number of voters' rather than 'total votes' given each party I am following the example of McCallum and Readman (p. 252), of deducting from the total votes received by the Conservative and Labour parties a figure representing the 'double counting' of two-member seats. Although my table is slightly different (for the reasons given above (p. 16), I have accepted the figures to be deducted as calculated by the authors, according to the method outlined on page 251. My figures (like those of McCallum and Readman) do not take account of the 'party support' of those electors in the three constituencies in which there was no contest. In any case, the fact that, according to their calculations, the party support was approximately evened out, preserves the significance of the figures for our purposes.

(*ii*) The margin against the Labour Party and its allies is calculated from Table II as follows: total non-Labour party voters (12,198,827) less total Labour Party and Allies voters (11,743,317) equals 455,510 – the margin which all other parties combined enjoyed over the Labour Party in terms of voters. McCallum and Readman's calculations (p. 252) produce a 'balance in favour of Socialism' of 65,880, but this figure has been achieved by including the votes of supporters of the Communist Party, Scottish Nationalists and 'Socialistic Independents' along with the Labour Party and its allies in a general category called 'Pro-Socialist'.

The Labour Party and its allies were supported by something more than 11·5 million people, or about 49 per cent of the total voters. The Conservatives and their allies received the votes of more than nine million people, or 41·5 per cent of the total voters. Despite the circumstances favourable to Labour in 1945, it is clear that the Labour Party and its allies failed – admittedly by a very small margin – to obtain the support of half the electorate. Another (roughly) 250,000 supporters drawn from the Conservative (or any other) party would have converted Labour's large *plurality* into a small *absolute majority*; approximately 450,000 votes was the margin by which the Labour Party and its allies failed to equal the support throughout the country of all the other parties combined.

The Conservative Party and its allies, although losing more than twenty per cent of their 1935 supporters, still held the support of a larger percentage of the electorate in 1945 than Labour and its allies had enjoyed in 1935 – and, indeed, larger than it had obtained in 1906 against the Liberals. Balancing this, it must of course be remembered that Churchill's Government was rejected by about three of every five voters at the 1945 general election.[18] But rejection of the Conservatives did not mean overwhelming acceptance of the Labour alternative: Labour's support in the country in 1945 was smaller (relatively) than that enjoyed by the Conservatives and their allies in 1931 and 1935![19]

If such a calm analysis of the results of the 1945 general election gave some hope to Tories long after the event, it hardly sufficed to compensate those Conservatives who had expected to continue their (one is tempted to add 'rightful') rule. Certainly most Conservative M.P.s thought that their party would win. This was the view of Earl Winterton. 'As before the 1906 and 1929 elections', he has written, 'few Conservative organizers foresaw or foretold in private how heavy our defeat would be. I met *only two men of importance* before the election *who believed we should be defeated*. One was Lord Templewood and the other the late Duke of Devonshire. [The latter] . . . thought we should have a defeat comparable to that of 1906.'[20] Oliver Lyttelton (now Lord Chandos) has recorded that only R. A. Butler from among his Cabinet colleagues at the time was pessimistic about the outcome.[21] Christopher Hollis, must have expressed the attitude of many of his colleagues in the Conservative Party when he wrote, about a month before the election: 'Whatever exuberant rhetoric may from time to time pretend, nobody seriously thinks that the Labour Party have any chance of gaining a clear majority at the election, and no one pretends even as a joke that the Liberals have any chance of obtaining such a majority'.[22] Nor was this view of the slim chances of the Labour Party confined to the Conservatives. A Mass Observation study in 1943 had found that the 'commonest single belief among politicians seems to be that at the next General Election, whatever Party or Group Winston Churchill heads will win'.[23] But the study continued with this warning. 'The common editorial and M.P. assumption of Churchill's post-war potency finds little support in studies of public, let alone private, opinion. Supremely popular as he is today, this is closely associated with the idea of Winston the War Leader, Bulldog of Battle, etc. Ordinary people widely assume that after the war he'll rest on his magnificent laurels. If he doesn't many say they will withdraw support, believing him no man of peace, of domestic policy, or human detail.'[24] The fact that the study *did not confirm* the likelihood of his post-war hold did not prevent journals and newspapers sympathetic to Labour from exhibiting extreme caution in predicting the election results,[25] or Churchill from assuming that he would win the election.

Before the election campaign – in fact before the end of the Coalition – his own party organization had given Churchill a sour forecast of the party's likely failure in a general election that year. At a meeting held at 24 Old Queen Street (home of the Conservative Research Department) Area agents reporting on the state of the party organization unanimously asserted that because of the party's poor organization it could not win that summer. When Ralph Assheton, the Chairman of the Party Organization, had totalled up the agents' estimates of seats which the party could win he announced that, on that estimate, the party would lose the election. When asked whether an autumn election would make a difference the agents agreed that although the party organization would be in the course of reconstruction there would be little difference in the anticipated result.

It was not unknown for Churchill to ask for advice of the Central Office and then proceed with his own ideas. On this occasion his resolve – or more privy counsel – prevailed and a summer election was called. Once the campaign began and his close advisers had evidence of the tumultuous response which he received at public meetings from the grateful people, confidence was restored. At a second meeting of Area agents it was agreed that the party could and would win the election. Only the few party officials who remained unconvinced by the turnabout were not surprised at the outcome. But Churchill, expecting victory to be his, was surprised and bitterly disappointed.

After the campaign had ended Churchill went on holiday in France, thence to attend the Potsdam conference. At dinner on 18 July Premier Stalin confessed to him that 'all his information from

Communist and other sources confirmed his belief that [Churchill] should be returned with a majority of about 80'.[26] Confident that he would be returning to the conference, Churchill went back to England to await the results; and encouraged by 'the latest view of Central Office that [he] should retain a substantial majority',[27] told King George, on the eve of the count, that he expected a majority of between 30 and 80.[28]

There can be little doubt that it was this optimism which made the result so crushing a blow for Churchill personally and for his party in general. Churchill was, by his own admission, 'deeply distressed at the prospect of sinking from a national to a party leader', and tendered his resignation without so much as a day's delay. There was no question of waiting for Parliament to reassemble: 'the need for Britain being immediately represented with the proper authority at the Conference . . . made all delay contrary to the public interest'.[29] The full impact of Churchill's disappointment – even bitterness – and his consequent desire to hasten the transfer of power is frankly revealed by the following comment in his memoirs of the Second World War written some time after the event: 'The verdict of the electors had been so overwhelmingly expressed that I did not wish to remain *even for an hour* responsible for their affairs.'[30]

Time was to heal the wounded pride of the famous war leader. But disappointment with the 1945 election result was to play a part in determining Churchill's attitude to party politics and his leadership of the Conservative Party in the immediate post-war years.

II

Some attempt must now be made to account for the result of the 1945 election and to examine, in particular, Conservative explanations of the defeat; for their diagnoses were inevitably related to the remedial measures prescribed.

It is unfortunate that the few 'scientific' studies of the 1945 election which were made are, for the most part, inadequate. Two studies by Americans published in the *Public Opinion Quarterly*[31] are unsatisfactory partly because of unproductive technique and partly because of the authors' incomplete appreciation of the background of British politics. Another, Mark Abrams' study,[32] rejected as statisically unprovable the idea that the swing can be explained by those 1945 voters who were too young to vote in 1935, but (after an examination of regional voting statistics) suggested in its place the no more acceptable explanation that the disproportionate ratio of seats to votes was due to 'the luck of the distribution of electors favouring the Labour Party' in Lancashire and Cheshire, the Northern Rural Belt, the Eastern Counties and Scotland.[33]

One sample survey conducted by Mass Observation has for all its deficiencies the merit of suggesting those sections of the electorate which might account for the swing.[34] By comparing the voting behaviour in 1935 and the voting intention in 1945 of respondents 35 years and older, three main discoveries were made:

> that there were as many ex-Labour voters intending to vote Conservative in 1945 as ex-Conservatives intending to vote Labour;
>
> that there were 'more ex-Conservatives than ex-Labourites who did not intend to vote';
>
> that 'a considerable number of those who failed to vote last time [were] this time voting Labour'.[35]

From this it was concluded that 'the large Labour majority did not arise from a change of opinion among those who had previously been Conservative supporters, but from the following three sources:

1. Young people who had not previously voted.
2. Older people who had a vote at the last general election but did not use it.
3. Conservative sympathizers who did not vote'.[36]

Although based on a sample too small to be of generalized validity, this study does produce plausible conclusions which at least do not conflict with those of most other observers. However, the Mass Observation survey offers no help in accounting for the reasons why the three crucial social groups identified by the study acted as they did. For this one must turn to the more impressionistic assessments of the 1945 result.

In addition to the coincidence of factors favourable to the Labour Party referred to above – the 'mechanical advantages' of the electoral system in 1945, and the natural 'swing of the pendulum'[37] – two further explanations have been given for the result in 1945: the residue of anti-Conservative discontent in the entire inter-war period which came to a head in the election,[38] and the Conservative Party's (and in particular Churchill's) disastrous conduct of the campaign itself.[39] Both explanations can be taken as complementary if it is argued that the Conservatives failed to counteract the long-term cause of their defeat (the prolonged resentment of Conservative policies) because of the ineffectiveness of the party's electoral campaign (the short term cause of the defeat). Something of this synthesized explanation is suggested by Mr John Wheeler-Bennett's surmise that 'only a brilliant *tour de force* on the part of Churchill could have saved the Conservatives from defeat'.[40] But while recognizing that the Conservative campaign was less than brilliant, he unfairly attributed the Labour victory *merely* to the triumph of 'suspicion' and 'distrust' of the Tory Party. Distrust of the Conservatives there certainly was – distrust which was hardly lessened by an official national campaign[41] in which affirmation of Conservative programmes for post-war recovery took a poor third place to a concentrated exploitation of Churchill's personality and a negative attack on the Labour Party[42] – but without public confidence in Labour's ability to carry out the expected social reform, distrust would not necessarily have been sufficient to bring Conservative defeat. Many Conservative candidates, especially the Tory Reformers, in their own campaigns 'took the Government programme quite seriously and while making the most of Churchill's association with the Conservative Party did their best to defend private enterprise on its merits'. There is good evidence,[43] moreover, that the main lines of voting opinion had hardened before the campaign ever began. While not dismissing the influence of the campaign altogether, it appears more reasonable to account for the Conservative defeat ultimately in terms of the failure of the Conservative Party to overcome the disaffection it had accumulated since 1935, and to present itself as the convinced reformer of the social system which general consensus seems to have demanded[44] and which the Labour Party appeared to satisfy. The people's efforts in the war were linked with the expectation of a restoration and improvement of national well-being after the war. Certainly Gallup poll surveys of the leading issues of the campaign revealed a predominate concern with the domestic (rather than foreign policy) issues of the campaign, and domestic issues described as 'domestic in the popular, non-political sense of the term'.[45]

III

Conservative explanations of the defeat have been many and varied. It is perhaps worthwhile to set out the most articulate general assessments of the causes of the Labour victory as seen by Conservatives – then and since.

The most frequent explanation of the Labour victory (and one which many leading Conservatives uncritically fall back on today) is that which sees the 1945 result largely in terms of the Conservative Party's relative organizational weakness[46] ('due to the party's loyal abstention from party politics during the war years') and the superior propaganda advantage enjoyed by the Labour Party as a result of the alleged left-wing bias of the B.B.C., and the supposed left-wing influence on the forces vote of the Army Bureau of Current Affairs. This point of view was expressed most completely by W. W. Astor:

> The primary cause of the Conservative defeat was the natural swing of the pendulum. But that the pendulum swung faster and farther than anyone expected was due to the pre-election propaganda victory of the Left. The Conservatives concentrated too fully on winning the war, while the Socialists did not scruple to attack and denigrate their too loyal partners in the National Government.[47]

Most observers agree that the Labour Party's constituency associations were better prepared than the Conservatives' for the campaign. R. H. S. Crossman has noted that in his constituency the Conservative party machine was 'in sad disarray', but added that only the Communist Party was fully organized.

But not all Conservatives sought to shift the onus of defeat from the party's own actions or inaction. Those who were most critical of the party's complicity in the defeat have tended to concentrate on two main factors: the ineffectiveness of the campaign (especially Churchill's ill-conceived 'Gestapo speech') and the inadequacy of Conservative policy. A letter to *The Times*, 31 July, 1945, regretted Churchill's policy-less campaign. 'A national party,' the writer believed, 'must have a national policy.' A further explanation of the defeat offered by a now leading member of the Conservative Government, is obviously influenced by current descriptions of the election battle as a competition of 'top people' – between a potential Prime Minister and his team of closest advisers. On this reading, Labour, with Attlee, Bevin, Morrison, and Cripps were seen to be a better team in 1945 than the Conservatives could put up. One Central Office official involved in the 1945 election is inclined to the view that the conduct of the campaign, like the timing of the election, was unimportant and that other factors – the better preparation of the Labour machine, the long period without an election, and the lingering resentment of Baldwin and Chamberlain – were more relevant causes of the Conservative defeat. One of the most outspoken and comprehensive assessments of the causes of the Conservative defeat of this type came from Quintin Hogg. 'The result of the election,' he wrote in his column in the *Daily Mail*, 'was not intended as a vote against Mr Churchill. It was not, as such, a condemnation of the idea of National Government, and it was not even primarily due to the mistakes in the conduct of the campaign itself. The decision can only be explained as the consequence of a long pent-up and deep-seated revulsion against the principles, practice and membership of the Conservative Party.'[48]

Hogg did not ignore altogether certain tactical errors in the campaign. 'The Conservative Party,' he wrote, 'completely misused the wonderful opportunity given by the B.B.C. Our programming of talks was never planned as a series on sound broadcasting principles.' Nor did Churchill's 'Gestapo speech' assist the Conservative cause: '[It] must be said, with great respect but quite firmly, that Mr Churchill's Gestapo speech was the greatest blunder of the campaign.'[49] But for him the failure of Conservative attitude and policy was crucial: the party had been restrictionist and not expansionist when faced with unemployment before the war; it had not realized that a planned economy could be reconciled with freedom; and the Tory leaders had allowed the party to get out of touch with the people.[50]

Hogg was not alone in fixing on the failure of policy as the key to the Conservative defeat. For Aubrey Jones 'the Conservative downfall was not just an unnatural accident. It was the result of influences which had been at work for a long time, chief among them the decline over several decades, of Conservative thought.'[51] The long power-hold by the Conservatives, assisted by 'the incompetence of Socialist administration', had nevertheless been an unnatural thing.

Although Conservatives might be welcomed 'as a refuge against mal-administration', they had failed, in his view, to develop positive principles of action – a failure which was revealed by the 1945 election campaign.

Professor W. L. Burn has added his agreement to the criticism of Conservative policy and has linked it forcibly with the ineffectiveness of the party organization as well:

> It is odd that Mr Churchill should have made the mistake of declaring war on opponents who were at least half mobilized when mobilization of his own party was scarcely begun. Bedevilled by years of pseudo-Conservatism, shaken in morale by the intellectual superiority which they had allowed the Labour Party to assume, ashamed of many of the things they believed in their hearts, the Conservatives lacked a doctrine. It was fatal that they should have lacked a method too.[52]

Apart from general complaints of the party's unsatisfactory attitude and policy during the inter-war years, it was possible to level criticism at party policy and doctrine at the time of the general election from at least three points of view. It might be held simply that there had been no attempt whatever to adjust Conservative thought to the changing conditions of Britain's national life. Others might recognise such attempts but write them off as pseudo-Conservatism; for them the Conservatives possessed no *acceptable* policy – and this they equated with no doctrine at all.[53] Thirdly critics might note – and appreciate – the attempts of such bodies as the Tory Reform Committee and the Post-war Problems Committee to give contemporary content to Conservative principles, but regret the failure of this body of thought to make any special impact in the official policy statements of the party before and during the election campaign. Such a view was endorsed by W. W. Astor:

> Looking back again, it is clear that whatever propaganda machine we had suffered from the lack of authoritative statements of party policy in the period previous to the election. I stress the word 'authoritative'. Before the election the Post-war Problems Committee's numerous reports, the 'Signpost' booklets, the various pamphlets produced by the Tory Reform Committee, were all good, but they were not authoritative. They did not bear the

imprimatur of the Prime Minister. There was no evidence that he had read them. They were not the themes of speeches of Cabinet Ministers, and the Election Manifesto, when it came, was swamped in the turmoil of side issues and largely ignored by both sides.[54]

There is considerable merit in this latter criticism. To support it, however, is not to elevate the conduct of the campaign to the crucial position in any account of the Conservative defeat. It is merely to acknowledge what we have noted before – namely, that the Conservative campaign was dominated by the eccentricities of the Churchill–Beaverbrook attack on the Labour Party – and to admit that such positive statements of Conservative policy as were developed before the election were relatively insignificant in the campaign. Some consideration will have to be given, however, to this half-concealed policy when we turn to an examination of the condition – both mental and physical – of the Conservative Party as it entered opposition.

REFERENCES

[1] *Onlooker* (London, April 1945), p. 2.

[2] R. B. McCallum and A. Readman, *The British General Election of 1945* (Oxford, 1947), pp. 1–23; Winston Churchill, *Triumph and Tragedy* (London, 1954), pp. 508 ff.; C. R. Attlee, *As it Happened* (London, 1954), pp. 132 ff.; John Wheeler-Bennett, *King George VI: His Life and Reign* (London, 1958), pp. 629 ff.

[3] McCallum and Readman, p. 21

[4] Churchill, *Triumph*, pp. 551, 513–14.

[5] Churchill, *Triumph*, p. 512.

[6] McCallum and Readman, pp. 240–1, for newspaper forecasts in the first days after polling day of a Conservative victory.

[7] McCallum and Readman, pp. 248 and 252.

[8] According to this arrangement the Government appears to have 413 seats: the Opposition 213, with 14 independents unaligned. The result is produced in this manner in The Times, *The House of Commons, 1945* (London, 1945), p. 281, and in *The Times*, 10 August, 1945.

[9] McCallum and Readman, p. 248.

[10] In excluding the Communists from the reckoning of the Labour vote we are following the practice of J. F. S. Ross in his *Elections and Electors* (London, 1955), p. 374; but our total of 397 seats for the Labour Party differs from his because of his inclusion of one other 'Labour' member and a 'Labour Independent'.

[11] McCallum and Readman, p. 252.

[12] The total given here for the Conservative Party and allies accepts without modification that given by McCallum and Readman, p. 248, but differs from that given by David Butler, *The Electoral System in Britain, 1918–1951* (Oxford, 1953), p. 173 (212 seats), and J. F. S. Ross, *Elections*, p. 374 (215 seats).

[13] Comparisons in absolute figures between dissolution and post-election representation must take account of the increase in the number of seats in the House – from 615 to 640 – as the result of the creation of 25 new seats by the redistribution of 1944. The Conservatives won only nine of the seats so created; Labour took the rest.

[14] Times, *Commons, 1945*, pp. 130 and 135.

[15] McCallum and Readman, p. 264, and Appendix III, pp. 279–92. The 'swing' is computed as the average of Labour gains and Conservative losses.

[16] H. G. Nicholas, *The British General Election of 1950* (London, 1951), pp. 327–33, and McCallum and Readman, pp. 287–8.

[17] David Butler, in Nicholas, *Election, 1950*, pp. 331–2. Butler discusses this 'bias' only in connection with the 1950 results, but it is reasonable to assume the disposition of the Labour Party to concentrate its majorities in safe seats rather more than the Conservatives was operating in 1945 as well.

[18] McCallum and Readman, p. 249.

[19] Roy Jenkins' comparison of the geographical distribution of Liberal seats in 1906 and Labour seats in 1945 is interesting. Jenkins considers Labour and Irish Nationalist seats as part of the Liberal total in 1906 and regards I.L.P., Common Wealth and Communist along with Labour in 1945. According to this arrangement he shows that the Liberals secured 74 per cent of the seats in what is now the United Kingdom as compared to only 64 per cent by the Labour Party in 1945. The comparison reveals that the Labour Party did better than the Liberals in the big towns and industrial areas (witness the breakthrough in Birmingham which the Liberals failed to achieve at all), and that although both the Liberals and Labour were relatively weak in the South of England (excluding the large towns) the Labour Party was 'a good deal weaker than the Liberals had been'. In general, he concludes that 'geographically, the Liberal Party was a good deal more broadly based than the Labour Party of 1945'. Roy Jenkins, *Mr. Balfour's Poodle* (London, 1954), pp. 196–201.

[20] Earl Winterton, *Orders of the Day* (London, 1953), p. 313. Cf. Lord Salter, *Memoirs of a Public Servant* (London, 1961), p. 284.

[21] Oliver Lyttelton, Lord Chandos, *Memoirs* (London, 1962), p. 307.

[22] Christopher Hollis, 'The Conservative Opportunity', *New English Review*, XI (June 1945), p. 109.

[23] Tom Harrisson, 'Who'll Win ?', *PoliticalQuarterly*, XV (January 1944), p. 22. Many Labour M.P.s apparently believed that, because of Churchill, the Labour Party would be denied victory until a second post-war election. *Ibid.*, p. 23.

[24] Tom Harrisson, 'Who'll Win ?', *Political Quarterly*, XV (January 1944), p. 24. Cf. Peter G. Richards, 'The Political Temper', *Political Quarterly*, XVI (January–March, 1945), pp. 57-56, for an analysis of the by-elections after 1935 showing the steady loss of confidence suffered by the Conservative Party.

[25] See, for example, the editorial 'So much for so few' in the *New Statesman*

and Nation, XXIX (2 June, 1945), p. 347, for the caution displayed in predicting the result. See also McCallum and Readman, p. 240, for similar treatment by the *Daily Herald* and *Mirror*.

[26] Churchill, *Triumph*, p. 549.

[27] Churchill, *Triumph*, p. 583.

[28] Wheeler-Bennett, p. 630.

[29] Churchill *Triumph*, p. 583.

[30] Churchill, *Triumph*. Cf. Virginia Cowles, *Winston Churchill: The Era and the Man* (London, 1953), p. 355. See also Chandos, p. 328.

[31] Frank V. Cantwell, 'The Meaning of the British Election', *Public Opinion Quarterly*, IX (Summer 1945), pp. 145–57, and William J. Newman, 'Patterns of Growth in the British Labour Vote', *Public Opinion Quarterly*, IX (1945), pp. 446–55.

[32] Mark Abrams, 'The Labour Vote in the General Election', *Pilot Papers*, I (1946), p. 7.

[33] Mark Abrams, 'The Labour Vote in the General Election', *Pilot Papers*, I (1946), p. 24. See the criticism of Abrams' study by David Butler in McCallum and Readman, pp. 291–2, and by H. Durant, *Political Opinion* (London, 1946), p. 8.

[34] Mass Observation, 'Post Mortem on Voting at the Election', *Quarterly Review* (January 1946), pp. 57–68. The investigation is based on a 'very limited sample' in one London constituency.

[35] Mass Observation, 'Post Mortem on Voting at the Election', *Quarterly Review* (January 1946), p. 61.

[36] Mass Observation, 'Post Mortem on Voting at the Election', *Quarterly Review* (January 1946), p. 62.

[37] *The Times* 'The People's Choice', 27 July, 1945, and W. W. Astor, 'The Conservative Party in Opposition', *New English Review*, XII (1946), p. 344. See also R. H. S. Crossman, *Labour in the Affluent Society* (London, 1960), pp. 3–4, and Richard Rose, 'How the Party System Works' in Mark Abrams and Richard Rose, *Must Labour Lose?* (London, 1960), pp. 61–63, for a critique of the concept of the swing of the pendulum.

[38] 'There had been no general election since 1935 and the great swing to the Left at the end of the war . . . was the outcome of tendencies and aspirations which had been fermenting for nearly a decade.' Times, *Commons 1945*, p. 14. Cf. Drew Middleton, *The British* (London, 1957), p. 56, and *Annual Register, 1945* (London, 1946), p. 53. McCallum and Readman, p. 44, noted that 'this election was a challenge . . . [to] the total record of all the governments of the twenty years between the wars . . .', and illustrated in their chapter, 'The Issues', the frequent Labour criticisms of the Tory record in the inter-war years.

[39] See especially *The Times* editorial 'The People's Choice', Cf. *Annual Register* p. 53; Middleton, p. 56, *New Statesman and Nation*, 'At the Hustings', XXIX (9 June, 1945), p. 367; Alan Campbell-Johnson, *Sir Anthony Eden* (London, 1955, p. 201.

[40] Wheeler-Bennett, p. 637.

[41] *Register, Annual* p. 49. R. H. S. Crossman noted during the campaign that local Conservative newspapers and candidates were embarrassed by the

Beaverbrook and Churchill campaign and were disaffiliating themselves from it. *New Statesman and Nation*, 'A Midland Election', XXIX (1945), p. 416.

[42] Cf. McCallum and Readman, Chapters IX and X, on the campaign. Important evidence of the disapproval which Churchill's first radio speech incurred is offered by Mass Observation, 'Post Mortem', *Quarterly Review* p. 65.

[43] See McCallum and Readman, pp. 268–9, for evidence from opinion surveys to this effect.

[44] See W. K. Hancock and M. M. Gowing, *British War Economy* (London, 1949), especially p. 541, for the idea that there was an implied contract between the Government and the people.

[45] McCallum and Readman (p. 150). A.B.I.P.O. poll printed in the *News Chronicle*, 18 June, 1945 (quoted in McCallum and Readman, p. 150) taken during the election campaign 'inquiring what questions do you think will be the most discussed in the General Election?' yielded the following result: Housing 41 per cent; Full Employment 15 per cent; Social Security 7 per cent; Nationalization 6 per cent; International Security 5 per cent. See also Lord Morrison of Lambeth, *An Autobiography* (London, 1960), p. 236, and Cowles, p. 353.

[46] Crossman, *New Statesman*, p. 416. See also, B. S. Townroe, 'Some Lessons of the Election', *National Review*, CXXV (September 1945), p. 210, and Jean Blondel 'The Conservative Association and the Labour Party in Reading', *Political Studies*, VI (1958), p. 103.

[47] Astor, p. 344 See also *ibid.*, pp. 344–5. Churchill presents a more moderate expression of a similar opinion in his memoirs, *Triumph*, pp. 508–9.

[48] Quintin Hogg, 'Defeat but not Disaster', *Daily Mail*, 30 July, 1945.

[49] Quintin Hogg, 'Defeat but not Disaster', *Daily Mail*, 30 July, 1945.

[50] Quintin Hogg, *Daily Mail*, 25 September, 1945.

[51] Aubrey Jones, 'Conservatives in Conference', *The Nineteenth Century and After*, CXLII (November 1947), p. 219.

[52] W. L. Burn, 'The General Election in Retrospect', *The Nineteenth Century and After*, CXLII (July 1947), p. 18. The decline of Conservative thought decried by both Jones and Burn is an echo of the lengthy moan by 'B', 'The Age of Innocence', *National Review*, CXXII (April 1944), pp. 285–91. '. . . Conservatism has allowed itself to be deprived of the intellectual leadership of the nation.' 'Save for a few stalwarts such as Mr Pickthorn, for a few publications such as the *Signpost* series and for a few groups such as that of the *Tablet* . . . Conservative doctrine has been largely allowed to go by default.' p. 286.

[53] Lord Balfour, 'After the Conservative Defeat', *The New English Review*, XI (November 1945), p. 588.

[54] Astor, p. 346.

CHAPTER II

The Conservatives Enter Opposition

ONE OF the main purposes of this study of the Conservatives in opposition is the consideration of the response of the party to Labour's post-war 'revolution'. It is necessary, therefore, to delineate, however tentatively, the orientation of Conservative thinking, at the time the party entered opposition, on those matters which would engage the energies of the Labour Government thereafter. If we are to make sense of the process of Conservative policy-reformulation and the party's position in Parliament in the later years it is essential to give some attention now to the frame of mind in which the party found itself in July 1945.

We must first look back to the war years to observe Conservative attitudes on a number of specific proposals for post-war reconstruction and to note the views of special groups within the Conservative Party – like the Tory Reform Committee and the Post-war Problems Central Committee – on Conservative policy for the post-war world. Next the party's official campaign literature must be examined along with views expressed by the party's leading officials. We are looking particularly – to put it most crudely – for the 'progressiveness' (or lack of it) in Conservative thinking at the time. The result, as might be expected, is no simple image; Conservatives then, as now, yield unwillingly to a single stereotype.

CONSERVATISM: A DOUBLE IMAGE

I

In at least two important aspects of the planning for post-war reconstruction – education and full employment – the Conservative Party revealed itself prepared to accept innovations of considerable proportions. The Education Act, which received the Royal Assent on 3 August, 1944, has been described as 'the first major piece of social legislation with a welfare state outlook in a number of respects'.[1] For all its deficiencies the Act may truly be regarded as a major item of progressive legislation in which R. A. Butler, the Minister of Education, firmly grasped a few nettles which Conservatives had hitherto been reluctant to approach. The statutory system of education was completely reorganized into three progressive stages; planning weapons were introduced in the notion of a development plan for 'primary', 'secondary' and 'further' education; the school-leaving age was to be raised (ultimately) to 16 years; and the emphasis in the overall responsibility for education was shifted from local to central authorities. Despite these extensive reforms the Act passed with very little Conservative parliamentary opposition. Indeed, the Bill received its roughest treatment at the hands of M.P.s on the left of the Conservative Party associated with Mrs Cazalet Keir's equal-pay-for-women-amendment, which had the support of the Tory Reform Committee.

The Conservative Party outside Parliament was equally receptive. Although the Central Council had complained of the inadequacy of the proposals relating to religious education in the White Paper,[2] the party conference held on 14 March, 1945, congratulated Butler 'on having secured such a broad measure of agreement on the principles embodied in his 1944 Act', and 'especially welcomed the opportunity for experiment, particularly in the post-primary field'.[3]

There was also much agreement within the Conservative Party (parliamentary and extra-parliamentary) – as there was between it and the Labour Party – on the value of the Keynsian proposals to achieve full employment embodied in the White Paper (Cmd. 6527) published on 26 May, 1944. The Conservative members of the National Coalition had, according to Attlee's recollection, 'accepted full employment as an object of any government'.[4] This acceptance was echoed by the Conservative Party at its conference in March 1945 and high-lighted by the party's *Notes for Speakers and Workers* as one of the key issues of the election.[5]

This is not to suggest, however, that Conservative views on full employment were a carbon-copy of Labour's. Conservative references to full employment always revealed a distinctive view of the place of public and private enterprise and controls within any policy by which full employment would be pursued. Although they might agree that it was 'the duty of the state to intervene in industrial affairs when national interest required that', they were careful to add that 'where it intervenes it must be watchful not to impair initiative . . . [nor] to impair the elasticity of industry to meet new situations'.[6] Nationalization of industry they rejected on grounds of its expected inefficiency;[7] and the removal of wartime restrictions and regulations was given an almost obsessive priority in the minds of many Conservatives.

It was the party's 'firm conviction' that free enterprise was 'the life-blood of a healthy and progressive industrial and commercial organism',[8] but it professed a belief in a flexible approach to particular situations: just as controls would have to be preserved in the transitional period from war to peace,[9] so Conservatives were 'not bound to oppose State or public ownership of anything at all times'. Even if it could be doubted 'whether the Conservative Party as a whole [had] yet appreciated the full implications of Keynsian economics',[10] it seems clear that the leadership of the party (and many of the party's followers) supported *in principle* the National Coalition's declaration that 'one of the primary aims and responsibilities of the British Government after the War would be the maintenance of a high and stable level of employment'.[11] But, as Wheeler-Bennett has observed, remarkable as it was that agreement in principle could be reached on the principles of post-war employment policy, 'the production of the White Paper on that question showed that there were limits beyond which it would be unprofitable to discuss post-war problems. The *differences were too great* – and these were matters on which compromise might well have given the worst of both worlds.'[12]

With respect to two other important questions of post-war construction – the Beveridge proposals for social insurance and workmen's compensation and the National Health Service – the picture of Conservative attitudes is less clear-cut. Although Lord Attlee has given it as his opinion[13] that the Government did not 'cold-shoulder' the Beveridge Report and that any delay was probably owing to Churchill's desire to introduce the legislation himself after the war, and although we have evidence of the party's commitment to the idea at the time of the general election,[14] it may still be argued that Conservative reactions to the Beveridge proposals were not always unambiguously sympathetic.

Support for the Beveridge Report was the *raison d'être* of the Tory Reform Committee. And, as early as May 1943, the Conservative

Party conference (and Central Council) gave the proposals qualified approval. The conference 'consider[ed] that [the Report] accord[ed] with sound principles for the improvement of the condition of the people within the framework of the existing economic and political system' but it insisted on 'contribution as a condition of benefit', and '. . . the obligation to accept work if available'. The motion with the following addendum – '. . . that this Conference is of the opinion that the existing Friendly Societies should remain part of our future social system' – was carried with only six voting against.[15] The Post-war Problems Committee also professed its enthusiasm – if a little belatedly – for the White Paper derived from the Report[16] in a pamphlet designed 'to show how the proposals in these schemes rationalize and round off the contribution made in the past by the Conservative Party in this field of political behaviour'.[17] The pamphlet defended the Government's rejection of the principle of varying benefit rates in accordance with changes in the cost of living (on ground of excessive complication and unworkability) and the downward adjustment of the children's allowance (on grounds of higher total expenditure by other means), but the main lines of the plans were fully supported. This applied to the proposals for industrial injury insurance as well. The Committee considered that these proposals would improve industrial relations, and make for long-term security.[18] 'Trusting our countrymen' the Committee stated, 'we believe the results will be psychologically good, and looking at the whole future we accept the redistribution of income involved as economically sound'.[19]

But this conviction was not shared by all Conservatives.[20] The three-way split in the vote on the second reading of the progressive Catering Wages Bill[21] served to focus attention on a not inconsiderable section of the Conservative parliamentary party for whom – as was also later revealed in the debates on the two White Papers on social insurance[22] – the party was moving too quickly in the direction of radical reform. Right-wing opposition within the party was bolstered (but who can say with what effect?) by persistent abuse of the Beveridge proposals by the right-wing Conservative *National Review*.[23] This journal pressed – with some real justification – the view that such proposals for social reconstruction (and in this they included the Education Act as well) depended 'upon matters very largely beyond our control' and were 'feasible [only] in an era of great prosperity and much gainful employment'.[24] But in such hands the argument was posed as a reason for doing nothing, for waiting until the war was over before discussing it.

Churchill appointed a secret committee composed largely of Conservative M.P.s to advise him personally on the Beveridge proposals before the Coalition White Papers were issued nearly two years after the original Report. But whether it was because the preservation of party unity necessitated caution or the longer-term tactics suggested by Attlee were the foremost consideration, the Conservative Party did not escape creating the impression – despite the efforts of Sir William Jowitt, R. A. Butler and Sir John Anderson – that their support of the Beveridge proposals was less than whole-hearted.[25]

The White Paper on the National Health Service (Cmd. 6502) published earlier in the year divided the Conservative Party rather less than the later 'Beveridge White Papers'. Leading Conservative members of the Coalition, no less than those from the Labour Party, responded to a combination of factors given particular import by the wartime experience which prepared the public for a major advance in the public health services. According to Wheeler-Bennett, Conservative and Labour members of the Cabinet were in agreement on the national health service plans, but there is some evidence to suggest that the 'Cabinet compromise' on the White Paper represented more a victory for the Labour Party's position – 'the result of political bargaining in which Labour and the S.M.A. [Socialist Medical Association] came out best'.[26]

If the Conservatives were less than fully committed to the proposals for a national health service as set out in the White Paper they revealed little displeasure with the principles involved in the two-day debate on the White Paper. Many Conservative back-benchers, it is true, expressed concern for certain specific features of the plan – especially the fear that voluntary hospitals would receive insufficient financial support to keep them going and that the special doctor-patient relationship would be destroyed by a salaried service – but very few attacked the desirability of the plan as a whole.[27]

As a result of negotiations with the British Medical Association which began in December 1944 a number of concessions were made – on what Henry Willink, Minister of Health, chose to regard as matters of administration rather than principle – which had the effect of meeting on nearly every count objections raised by Conservative back-benchers in the earlier debates (and presumably by the B.M.A. in negotiation). The concessions were bitterly attacked by the Labour Party in the House and at the party's annual conference in March 1945.

The Conservative Party conference meeting in March 1945, after a brief but, for some, potentially disastrous flirtation with reaction, 'welcom[ed] the Government's decision to make a comprehensive National Health Service available to all'.[28] An amendment declaring that the principles incorporated in the White Papers were 'a negation of the liberty of the individual' had the support of a few constituency representatives at the conference, but the participating M.P.s – including Samuel Story who had criticized the White Paper in the earlier Commons debate, and especially Quintin Hogg – succeeded in getting the amendment defeated by a large majority.

Having the support of the party conference, the parliamentary party and the medical profession itself, it seems clear that the Conservative Party meant to bring in legislation. They would, Dr John Saloma believes, 'have initiated a National Health Service, although probably in stages, but for the change of parties at the General Election'.[29] It would have been, however, a different health service from the one visualized in the Coalition White Paper.

II

Since no survey of Conservative thinking before the 1945 election would be complete without it, some consideration must now be given to the contributions of the Post-war Problems Central Committee and the Tory Reform Committee. The Post-war Problems Central Committee was also known as the Central Committee on Post-war Reconstruction. It must not be confused with another body – the 'Post-war Policy Group' – headed by Sir John Wardlaw-Milne and composed mainly of Conservatives, whose main concern was the treatment of Germany after the end of the war. The first steps towards creating this Central Committee were taken by the Executive Committee of the National Union on 14 May, 1941, to fulfil 'Mr Churchill's desire for the preparation of practical measures of reconstruction and social advance to enable the country to recover from the War'.[30] By the end of the summer a Central Committee headed by R. A. Butler (Chairman) and Sir David Maxwell Fyfe[31] (Vice-Chairman) had been established and empowered to set up sub-committees which would report first to the Central Committee. This central body then transmitted reports to the Leader of the Party and 'to Ministers who [might] be interested in the subjects covered by them'. By early 1943 there were 10 sub-committees at work with an average membership on each of about 12, Conservative M.P.s on most committees being in a minority. By 1945 the number of committees had grown to about 16.[32]

The committees 'were given wide terms of reference and were left free to tackle their problems with open minds and without regard to the party's pre-war policies',[33] but it was made perfectly clear that the responsibility for the creation of party policy remained solely with the Leader of the Party.[34] Moreover, for all the sub-committees at work and all the topics considered the *published* results of the efforts of the Post-war Problems Central Committee appear rather slight. A few reports including those on demobilization and resettlement, housing, controls, agriculture, and employment made reasonable technical contributions and these found their way into the party's official campaign literature.[35] Others – the three reports of the Education Sub-committee, which appeared before Butler's Education Bill – varied little (not surprisingly) from the officially expressed views of the party in the parliamentary debate.[36] How influential these reports may have been in bringing Conservative opinion around to general support for the Bill it is impossible to say; but it seems fair to assume they had some favourable impact on party thinking, which, if it were the case, would more than justify the committee's endeavours.

In general, however, the sub-committees dealt with what might be considered the marginal problems of post-war reconstruction: electoral reform; agriculture; constitutional reform; forestry; even the social services. Like those of the Sub-committee on Demobilization and Resettlement, the proposals of the sub-committees '[were] framed on the assumption that the paramount consideration when the war ends must be the reorganization of our finance, industry and commerce on a sound basis',[37] without giving any real indication of how this 'sound basis' was to be achieved. The most extensive consideration of the problem was given by the Sub-committee on

Industry, under the chairmanship of Henry Brooke, but it went little beyond vague acceptance of the duty of the state to intervene when the nation's interest required it. And even this conclusion was cushioned in traditional Conservative warnings about the dangers of controls and the necessity to preserve the spirit of private enterprise.

One of the last of the publications issued under the name of the Post-war Problems Committee – *Forty Years of Progress* – characterized as it was by the complacency with which it reviewed the record of previous Conservative governments rather than the originality of its suggestions, had the flavour of pure election propaganda. After examining the last forty years to see how the British system 'so largely centred upon free enterprise' had done for the country, the Committee's report concluded:

> Those who would condemn out of hand the record of these years and would replace by a few swift Acts of Parliament the system which has provided such solid gains by another, as yet untried in these Islands, may well pause to ask whether it is possible to create quickly or by legislation, a system even to match, still less to better, the past achievements of our present system, or its developing promise for the coming peace.[38]

Not much evidence here, at least, of the conviction and the zeal required to reconstruct a land fit, if not for heroes, at least for ordinary men and women wearied by the war.

The significance of the existence of the Post-war Problems Central Committee, it seems fair to say, was not in any startling contribution it made to progressive – or reactionary – Conservative thought. Its real importance lay in the machinery which it provided for the continuation of policy consideration by the party after the defeat in 1945. The Tory Reform Committee was certainly much more important as a source of Conservative ideas before the end of the war, and especially was it important for the image which the Tory Reformers presented of a Conservative Party clearly prepared to face the problems of post-war construction in a progressive manner.

'The Committee was originally formed in February 1943', the group's first official publication stated, 'with the object of encouraging the Government to take constructive action on the lines of the Beveridge Scheme'.[39] Some 41 signatories of the Conservative amendment calling for the immediate creation of a Minister of Social Security to give effect to the principles of the Report, joined together under the chairmanship of Lord Hinchingbrooke (now Lord Sandwich), with Peter Thorneycroft and Hugh Molson (now Lord Molson) as Joint Secretaries. With the assistance of F. C. Hooper's[40] Political Research Centre they were soon pushing well beyond their original concern with the Beveridge Report to present ideas on such matters as the Catering Wages Bill, post-war reconstruction, civil aviation, agriculture, education and war pensions.

If the sole claim to fame of the Tory Reform Committee had been based on its first publication – *Forward – By the Right!* – its appearance on the political scene would undoubtedly have had little lasting impact, for there is much truth in the following criticism by a commentator at the time:

> The political layman who reads *Forward – By the Right!* is chiefly impressed by the thought of how completely out of touch with the modern citizen the Tory Party must be, if those who penned this 16-page pamphlet are regarded by the rest of the party as rebels and progressives. It contains only one original proviso. That is the compulsory service recommendation.[41]

But its efforts did not end with this one publication. It continued to stress in its criticism and its proposals one main theme of the original document which set it apart from many others in the Conservative Party: it accepted fully the need for both national planning and public control in a post-war system in which both private and public enterprise would have to be used.[42] It also 'criticized the Government whenever [it] felt that reactionary influences or internal dissentions were preventing the adoption of reforms which were reasonable and beneficial'; 'whenever it was thought that the party's policy was reactionary it developed policies of its own.'[43]

In adopting their radical reforming posture the Tory Reform Committee members were continuing the respected tradition of Disraeli and Lord John Manners's Young England, Randolph Churchill, Drummond-Wolff and Gorst's Fourth Party, and F. E. Smith's pre-1914 Social Reform Committee, movements involving the Tory progressives in the party's history.[44] The central notion linking members of the Tory Reform Committee was the rejection of the values and policies of business Conservatism, of doctrinaire *laissez-faire*. Like some aristocratic party spokesmen outside the Committee,[45] Tory Reformers stressed the necessity of accepting state action and private enterprise as complementary. Quintin Hogg's description of the 'New Conservative' seems typical of the attitude of the members of the Committee:

> He will not engage in the dispute between Nationalization and Private Enterprise. He sees in the modern extra-political forms of public control a nationalization which has lost its terrors, and in the larger joint-stock companies with limited liability a private enterprise which has lost its meaning. He is not impressed by the fear of schemes for social security as destructive of enterprise. On the contrary, he sees in them the basis for social stability necessary to the restoration of industry. He recognizes that privilege based on birth or wealth has served its ends, and he looks forward to a classical democracy in which differences of education and technical skill have taken their place.[46]

The Tory Reformer, as Dr Saloma has put it, fused the new economic thought typical of Harold Macmillan and the economic nationalists 'with older strains of Tory social concerns'.[47] But his acceptance of nationalization did not extend very far (a Committee report, *A National Policy for Coal*, for example, rejected nationalization as 'irrelevant to the coal industry'[48]) and private enterprise continued to hold for him an important rôle in society provided it was integrated with the national interest.[49]

III

This general survey of Conservative thinking in the war years makes it clear that there existed within the party – both officially and semi-officially – a considerable body of progressive thinking. The parliamentary party, it is true, still contained its fair share of what Hogg once called the 'reactionary rump' – men seemingly incapable or unwilling to accept the extensive social reforms on a broad front which others accepted as necessary for the reconstruction of a war-torn Britain. But perhaps more surprisingly it has emerged that that part of the Conservative Party – the party conference – which has most frequently been associated with reluctant acquiescence in radical change was at this time generally favourably disposed to innovation. (Although it may be worth noting that in at least two important cases[50] the party conference was retrieved from – or encouraged to desist from assuming – a reactionary position because of the skilful pleading of the Tory Reformers present.)

On several important issues there were crucial differences of emphasis as between the Conservative Party and the Labour Party – especially over the health service, the rôle of public enterprise in post-war Britain, and perhaps also the full implications of post-war employment policy[51] – but in the main there was considerable agreement between the two main parties. Indeed, it was not surprising that Mark Abrams should have concluded that 'from an examination of the campaign literature officially provided by the headquarters of the Parties, it was difficult to discover any basic conflicts separating the Left from the Right'.[52]

But such agreement as existed between the parties and much of the really progressive content of Conservative thought was largely obscured by the character of the election campaign. 'From the opening sentences of Mr. Churchill's first national broadcast it seemed,' to Mark Abrams as to many other observers of the election, 'that he and Conservative headquarters had decided that the 1945 election, as the issues facing the British people, was essentially a continuation, indeed a repetition, of the inter-war scene.'[53] It was a fundamental misjudgement to look back to the fears of the earlier decades when minds were concentrated on the problems of reconstruction for the future. It killed 'the leavening in the Tory lump' provided by the Tory Reformers and the result was electoral disaster. But if the election campaign was lost, the battle to recover power still lay ahead. In this the progressive notions already developed in the party would have time to push their way to the forefront.

THE STATE OF THE PARLIAMENTARY PARTY

I

The defeat of Churchill's Caretaker Government was serious enough from the point of view of the number of seats lost;[54] in terms of the quality of the membership of the party left to form the Opposition in the Commons the result appears at first sight to have been even more calamitous. In all, no less than 32 members of Churchill's second administration lost their seats: five had been members of the Caretaker Cabinet, eight had been ministers of Cabinet rank, and 19 had been under-secretaries.

Of the 213 Conservatives and allies elected in 1945 78 had not been members of the previous House. In fact with the exception of two of this number – C. W. H. Glossop who had been M.P. for the Penistone division from 1931–35 and Sir Hugh Lucas-Tooth who had represented the Isle of Ely from 1924 to 1929 – none had ever served in the House before. But despite the loss of many ministers and under-secretaries and the acquisition of a largely inexperienced back-bench, the Conservative Party was not for this reason at a great disadvantage as compared with the Labour Party. On the Government side most members with experience in the Coalition Government had survived the election; but the back-benches of the Labour Party were also dominated by M.P.s with no previous experience of the House. There were 244 new Labour M.P.s. J. F. S. Ross has noted that 'in one respect this new House [was] unique in modern times, in that more than half its members – 324 out of 640 – when its first session opened had no previous experience at all of parliamentary life'. His comparison of the average ages of new members of both parties is interesting: Conservatives 41 years 4 months; Labour 45 years 6½ months.[55]

Nor were the Conservative Party devoid of experienced parliamentarians. In addition to three former members of the War Cabinet – Sir John Anderson, Winston Churchill and Anthony Eden – there survived 22 other Opposition M.P.s with considerable governmental experience, including Sir David Maxwell Fyfe, R. A. Butler, Capt H. F. C. Crookshank, R. S. Hudson, Oliver Lyttelton, H. U. Willink, Col Oliver Stanley and W. S. Morrison. Moreover the severity of the defeat of the former ministers in the general election was soon greatly mitigated by the return of a number of them in by-elections later in 1945. Death removed two Conservative M.P.s, Sir E. T. Campbell and L. R. Pym, before the House had met and the elevation to the peerage of three 'sturdy knights', Sir G. Broadbent, Sir W. Davison and Sir Leonard Lyle in the Resignation Honours, created valuable openings in three more relatively safe seats. The opportunity afforded of strengthening the Opposition front bench was promptly seized, and before the year was out Harold Macmillan, Brendan Bracken, Ralph Assheton, Richard Law, and Peter Thorneycroft were back in the House, adding their weight to the Conservative cause. Later, in 1946, Henry G. Strauss (formerly Parliamentary Secretary in the Ministry of Town and Country Planning) and Walter E. Elliot (who had served as Minister of Agriculture and Fisheries) were returned to the parliamentary fold. In 1947 Malcolm S. McCorquodale (formerly Parliamentary Secretary in the Ministry of Labour and National Service) was also returned in a by-election.

However, some Conservatives were not so much concerned about the quality of the front-bench spokesmen as they were about the abilities of the back-bench supporters. Earl Winterton believed that the party had a 'better intake of new young members, men of brilliance and achievement in many fields' in 1945 than in 1906.[56] But one leading Conservative official expressed the view, after the 1945 election, that two-thirds of the occupants of the Conservative benches were useless.

Comparison of the successful Conservative candidates in 1945 with their opposite numbers during the inter-war period confirms the view that the 1945 defeat fell hardest on those Conservative M.P.s whose education, occupation, and social rank were more typical of the social composition of the British society as a whole. Conservative representation in the House has always been unrepresentative of the electorate, but the survivors in 1945 were even less representative than previously.[57]

There can be no doubt that the system of candidate selection in use in the inter-war period – one in which 'those who were willing to pay all their election expenses (anything between £400 and £1,200) and to subscribe between £500 and £1,000 a year to the local Association' always had 'an excellent chance of being adopted' while those 'unable to pay anything towards their election expenses and only able to subscribe £100 or less to the local Association' had 'hardly any chance at all'[58] – meant that the safest seats had gravitated to the wealthy (and usually aristocratic) members of the party. In a decisive defeat like that in 1945 the party was left with a high proportion of safe-seat candidates and, as another Conservative has noted, the men with the safest seats were not often the ones with the most to contribute to the House.

In 1944 'Onlooker', writing in the *National Review*,[59] referred to some 29 Conservative M.P.s then on the back-benches who showed considerable promise for the future. His selection of party talent ranged from Sir Herbert Williams on the right of the Conservative Party to Quintin Hogg, one of the most progressive young Tory Reformers, but was more heavily weighted on the side of the more conservative Conservatives. It is interesting to see how well these back-benchers fared in the election and how their success compared with that of Conservative M.P.s as a whole who put themselves forward as candidates in 1945. Three hundred and twenty-five Conservative M.P.s[60] stood as candidates in 1945; of these 189 – or 58·8 per cent were elected. By comparison 'Onlooker's' candidates did not do so well: only 12 of the 29 candidates were successful – or about 41·4 per cent of the total.

If we take the Tory Reform Committee members before 1945 as representing some (if not all) of the more progressive Conservative M.P.s and compare their success at the general election with Conservative M.P.s in general we find that, although they did slightly better than the 'Onlooker' group, their failure rate was nevertheless higher than for Conservative M.P.-candidates as a whole. Only 19 Tory Reformers from a total of 41 – or 46·3 per cent – were elected in 1945. This figure includes two successful candidates – Quintin Hogg and Hugh Molson – who were also listed in 'Onlooker's' group. It excludes, however, Peter Thorneycroft who was defeated in the general election but returned in a by-election later that year.

These statistical comparisons can hardly *prove* anything about the composition of the Conservative Party after the election in 1945. They do, however, help to substantiate the concern of several leading Conservatives that the old candidate-selection system was not one designed to leave the party after a decisive defeat in the strongest possible position for recovery. For example, 35 Conservative M.P.s who voted for Sir Douglas Hacking's amendment to the Catering Wages Bill were elected in 1945. Two of these M.P.s did not take their seats on the back-benches because they were raised to the peerage before the House met. The – to many – unfortunate state of the Conservative 'rump' after the 1945 defeat made a profound impact on party thinking and became, as one Conservative put it, 'the most powerful reason' for attempting to break the old system in following years. If landslides were to hit the party again in the future they must, many thought, safeguard their best material more carefully.

Earl Winterton, comparing the state of the Conservative Party in

1906 and 1945, has given it as his opinion that the party came out better from the latter election:

> The defeat of our party, though heavy enough, was proportionately less severe in 1945 than in the 1906 election; we were united under a great leader; and we had two excellent Chief Whips in the person of Mr James Stuart and afterwards Mr Patrick Buchan-Hepburn. They and their assistants were, in the main, a more efficient team than their Conservative predecessors when the party was in Opposition from 1906 to 1914. Moreover, in 1906 Mr Balfour's leadership was disliked by many of his followers, and the party was divided between tariff-reformers and free-traders.[61]

If the retention of political power assists party unity, loss of that power has imposed strains on Conservative Party unity no less than on any other party. Despite the supreme position of the Leader of the Conservative Party (seemingly under all conditions) and the high premium set upon party loyalty, the authority of the Leader of the Conservative Party is unquestionably less potent in opposition than in power. Winston Churchill, like Balfour,[62] experienced some difficulty in making the adjustment from Prime Minister to Leader of the Opposition. But there can be no doubt that Churchill was far more secure in his leadership of the Conservative Party after July 1945 than Balfour had been after his defeat in 1906.

Under Balfour, party unity had already weakened greatly while the party was still in power, and, indeed, it had been his inability to reconcile differences between the tariff-reformers and free-traders within the parliamentary party which had caused him to resign without calling for a dissolution in 1905. In 1906 the Conservatives fought the election as a divided party; they emerged from the election an even more badly divided party. That Balfour should have lost his seat along with many others in the rout, could not have assisted his attempts to impose authoritative control over the warring party groups.

The contrast with Churchill's position is striking. Churchill entered the 1945 election campaign at the apogee of his great fame as a war-leader and leading a united party. Although his party was defeated, he emerged from the election a figure of incomparably greater respect and prestige than Balfour (perhaps ever) had enjoyed.

His party was still fundamentally united – no powerful Duke of Devonshire threatened a separate course of action from the Leader's. And several Conservative M.P.s must have felt a special debt to their Leader for their very presence in the House: without his 'coat-tail', some must have wondered, how many would have been spared?

But if the Conservative Party during and immediately after the election in 1945 was in no sense the divided party it had been in 1906, it was not true that Churchill's leadership of the party was thereafter beyond question or that no differences over policy arose within the party. In fact, attitudes towards Churchill's leadership and policy questions were often closely linked. Those Conservatives, either in the House or in the country, who explained away the 1945 defeat in terms of 'pendulums' or Labour disloyalty or an electorate 'deluded by visions of a Socialist Utopia' saw little need for radical reform of the party's policy. Those, on the other hand, who rejected this comfortable view were firmly convinced that party salvation could and would come through a thorough reformulation of party policy. In general, those Conservatives most anxious for policy reformulation were also most critical of the absence of progressive policy statements in the election campaign, and among these Churchill's reluctance to accept the idea of policy restatement did not go uncriticized. Differences in party opinion on the question of policy reformulation and criticism of the party leadership will be examined in detail at a later stage; I mention them at this point merely to avoid exaggerating the unity which existed within the Conservative Party as it entered opposition in 1945.

At the same time, however, it is necessary to emphasize two vital differences between 1906 and 1945 as regards criticism of the party leadership and party differences over policy. In the first place criticism of Churchill never – not after the election nor at any time during the six years of opposition – reached the peak of violence shown against Balfour, or against Baldwin for that matter.[63] Churchill began his period as Leader of the Opposition in a stronger position than Balfour and had much weaker sallies to repel. Secondly, while noting the existence of policy differences within the Conservative Party after 1945, it is essential to underscore the point that such differences of opinion were by no means as profound as those which had earlier separated tariff-reformer from free-trader.

II

In the foregoing I have tried to capture the essential character of the Conservative Party as it embarked upon its six years as the Opposition. It is necessary now to animate the scene and follow the actions of the party in the following years. There is, fortunately, a natural boundary and a natural contrast to the point from which we began which is set by the party's return to power in 1951. We are bound, throughout the survey of the Conservatives in opposition, to seek to discover in what ways and to what extent the actions of the party helped to assist its recovery of political power.

Most leading Conservatives today point to three crucial factors for which the party was itself responsible – there are others, of course, quite beyond its own influence – which contributed to the recovery: the extensive party reorganization after 1945; the policy 'rethink' – i.e. the reformulation of a clear Conservative policy adapted to post-war conditions; and the effectiveness of its parliamentary opposition. It is to these matters to which we now turn our attention.

REFERENCES

[1] Dr. John Saloma, *British Conservatism and the Welfare State*, unpublished Ph.D. thesis, Harvard University, 1961, p. 280. See his Chapter IV for a full treatment of the Conservative Party and educational reform in the twentieth century.

[2] See the National Unionist Association of Conservative and Liberal Unionist Organizations: Council Minute Book, July 1917–March 1945 (hereinafter cited as Council Minute Book, I), 7 October, 1943, pp. 394–5.

[3] *Notes on Current Politics* (Conservative Central Office [C.C.O.], April 1945), p. 13 (hereinafter cited as *N.C.P.*).

[4] C. R. Attlee, *As it Happened*, p. 175. Cf. his letter to Harold Laski cited by Kingsley Martin in *Harold Laski, 1893–1950* (London, 1953), p. 160.

[5] *Notes for Speakers and Workers* (Conservative Central Office, 1945), pp. 13 and 38–45.

[6] Extract from a 'summary of the main principles' of the report of the Sub-committee on Industry (Post-war Problems Committee) p. 45. See Council Minute Book I for a conference resolution on full employment passed in March 1945.

[7] Extract from a 'summary of the main principles' of the report of the Sub-committee on Industry (Post-war Problems Committee), p. 45. Cf.

also the 1945 party conference resolution on 'Bureaucratic Control and Nationalization', *N.C.P.*, April 1945, p. 12.

[8] For Conservative views on controls see the resolution on 'Freedom of the individual' passed at the 1945 party conference, and *Notes for Speakers*, pp. 19–20 and 196–7.

[9] Cf. Churchill and Lord Woolton on the preservation of controls Council Minute Book I, p. 196, and extracts from *Work*, the report of the Sub-committee of Industry, *ibid.*, p. 197.

[10] Hugh Molson 'Election Issues', *The Contemporary Review*, July 1945 [reprint], p. 3. Cf. Molson, 'The Tory Reform Committee', *New English Review*, XI (July 1945), p. 252.

[11] *Notes for Speakers*, p. 13.

[12] Wheeler-Bennett, p. 629

[13] Francis Williams, *A Prime Minister Remembers* (London, 1961), p. 57.

[14] *Notes for Speakers*, pp. 58–78, and especially Churchill's and Eden's pledges to support 'this great social programme of reconstruction, irrespective of the consequences of the election', p. 77.

[15] Council Minute Book, I, pp. 386–7.

[16] Cmd. 6555, 6551 (London, 1944).

[17] *The National Insurance Plan* (Post-war Problems Central Committee, London, June 1945), p. 6.

[18] *The National Insurance Plan* (Post-war Problems Central Committee, London, June 1945), pp. 18–19.

[19] *The National Insurance Plan* (Post-war Problems Central Committee, London, June 1945), p. 12.

[20] It was not shared by all Labour members either. 'Reservations or outright objections to the plan tended . . . to break along the lines of generations. . . ', Dr Saloma has noted (p. 387). Ernest Bevin was noticeably cool to the Beveridge plan, making the comment: 'Man cannot live by Beveridge alone.'

[21] The Bill was designed 'to establish a statutory commission for regulating the remuneration and conditions of employment in the catering trades'. In the vote on the second reading (9 February, 1943) 107 voted for the Coalition motion, 111 voted against, and 135 abstained. See 386 *H.C. Deb.* 5S., cols. 1196–1286.

[22] *Hansard* 404, cols. 979–1093; 1106–1210; 1387–1498; 1555–1649. Most Conservative critics attacked the proposals on two main grounds; (1) The desirability of retaining the Friendly Societies in the operation of the Scheme; (2) The cost to the country. Conservative objections to Part II of the Bill dealing with industrial insurance were much less vehemently expressed, the major objection being non-reference to the Courts.

[23] *National Review* January 1943, pp. 19–20; March 1943, pp. 177–8; January 1944, p. 17; March 1944, p. 194. Cf. *Truth*, 15 October, 1943.

[24] *National Review* (March 1944), p. 194; Cf. *National Review* (January 1944), p. 17.

[25] Dr Saloma has written that 'there is little room for doubt that the party's lukewarm and hesitant acceptance of social insurance contributed to Labour's subsequent victory' (p. 392).

[26] Saloma, p. 399. See the suggestion by Dr S. Murray of the S.M.A. at 44th Annual Labour Party Conference.

[27] *Hansard* 398 cols. 427–518; 535–633.

[28] *N.C.P.*, April 1945, p. 12.

[29] Saloma, p. 407. See p. 408, for a citation from a letter to the author from Dr Harry Eckstein in which the latter (a close student of the history of the N.H.S. Act) stated that 'there cannot be the slightest reasonable doubt that the Conservatives would have barged ahead with the project'.

[30] *Looking Ahead* (An account of the proceedings of the Meeting of the Central Council . . . 2 October, 1941), National Union of Conservative Associations, 1941, p. 1.

[31] Now Lord Kilmuir.

[32] National Union Reports to the Central Council, 1919–45 (hereinafter, *Reports*), London, National Union of Conservative and Unionist Associations, 7 October, 1943, p. 5; and 14 and 15 March, 1945, p. 7.

[33] *Looking Ahead – Demobilization and Resettlement* (Central Committee on Post-war Reconstruction, September 1943), frontispiece.

[34] See *Reports*, 20 and 21 May, 1943, p. 13.

[35] See *Notes for Speakers*, pp. 45, 98–99, 110, 197, 225.

[36] According to Dr Saloma, p. 270, *Educational Aims* (the sub-committee's first interim report) was a 'clearly progressive document'. He noted that this and the second interim report were criticized by the Central Council in October 1942 for their emphasis on 'the state'. 'Nation' was substituted for 'state' in *Looking Ahead. The Statutory Educational System* (third interim report), January 1944.

[37] *Demobilization and Resettlement* (Central Committee on Post-war Reconstruction, 1943), p. 13.

[38] *Forty Years of Progress* (Post-war Problems Central Committee, June 1945), pp. 10–11.

[39] *Forward – By the Right!* (London, 1943), p. 1.

[40] Now Sir Frederick Hooper. The link with Hooper lasted until May 1944, when the Tory Reform Committee set up its own research staff, drawing some from Hooper's Political Research Centre. *Observer*, 'Tory Reform M.P.s to have own Research', 28 May, 1944.

[41] Olive Moore 'Can the Tory Reform', *Persuasion*, Summer 1944, p. 20

[42] *Forward – By the Right!*, pp. 10–11.

[43] Quintin Hogg, *One Year's Work* (London, 1944), p. 127. See *Tools for the Next Job* (London, 1945) for the Committee's lengthy exposition of the case for an expansionist government policy centred on the re-equipment of industry.

[44] See Harvey Glickman, 'The Toryness of English Conservatism', *The Journal of British Studies*, I (November 1961), p. 117.

[45] Cf. Lord Salisbury, *Post-war Conservative Policy*, p. 4; pp. 5–6: Earl of Selbourne, 'On Conservative Policy', *National Review*, CXXIII (July 1944), p. 61.

[46] Hogg, *Work*, pp. 43–44. Cf. Viscount Hinchingbrooke, *Full Speed Ahead: Essays in Tory Reform* (London, 1944), pp. 7–8, 20–21, 30–34; Captain L. D. Gammans, 'A Tory Reformer Replies', *Manchester Evening News*, 23 November,

1943; Peter Thorneycroft, 'Tory Reform: What we are after', *Picture Post*, 29 April, 1944, p. 10.

[47] Saloma, pp. 391–2.

[48] Cited in *The Times*, 'Policy for the Coal Mines', 4 April, 1944; cf. Gammans. Tory Reform Committee publications during the election campaign could be viciously anti-nationalization and anti-socialist. See *What is a Tory?* (Tory Reform Committee, London, [1945]), p. 2, and *Nationalization or National Government* (Tory Reform Committee, London, [1945]).

[49] Hinchingbrooke, *Ahead*, p. 20. Thorneycroft, p. 10.

[50] See Council Minute Book, I., 7 October, 1943, p. 396, and Molson, 'The Tory Reform Committee', p. 247, for details of Sir Alfred Beit's amendment to a Central Council motion depreciating 'Government control of private enterprise unless a clear case was made out of a monopoly detrimental to the interests of the community . . .'

[51] Wheeler-Bennett, p. 628.

[52] Abrams, 'Labour Vote', p. 16. Cf. Lord Lindsay, 'Britain's New Labour Government', *Virginia Quarterly Review*, XXII (Spring 1946), p. 258.

[53] Abrams, 'Labour Vote,' p. 16.

[54] McCallum and Readman, p. 266, ventured the opinion that the Conservative Party might be in a weaker position for recovery than after 1832 or 1906.

[55] J. F. S. Ross, *Parliamentary Representation* (London, 1948), p. 247. There were 244 new Labour M.P.s, p. 240.

[56] Winterton, p. 316.

[57] Ross, pp. 253, 258, 271 and 273.

[58] Ian Harvey, A Memorandum in Ross, *Representation*, p. 297.

[59] 'Onlooker', 'Conservative Party Talent', *National Review*, CXXII (February 1944), pp. 113–22.

[60] For purposes of this comparison only Conservative Party candidates are considered. The figure includes former front-bench Conservative candidates as well.

[61] Winterton, pp. 315–16. See also Nigel Birch, *The Conservative Party* (London, 1949), p. 39.

[62] On Balfour's leadership see R. T. McKenzie, *British Political Parties* (London, 1955), pp. 75 ff. On Churchill as Leader of the Opposition see below, pp. 266–9.

[63] See L. S. Amery, *My Political Life* (London, 1955) III, pp. 22–39, for an account of pressures on Baldwin's leadership of the party.

CHAPTER III

Party Reconstruction: The First Year

THE TRADITIONAL response of the Conservative Party – or any party – following defeat in a general election has been to look primarily to the organization of the party for a scapegoat. R. T. McKenzie has referred to the 'extraordinarily cyclical process' by which party reorganizations have taken place within the Conservative Party in the past, and has noted that the general theme of these half-dozen major party reorganizations has been 'to make the organs of the National Union more broadly representative of the party membership or to provide more effective channels of communication between the party organization outside Parliament and the party leaders in Parliament'.[1] More specifically, the tendency has been that:

> Defeat in a general election traditionally leads to more or less vociferous demands on the part of party supporters for a reorganization of its structure; the leaders in Parliament (or the National Union itself) appoints a committee of inquiry which recommends more or less extensive modifications in party structure without ever seriously suggesting a redistribution of power between the three main sections of the party organization.[2]

Having suffered an electoral defeat comparable only to the 'disasters' of 1832 and 1906, the Conservative Party responded more positively in 1945 to the challenge of defeat than ever before. Immediately the results were known important changes in what Professor Beer has called 'the structure of action' began to occur. If some members of the higher circle of the party were slow to respond to the post-war necessity of developing new party policy, careful attention *was* quickly paid to the means whereby a new policy – which many argued must come – could be formulated, discussed and disseminated.

To some extent prompt action in reorganizing and revitalizing the party was motivated by the unsatisfactory position into which the traditional party structure had slipped as a result of the war and the so-called 'political truce'. The party had continually emphasized its patriotic behaviour during the war implying strongly that it, at least, was willing to sacrifice the party's interest for the nation's good. There is no doubt that the constituency organization of the Conservative Party at the time of the general election in 1945 was vastly inferior to that of the Labour Party; there is no doubt either that this was only partly due to a special interpretation of the 'electoral truce'.

Under an agreement reached between the three major parties on 26 September, 1939, 'each party undertook not to nominate candidates at by-elections against the candidate of the party who held the seat at the time of the vacancy. The agreement was to hold good during the war, or "until determined on notice given by any one of the three parties signatories thereto".'[3] The Conservative Party, it is said, read more into the electoral truce and went so far as to consider 'that it involved a complete lapse of political activity in the constituencies', even, the Nuffield study suggests, 'to the point of disbanding the staff of their local organizations'.[4] The exact meaning of McCallum and Readman's statement is not entirely clear, but if it is intended to mean that the Conservative Party encouraged, as a matter of policy, the disruption of its constituency organizations, then it seems to me this interpretation is open to doubt; for there is ample evidence to suggest that this extreme interpretation of the electoral truce had no support whatever from the party's leaders. It must not be thought that the party, either its Leader, his advisers or the National Union itself, waived serious interest in the party organization during the war years. Indeed, their concern was, if anything, more pronounced.

Partly, therefore, to amend the conventional impression of the party's attitude towards its organization during the electoral truce, and partly to place the post-election changes in their proper perspective, it is necessary to examine first those developments in the party organization which occurred during the war years. Because it has often been held by party officials, the press, and academics alike that the key to the Tory revival during the opposition years lay in the effectiveness of its thorough party reorganization, consideration of the party structure and its evolution is of real importance. It will be necessary, therefore, to analyse changes in the party organization

– the spectacular and the relatively unnoticed – and attempt to assess their rôle in the broad context of the party's revival.

THE WAR YEARS

The assertion made, for example, by McCallum and Readman that, while the Labour Party continued to hold annual conferences, the Conservatives 'considered that the activities of the party itself should be curtailed by reason of the political truce', and for this reason 'held no party conference during the war years until 1943', is highly misleading. The Labour Party had (and still has) no meeting of its mass membership comparable to those of the Central Council of the National Union – meetings which were in fact attended by an average of about 400 representatives no less than eight times during the war years.[5] Moreover, it is not altogether certain that the party's decision to cancel the conferences was not based more on a realistic assessment of the number of constituency members that might be expected to attend than on a matter of principle derived from the electoral truce. At any rate, important meetings were held during the war years by the Conservative Party, and it is clear from a survey of the Council minutes and Reports of the Executive Committee to the National Union that the National Union was deeply concerned both with the maintenance of the constituency associations and with the development of new institutions within the party structure.

A report of the Executive Committee to the Council meeting on 30 March, 1939, referred to the establishment of a Treasurer's Department at Central Office 'to deal with the collection of funds for Headquarters, and the giving of advice where requested to Area councils and constituencies in organizing their own financial methods and procedure'.[6] Reference was also made to the 'progress made by constituency associations in carrying out the proposals for bringing the Junior Imperial League into full partnership in the party organization'. Following the recommendation of the Executive Committee, the Central Council amended the Rules of the National Union to provide that 'the Chairman and Secretary of the Central Education Sub-committee and the Secretary of the Central Labour Sub-committee be *ex-officio* members of the Central Council'.

Although most constituency associations continued to resist all efforts to integrate the youth organization with the senior membership of the party, the National Union's executive was already aware of a factor which was to assume great significance in the post-war years – the rôle within the mass party of youth and the party's youth movement. The attempts to improve the party's financial machinery, still-born at the outbreak of the war, were to be revived towards the end of the war and, with even greater determination, during the years of opposition.

At the Central Council meeting later that year in June another minor change was effected in the party organization, the full implications of which were not drawn or developed until the last years of the war. The revision which made additions in the representation of the London Area (formerly the Metropolitan Area) to the Area council, arose out of a report of a committee set up by the Leader of the Party. 'National and municipal politics,' it was held, 'could not be separated, and the addition of municipal representatives to the Area council would enable all the Conservative forces in London to be brought together in order to stem the Socialist tide.'[7] Further development of this notion had to await the end of the war and the Labour victory in the general election, until the Conservative Party could be persuaded to contest local elections with the same thorough political-machine approach that was used in parliamentary elections. The report of 1939 was a mere taste of things to come.

When the Central Council met again in April 1940 the war had begun and the agreement over an electoral truce had been reached. It was at this meeting that a resolution was passed requesting a suspension of 'party strife' in the interest of national unity.[8] At the same time, however, another resolution was passed unanimously urging:

> that constituency associations should use every means to maintain their organizations at full strength, in order to provide facilities for members of the party to make such contributions as they [could] to the great war effort of the nation.[9]

The report of the Executive Committee to the Central Council indicates that the Executive had already sent, under the authority of Sir Eugene Ramsden, its chairman, a more strongly-worded resolution to every constituency. The resolution, passed unanimously by the Executive Committee, stated that: ' . . . the members of the

Executive Committee . . . strongly urge the necessity of maintaining the organization in every Parliamentary Division in as complete a state of efficiency as present circumstances will permit . . .'.[10]

Also, and despite the chairman's warning that it was contrary to the intention of the earlier motion calling for a party truce, a resolution was passed by a small majority requesting the Executive Committee 'immediately to take the necessary action to counteract Socialist propaganda which [was] being made use of in the Houses of Parliament, over the radio, and in the press'.[11] The patriotism of at least the majority of representatives present was tempered with a little political realism.

Again, the report of the Executive Committee the following year is informative. The Central Council meeting of 27 March, 1941, was told that:

> The reports reaching the Headquarters of the Party indicated that in many constituencies an efficient organization is being maintained. In the early months of the war a small number of constituency associations either closed down or practically ceased to exist.[12]

But the report then assured: 'There are now only a very few divisions in which the constituency association is completely inactive.'[13]

One further reference to the party organization was the resolution at the Council meeting in October 1941 noting the necessity 'to retain the interest and support of the rank-and-file members through periodical meetings and social events';[14] another in 1943 welcomed the suggestion of the Central Office to create 'Looking Ahead Circles whereby small groups of supporters [could] meet together regularly for the express purpose of considering post-war proposals';[15] and there was the direct appeal to the constituency associations by Winston Churchill. This appeal was sent out under his name (and is, therefore, the most official that has been discovered) and is most revealing of the Conservative Party's attitude towards the maintenance of the constituency organizations: 'It is not too much to say . . . that in the national interest and not merely for party ends, it is vitally important that, side by side with our war effort, ways and means should be found of keeping the Conservative Party organization in being and ready to be tuned up when the time comes. . . .'

'. . . [T]here seems to be an impression in some Conservative quarters that nothing need be done to keep the constituency organization together and to employ them on useful wartime activities.' And later: 'Confronted with the activities of both the Communist and the local Labour Parties some constituency associations unfortunately ceased to function. Others have felt compelled to dispense with the services of their staff, and where the staff have joined the Forces there has been hesitation on financial grounds, to engage wartime deputies . . . No one would minimize the wartime difficulties facing the associations. . . . It is essential, however, that every possible effort should be made to keep an organization in being.'[16] Often the 'country-before-party' theme was mixed with an appeal to strengthen the party organization for the future. For example, Major Dugdale speaking at Truro on 10 April, 1943, said: 'In no event must we attempt in the difficult times of war to compete with the Socialists in bribing the electors. I ask you to build up your organizations and have them ready for use when the proper time arrives.' All these factors reveal a deep concern with the maintenance of an organization whose roots had deteriorated from the state described in the spring of 1941.

Much as the National Union and the Central Office might encourage, the responsibility for the condition of constituency organizations remained the domain of the associations. Many party officials in the divisions volunteered for or were conscripted to the war effort; agents (where they existed) were in most cases past retirement age and not easily able to bear the extra burdens of wartime organization, and the management of the party's constituency organizations was usually left to women's groups which were more social than political. Under conditions such as these it is not surprising that many associations were disbanded, and that at the time of the general election there was, according to party officials, no constituency association which was fully active. But it is evident that such action was the result of circumstances and not the product of a conscious policy on the part of the party or its leadership. Indeed, as Churchill's appeal made so plain, although some constituency associations might decide to disband, such action was criticized at the time.

But party activity during the early 1940s was not restricted to attempting to maintain the existing party organization. The party began as early as May 1941 to set up the Post-war Problems Central Committee which was to be of some importance in the remaining years of the war. Then the Council meeting on 20 May, 1943, passed an important resolution requesting that 'steps should be taken as soon as possible to revive the Conservative and Unionist Junior Movement which was suspended at the outbreak of the war', as it was felt desirable that 'contact should be maintained with its former members, and that facilities should be provided now for young people who desire to be associated with the party organization'.[17] At the same meeting the Chairman of the Party Organization, Sir Thomas Dugdale, announced that he had already set up a committee to inquire into the Junior Movement of the party. This committee, under the chairmanship of Gerald Palmer, M.P., was appointed to:

> . . . consider and report as to what action should be taken to re-establish the Junior Movement of the Conservative Party, with recommendations as to the basis upon which it should be organized: (1) for such activities as [could] be undertaken during the war, and (2) as a permanent fraternity of youth after the war.[18]

After due consideration a report was presented to Sir Thomas in the spring of 1944, and at his suggestion it was subsequently discussed and unanimously approved by the Executive Committee. It was recognized in the report that 'as a result of the war conditions the Junior Imperial League had ceased to function in many parts of the country, and that with the passage of time the majority of the pre-war members would no longer be eligible for membership once the war was over'. 'It may well be,' the Executive's report noted, 'that young people returning from the forces . . . will demand a different set-up.'[19]

The Palmer Committee report recommended the reconstitution of the Junior Imperial League as the Junior Branch of the National Union, herein deliberately implementing and developing the recommendations of the pre-war Fraser Report which stressed the need for closer co-operation between the senior and junior organizations with equality of status and shared responsibility at all levels. The new plan, the Executive explained:

> . . . contemplates that there should be, in every constituency, a Junior Branch of the local association; in every area, an area

> Youth Council with adequate representation on the area council and the area executive; and at Headquarters a Junior Central Advisory Council with its own elected chairman, and with adequate representation on the Executive Committee of the National Union. The Youth Movement will thus, for the first time, be placed on a footing of complete equality with the Women's organizations [at every level]. . . .[20]

The Executive's recommendation that the Draft Rules giving increased representation to the youth movement be adopted was unanimously accepted by the Central Council on 14 March, 1945, less than four months before the party's defeat in the general election.

Two other matters arising during 1943 and settled in the next two years were reported on by the Executive Committee to a joint meeting of the Central Council and the party conference on 14 March, 1945. The reports of both the Special Finance Committee and the Post-war Problems Central Committee, forwarded to the conference for its approval at this time, contained important recommendations affecting the party organization which deserve attention.

A Special Finance Committee had been set up in 1943 upon the recommendation of a joint-committee comprised of representatives of the Executive Committee and the Emergency Committee of the Society of Agents 'to examine, on a broad basis, how the maximum income [could] be secured after the war for efficiently carrying on the work of the party throughout the country'.[21] The committee, with Sir Eugene Ramsden as its chairman, held fourteen meetings, examined numerous witnesses, and had access to 'valuable sources of information'. Its report received the general approval of the Executive Committee, a specially convened meeting of Area chairmen, and the Leader of the Party.[22]

Four main causes, the committee considered, rendered necessary an overhaul of the financial machinery of the party: the restricted financial resources of the Conservative Party as compared with 'the vast resources which the Socialists [could] command for political purposes'; the desire to assure that no person possessing the necessary qualifications and ability should be prevented from standing as a parliamentary candidate for the party; the growing recognition that 'strong central funds [were] more than ever necessary in order to provide for propaganda in all its forms'; and the need to provide the centre with funds sufficient to support adequately those constituencies, often electorally the most important, in which special difficulties existed. Every constituency, the report affirmed: '. . . should regard it as an obligation of honour to contribute to the party need in accordance with its ability to pay'.[23] In order to achieve closer financial co-operation between the centre and the Areas, the report recommended that the Areas should unite with the centre in the collection of Area and central funds. To this end it recommended the establishment of a National Board of Finance for the constituencies, to integrate finance, on which the Areas were to have substantial representation.

A joint sub-committee representative of Central Office and the National Union was subsequently set up to consider the best means of implementing the proposals. Although the Central Board of Finance (as it was then to be called) was not in fact operating until 1946[24] a beginning had been made before the electoral defeat in 1945 towards the integration of the party's financial structure from top to bottom – a tendency which the Maxwell Fyfe Committee on Party Organization further refined and elaborated.

The report of the Special Finance Committee also made another recommendation, one dealing with the treatment of agents and party organizers, which was elaborated and finally settled by the *Interim Report of the Committee on Party Organization.* The Executive Committee's report to the meeting of the Central Council and the party conference in May 1945, stated that '. . . a number of proposals [were] made for improving the condition and status of the Agent's profession, including the provision of increased financial help from the Central Funds for the training of agents and organizers, so that trainees [might] be adequately paid during their period of training'. The details of the plan were not drawn out in the Executive's report to the Central Council. The full report of the committee was presented as a confidential document to the Executive Committee, which, the Executive stated, 'it [did] not propose to publish'.[25]

The report of the Post-war Problems Central Committee, grew out of a resolution submitted to, but not reached at, the party conference and Central Council meeting in May 1943. This resolution noted:

> That in view of the increasing importance of local government, some reorganization of the party machinery is necessary in order:
>
> (*a*) In general, to assimilate party action and policy in relation to national and local government, and
>
> (*b*) To provide closer constituency and inter-constituency consultation and action on the basis of local government areas.[26]

These proposals were subsequently considered by the Post-war Problems Central Committee which made certain recommendations to the Executive Committee. The following recommendations were approved by the Executive Committee on 24 April, 1944:

> That a wholetime officer directly responsible to the General Director for local government matters should be appointed at Headquarters.
>
> That a Local Government Advisory Committee should be set up, and that the Committee should meet at regular intervals. The Committee should be kept informed as to new and impending legislation and should be entitled to make representations to the Executive Committee of the National Union.[27]

In accordance with the second recommendation a Local Government Advisory Committee was established, comprised of three representatives chosen in each of the twelve Areas. At its first meeting in December 1944, Geoffrey Hutchinson, M.P., was elected chairman. The Committee began immediately to plan Area conferences on local government problems which were to take place during the summer of 1945; but the general election intervened, and the conferences had to be cancelled.

* * *

None of the changes in the structure of the Conservative Party between 1939 and 1945 – as indeed is true of most other periods in the party's history – was major in nature. Nevertheless, from this review of the war years it has been possible to extract a few main themes. The Conservative Party is seen to have been concerned during these years not only with maintaining its constituency associations, but also with expanding and elaborating the party organization. Fundamental in this respect were the development of the party's youth organization; the beginning of an integration of the politics of local government with the party machinery at all levels; and the extension of the agencies of consultation dealing with party finance. Also of importance was the establishment of the Post-war Problems Central Committee and its sub-committees as research and advisory bodies. All these themes assumed a greater importance in the period from 1945 to 1951 when the Conservative Party concerned itself more carefully than ever before with a close analysis of its party organization. The post-war developments appear less 'revolutionary', however, when seen in the light of their well-defined roots planted during the war years.

THE PARTY IN OPPOSITION, JULY 1945–JULY 1946

Much of the credit for the Conservative Party's post-war reorganization has usually been given – quite rightly – to Lord Woolton, the great Chairman of the Party Organization. But it is remarkable how extensive were the plans for (if not always the full implementation of) measures of party reconstruction before Lord Woolton appeared on the scene. Without attempting to detract from the ability of this superb organizer to whom credit enough is due for the things he *is* responsible for, it is nevertheless worthwhile to appreciate the extent of the development of the party organization under his predecessor, the Rt Hon Ralph Assheton. Assheton had become Chairman of the Party Organization after the death of Sir Thomas Dugdale, and served from October 1944 to July 1946. Some newspapers speculated, immediately after the election, that Sir Andrew Duncan would be charged with the responsibility of investigating the state of the party organization throughout the country and the reorganization of the Conservative Central Office, but this came to nought.[28]

On 5 October, 1945, a meeting was held in London under Assheton's chairmanship, to which defeated candidates were invited to discuss the reasons for the party's electoral defeat. The official statement released by the Central Office after the meeting reported that 50 of about 200 people who attended had had an opportunity to discuss the matter for five hours and that 'a large number of constructive suggestions for the future were put forward'.[29] 'The main impression left by the conference upon some of those present,' according to *The Times* correspondent's report, 'was that there was little if any recrimination or bitterness about the Conservative defeat in July, and that the speakers . . . were concerned almost entirely with the policy and other means by which the Conservative Party [could] hope to make a more successful appeal to the country in the future.[30] Tom Driberg's account of this same meeting, however, does not support this picture of sweet reasonableness. He refers to the attempts of Spencer Summers and Ian Harvey, among others, who sought to pin the blame for the election defeat on Lord Beaverbrook. 'Mr Whiteside (Wembley South) called for his expulsion. Sir Derrick Gunston said: "I believe there is no man more detested throughout the political world than Lord Beaverbrook."'[31]

But even if most of the defeated candidates were able to avoid personal indictments for the party's failures in the recent past, they could scarcely conceal their desire for radical innovations in the policy and structure of the party. Before a decision had been taken not to debate resolutions, one was put before the meeting calling for an overhaul of the constitution, organization, and machinery of the party 'to be undertaken forthwith on democratic lines by a body representative of all shades of opinion favouring the increase of national wealth and prosperity on the basis of personal freedom and individual initiative.'[32]

Members of the Central Council were not without their own reasons for the party's election defeat and suggestions on how the party organization might best be rearranged to ensure future success; at the meeting of the Central Council on 28 November, 1945, some of these ideas were discussed. A resolution was moved deploring the lack of propaganda machinery and which urged 'the necessity of improving the existing machinery for presenting [the party's] point of view and for acquainting itself with current trends of feeling and opinion . . .'.[33] The resolution, passed unanimously, also requested the Executive Committee to submit a full report on these matters for consideration at the next Council meeting.

The Central Council also had something to say about the constituency associations. A resolution was moved recommending: 'that it [was] in the best interests of Conservative associations that officers of the associations [should] be elected annually by ballot, and in general no officer [should] hold the same office for more than three consecutive years . . .'. Further it urged the Central Council to call upon associations:

> . . . to take immediate steps so that officers, councils, executive committees, and ward and district polling branches are fully representative of a cross-section of the community, including wage earners, with a view to securing such representation in the House of Commons.[34]

But this particular suggestion was by no means acceptable to the bulk of the members present, for, as the minutes record:

> After a show of hands, the Chairman declared the voting for and against was so equal that it was difficult to decide, and suggested that instead of a ballot being taken, and in order not to hold up other business, the issue should be left undecided, though the resolution should be circulated to associations together with an indication of the large measure of support which it received.[35]

At the next Council meeting on 27 March, 1946, the Executive Committee reported briefly on the subject of propaganda machinery. As far as it was concerned 'machinery for ascertaining current trends of opinion already [existed] on a substantial scale in the constituencies'.[36] There were many opportunities provided in the numerous agencies of consultation from the branch meeting to the National Executive, and Butler's educational programme, they deemed, 'also provide[d] for a two-way exchange of ideas'.

The Harrow West Division Conservative Association appears to have remained dissatisfied with the steps that had been taken so far and placed a resolution on the agenda for the meeting on 27 March, 1946, which it had submitted and later withdrawn at the November 1945 meeting, demanding closer co-operation between the Central Office and the constituency associations 'as essential for the effective organization of the party'.[37] But this resolution like another demanding 'that the higher organization of the party [be] remodelled on modern lines' and that 'the ablest and most progressive officers [be] employed' was withdrawn, presumably after the Executive Committee's assurance in its report that everything that could be done was being done. Two other resolutions, one requesting visual aids for political education and propaganda, and another urging that constituency associations should revive interest in the Young Britons as 'a valuable means of propaganda for the party' were forwarded to the Executive Committee for consideration and report.

A few members of the Central Council thought that the Council itself had a greater rôle to play in the party's future. A resolution was therefore moved by C. H. Tyson and John Hay, a young Conservative, demanding more frequent meetings of the Central Council. 'In view of the urgent need of permitting the fullest exchange of ideas and information between the Leader of the Party and the members of it in the country . . .',[38] they called for quarterly meetings of the Council and an annual conference of the party of three days' duration. The motion was, strangely enough, defeated; but following the meeting an *ad hoc* committee was appointed to review existing procedure at Central Council meetings and to suggest improvements.

In reporting to the Executive Committee the committee expressed the opinion that the difficulties experienced at previous Council meetings, owing principally to a lack of time, might be overcome in future by holding not less than two meetings a year (in addition to the party conference which it also recommended should be a three-day affair), and by limiting the number of motions discussed. 'In order to test the value of these suggestions', the committee recommended *inter alia* that, as an experiment:

> . . . there should be a meeting of the Central Council in December and that it should be held on a Saturday.
>
> That the General Purposes Committee should be given power to limit the number of motions on the agenda. . . .
>
> That the General Purposes Committee should have the power to arrange for part of the time of the Central Council meeting to be devoted to considering important subjects not covered by motions, and without taking a vote.
>
> That the Executive should again review the procedure at the end of the present year.[39]

Although the Executive Committee approved the recommendations of the report, most of the suggestions were, in fact, ignored. Discussion of 'important subjects' in the manner recommended by the Committee's report was never implemented during the party's period of opposition. The report of the Executive Committee to the Central Council on 8 March, 1951, did recommend that: 'the decision of the Central Council in 1946 [*sic*], giving the General Purposes

Committee power to arrange for a part of a Central Council meeting to be devoted to considering important subjects not covered by motions and without taking a vote, should be put into effect.'[40] The Executive Committee's recommendation in March 1951 was put into effect only once – in 1955. Its reference to the *decision of the Central Council* of 1946 can refer only to the *recommendations* of the report of the *ad hoc* committee of 1946. It is remarkable that, in the light of the committee's desire for more Council meetings and for greater opportunities for discussion, the number of Council meetings was actually *reduced*. The Central Office publication of March 1945, *The Party Organization*, stated that 'the Central Council usually meets twice yearly in London',[41] and this was certainly the practice (with the one exception noted) during the war years. But without any formal announcement – for there was no decision by the Central Council itself, the rule-making body – the practice developed after 1945 of holding only annual meetings of the Central Council. The unofficial decision to cut the meetings to only one a year must have been taken even before the *ad hoc* committee had been appointed, for, in contrast with the publications for both Council meetings in 1945, the booklet containing the agenda and resolutions for the 1946 meeting bore the title *Central Council Annual Meeting*. The revised edition of *The Party Organization* of March 1946, also noted only that 'the Central Council meets in London . . .'.[42] With a degree of subtlety characteristic of the Conservative Party in matters of this kind a new 'convention' was quickly established which quietly ignored the wishes of one section of party opinion.

The Central Council was not alone in its concern for reorganization of the party. The Executive Committee of the National Union and leading officials of the party at Central Office had also been doing some hard thinking along these lines. But party headquarters, it seems, laboured under a number of severe handicaps. In August 1945 Sir Harold Mitchell had resigned from the position of Vice-Chairman of the Party Organization which he had held since 1942 and had been replaced by J. P. L. Thomas.[43] In September 1945 Sir Robert Topping had relinquished the General Director's job which he had held at Central Office since February 1931 and had been replaced by Lt-Col S. H. Pierssene. The position of Chairman of the Party Organization was filled by the Rt Hon. Ralph Assheton who, at the time of the election defeat, had less than a year's experience in his new job. To compound the difficulty the party's headquarters was understaffed and overcrowded. 'Expansion to a normal peace-time establishment [was] still delayed', the Executive Committee explained, 'by lack of suitable accommodation . . .'.[44] Despite these limitations the foundations were laid, during Assheton's term as chairman, for the rapid reconstruction that came with Woolton's accession to the position. Lord Woolton was not the party's sole innovator; many important developments were well under way by the time Assheton resigned.

It was noted that considerable interest in local government had developed within some sections of the party and that steps were being taken to integrate local politics more closely into the party machine, culminating in the appointment of an advisory body for local government which was represented on the Executive Committee. The formation of the Advisory Committee on Local Government merely served to quicken interest, and a great deal of time was devoted to consideration of contesting local government elections on party political lines, thereby using the full weight of the party machine against the Labour Party. A resolution which was finally agreed on was adopted by the Executive Committee, and a circular letter conveying the advice of the advisory committee was addressed by the Chairman of the Executive Committee to all constituency chairmen. The resolution stated that:

> . . . as the Socialist Party have now made it impossible to exclude party politics from local government elections, the Conservative Party organization should take a full and effective part in all contested local government elections; and that whilst the Conservative Party does not seek to control the independent judgement of the candidates when elected to local authorities, it is as a general rule desirable that candidates receiving the support of the party should stand as Conservatives or as members of parties co-operating with the Conservative Party.[45]

The borough elections of November 1945 provided the Advisory Committee with its first opportunity to experiment. An executive was appointed to co-operate with the Publicity Department at Central Office, and as a result a series of publications were prepared and issued by Central Office for use in the election. The literature, the preparation of which was an entirely new departure for the

Central Office, included a handbook for the use of candidates, a broadsheet, a collection of draft leaflets and posters, and a series of occasional notes to be issued periodically before the election.[46]

The entry of the Advisory Committee and Central Office into local elections was a qualified success. The report of the Executive Committee to the Central Council prepared for the 1946 Conference advised that it had been considered that the election material issued by the Central Office in the form of notes and the handbook, *Your Election Questions Answered*, had been most useful, but that the broadsheet had not been equally successful. In general, it was thought that 'assistance from Central Office should take the form of suitable material which [could] be adapted to local circumstances rather than leaflets and broadsheets printed ready for distribution'.[47] But the November elections were only the beginning, the beginning of a process which was to acquire much greater attention and interest in the following years.

The Central Office matched the interest displayed by the National Union by appointing Herbert Brabin as its Local Government Officer. Mr Brabin, when introduced to the Advisory Committee in June 1946, was appointed (according to the usual practice) Honorary Secretary of the body, and outlined suggested plans for developing the department. Under the aegis of these two bodies, Area conferences on local government problems were begun, to provide an opportunity for serving Conservative councillors (and others) to give expression to their views and, as the Council's Report put it, '. . . to feel that those views were sought and valued'.[48] At the party conference in October 1946 it was reported that successful area conferences had been held at Leeds, Birmingham, Cambridge, and Manchester. It was intended to cover the country in a similar manner, and thereafter to organize periodic conferences in order to maintain direct contact between councillors and the Local Government Department at Central Office.

Early in 1946, in response in part to the Labour Party's determination to repeal the Trades Disputes Act of 1927, *ad hoc* meetings were held between Central Office officials and some members of the pre-war Labour Committee movement to consider the party's future relations with organized labour. The problem was later put forward in meetings between Central Office officials, certain Labour Committee members, and Conservative M.P.s (including R. A. Butler,

W. S. Morrison, Quintin Hogg, and Henry Strauss). It was recognized by those concerned that 'all wage-earners were not members of Trade Unions, and that Trade Union strength [was] related to location of industry rather than to existing constituency boundaries'.[49] The Executive Committee consequently recommended that constituency and Area Labour Advisory Committees should be continued for the time being on the existing basis, but that 'their work should be supplemented by the establishment of Conservative Trade Union Councils, composed exclusively of active trade unionists, in those localities where industrial conditions [made] their creation desirable'. It also suggested that the present Central Labour Advisory Committee be replaced by a Central Trade Union Advisory Committee. Eric Adamson was charged with organizing the Area advisory committees and constituency organizations through his Central Office department, and, well before the party conference in 1947, advisory committees had been formed in all Areas, which in turn had chosen a Central Advisory Committee.

One of the most important reactions to the election defeat was the Conservative Party's new emphasis on research, policy formulation, and political education. At the meeting of the Central Council on 28 November, 1945, a very important step in this direction was taken with the reconstitution of the Post-war Problems Central Committee under the name of the Advisory Committee on Policy and Political Education. Because the nature and function of this committee will be of considerable importance when the changes in its structure (resulting from the Maxwell Fyfe Report) are discussed later, it seems worthwhile to consider carefully the details of its formation.

At the Council meeting, Henry Brooke, on behalf of the General Purposes Committee, moved:

> That warmly appreciating the work that was carried out by the Post-war Problems Committee . . . the Central Council resolves as follows:
>
> (1) A vigorous effort is immediately necessary to associate members of the party throughout every parliamentary constituency in the country with the formation of ideas as a basis of policy, and with spreading political education.
>
> (2) With that object in view, the Post-war Problems Central Committee should be *reconstructed under the same chairman* [Mr

Butler], with the title of Advisory Committee on Policy and Political Education, and should be given the widest possible powers to develop quickly a scheme which will promote the study and preparation of reports on suitable subjects for the benefit of the party organization . . . and to set up a political education movement.

(3) As in the case of the Post-war Problems Central Committee, the members of the reconstituted Committee should be chosen, not as representatives of any particular sections of the party organization; but because of their knowledge of the questions to be considered. It *should be appointed by the Executive Committee of the National Union*, and, if possible, at its next meeting.[50]

An addendum was moved by Hugh Molson, M.P., to the effect that the committee should be provided with the necessary research and secretarial facilities, and 'that arrangements should be made to co-ordinate its policy with the day-to-day activities of the parliamentary party in the House of Commons'. The amended resolution passed unanimously.

It should be clear from this resolution that the Advisory Committee on Policy and Political Education – in sharp contrast with the later Advisory Committee on Policy – was strictly speaking a committee of the National Union. Although in practice the Executive Committee did not appoint the members of the Committee – the choice was left to R. A. Butler and then approved by the Executive Committee of the National Union – the appointment of Butler as chairman of the committee was clearly made by the Central Council.

At the time of the Central Council meeting of 27 March, 1946, the Executive Committee was able to report that, with the agreement of the Chairman of the Party, two sub-committees were in the process of being set up.[51] The two sub-committees, the Political Education and the Publications sub-committees, under the general supervision of the Advisory Committee, were to be assisted by the expanding Research Department. Thus, despite the reluctance of Churchill to consider demands for explicit statements of policy, a body was formed soon after the election which was to be of value to the party when the decision was finally made to produce policy statements on a wide range of subjects. But it must be noted, as the Executive Committee pointed out, that: 'It was not intended that this Committee should lay down party policy, but it should help to provide the necessary material on which long-term policy could be based.'[52]

Two further results of the party's renewed interest in policy formulation and political education were the revivification of the Research Department and the creation of the Conservative Political Centre. The Research Department, established at 24 Old Queen Street in 1929 with Sir Keith Ball and Henry Brooke as joint-directors, was the inspiration of Neville Chamberlain. The party's ill-preparedness for the general elections of 1923 and 1929 had convinced Chamberlain that the party required the services of a body of thinkers independent of the Civil Service. Although the staff of the Research Department at this time was small compared to modern standards, it set to work on a number of projects – in particular plans for agriculture, employment, and tariffs[53] – which were the objects of legislation in the following years. At this time the Research Department shared with the Library and Information Department at Central Office the responsibilities for long-term research.

During the war the Research Department had ceased to function; but in late 1945 Winston Churchill decided to revive it and appointed R. A. Butler as its chairman. Mr Butler began immediately to draw around him a body of high-quality personnel – 'men of a different stamp than are usually brought into the party organization: university lecturers, ex-army officers, men who were setting out to be professional politicians' – who were to undertake with him a major re-examination of the party's policy. At the same time a Parliamentary Secretariat was established under the direct control of Churchill to work alongside the shadow cabinet[54] preparing briefs on day-to-day issues arising in Parliament. Meanwhile, the Library and Information Department continued a separate existence at Central Office. The Research Department, Parliamentary Secretariat, and Library were not amalgamated until 1948.

The Conservative Political Centre (C.P.C.) was established in December 1945, on Butler's initiative, 'to revive and extend the educational work which between the wars had been undertaken by the Central Education Department of the Conservative Party'.[55] Although the C.P.C.'s own publications describe the organization as 'closely linked with the Central Office'[56] and as a 'department of

Central Office',[57] Lord Woolton's assessment of its relationship to the party bears a closer relation to reality. The C.P.C. 'was independent of Central Office except when the bills came in', Woolton wrote: 'there was no connection between [the propaganda department at Central Office] and the Political Centre except through the Chairman of the Party'.[58] The C.P.C., also under the general control of R. A. Butler, was the most independent of any organization within the party structure, for in practice there was very little control by the Central Office over its expenses.

The C.P.C. was not concerned with duplicating the propaganda functions of the party's Central Office; rather it sought through its publications, conferences, and study groups 'to present the results of factual research and to stimulate discussion and ideas'.[59] 'The terms of reference given to the Conservative Political Centre,' according to C. J. M. Alport, '. . . were to create a system of adult education for the party and to provide it with the equipment needed to wrest the initiative of the battle of ideas from the Socialists.'[60] Because the C.P.C. and particularly its 'Two-way Movement of Ideas' programme was of some importance in the party's process of policy reformulation, further attention will be given to it later. For the moment it is enough to understand that the formation of the Advisory Committee of Policy and Political Education in November 1945 was the signal for several important developments within the party and that these developments had proceeded rather far by the time Lord Woolton came into the party organization.

At the party conference in 1946 the Executive Committee reported:

> Since the education movement of the party was restarted in November 1945, the area committees and about 120 constituency education committees have been formed. Area education officers have been appointed for eight of the twelve areas, and further appointments will be made this autumn as suitable candidates become available.[61]

Areas and constituencies were being encouraged, the Executive's report continued, to set up local C.P.C.s in the large population centres with the object of providing facilities for the training of discussion group leaders and 'to act as a focal point for local educational activities'.[62]

By this time also, a series of Area and county political education conferences had been held along the lines of the first post-war conference on political education which had taken place in London on 30 March, 1946. In a number of constituencies one-day and week-end conferences had been held. The Executive Committee announced, too, that the C.P.C. had made a survey of organizations interested in adult education and was maintaining contact in particular with the Bureau of Current Affairs, extra-mural departments of the universities and the Workers' Educational Association. In addition, the Political Centre had begun to make plans to open bookshops in London and other large urban centres – plans which had come to fruition before the next party conference in 1947.

It will be recalled that, in the two years before the end of the war, the Conservative Party had taken steps to create a new youth organization for young men and women between the ages of 15 and 30. Following the recommendations of the Palmer Committee the rules of the National Union were amended to take account of the new organization – variously called the Junior Organization[63] and the Young Conservative Union[64] between November 1945 and March 1946 – but finally named the Young Conservative Organization.[65] The rules of the National Union as amended in March 1945 provided for:

> A Central Committee of the Organization, to consist of:
> (1) the members of the Organization on the Executive Committee of the National Union;
> (2) the Chairman of each area committee of the Organization;
> (3) co-opted members not exceeding ten.[66]

This Central Committee was to act in an advisory capacity to the Executive Committee, and was to elect its own officers. In addition it was to have 'the same representation on the party conference and the Central Council, and on all Area councils and committees of the National Union as . . . accorded to women'. At the Area level 'a committee was to be set up . . . consisting of one or more representatives of each divisional branch of the organization . . . to act in an advisory capacity to the Area Executive . . .'. In the constituencies the divisional branch of the Young Conservatives was to be the basic unit 'entitled to one-third of the representation on the Executive Council and committees of the association'.

At the Central Council meeting on 28 November, 1945, the status of the Young Conservatives was reviewed, and a motion was put forward requesting that 'every effort should be made to support and encourage its activities'.[67] A few members were not satisfied with existing arrangements and moved an addendum to the resolution regretting 'that the upper age limit of the Junior Organization [had] not been fixed at 21'. After a short discussion the suggestion was defeated 'by an overwhelming majority'. John Hay, the Young Conservative from Brighton, then moved an amendment calling for a grant not exceeding £50 to be made to each Young Conservative branch or prospective branch from the funds of the National Union. His amendment was withdrawn after the Chairman of the Executive Committee, Major R. G. Proby, promised to consult the Chairman of the Party about the matter.

In order to put the new plan into effect a complete reorganization of the old Junior Movement at the constituency level was necessary to integrate the branches of the Young Conservative Organization fully with every constituency association. As a first step a subcommittee was chosen by the Chairman of the Party Organization to act as a central headquarters for the movement. Major J. Lillie-Costello held the position of Organizing Secretary for about a year. He resigned in March 1946 and was replaced by Lt-Col S. B. H. Oliver, who was then working in the Speakers' Department of Central Office. Oliver shared with J. P. L. Thomas, the Vice-Chairman of the Party, the responsibility for the development of the Young Conservatives in the following years.

Organizers were trained and made available to Area agents. Then the affairs of the Junior Imperial League were wound up at a special meeting of the existing members under the chairmanship of Lord Dunglass (now Sir Alec Douglas-Home). The next move was to appoint a leader in each provincial Area whose main object was to create Young Conservative activity in the constituencies. But these leaders were deliberately to make no attempt to develop large branches, for it was felt that the first essential 'was to form efficient branches of working members who, in their turn, were prepared to develop their own branches on sound political lines in the constituencies'.[68] Secondly, the object was to form a Co-ordinating Committee in each Area, and then to appoint a Central Committee to advise the Executive Committee on Young Conservative activity.

By July 1946, all Area advisory committees of the organization had been created, and a meeting was held on the sixth of the month to elect a Central Committee. Anthony Eden was chosen President, Anthony Nutting Chairman, and Peter Welch Vice-Chairman. This election was solely a matter for the representatives of the youth organization from the Areas, although Mr Eden had already been asked in advance by J. P. L. Thomas and Anthony Nutting's election was undoubtedly 'inspired' by Central Office. Thomas presided at the first meeting, and reviewed the work of the organization during the past year. He was able to announce that 'a Co-ordinating Committee had been formed in each of the 12 Areas, and that there was activity in 429 of the 534 English and Welsh constituencies, with 795 branches'.[69]

The emphasis, thus far, has been on what might be considered the major developments in the party's structure which occurred after the general election and before Lord Woolton took over as Chairman of the Party Organization: the slightly diminished rôle of the Central Council; the interest of both the National Union and the Central Office in the politics of local government; the establishment of new bodies to deal with the party's quickened interest in trade union affairs; the creation of the important Advisory Committee on Policy and Political Education, with the related revival of the Research Department and the founding of the Conservative Political Centre; and, finally, the rapid expansion of the Young Conservative Organization at all levels of the party structure. The account would be incomplete, however, without at least a brief glance at developments at Central Office in the first year of opposition.

The structural changes were not as extensive as might be inferred from a comparison of the March 1945 and March 1946 editions of the party's publication *The Party Organization.* This is not to imply that Central Office was being deliberately misleading. The functions of Central Office as outlined in the 1945 edition were severely summarized; the outline of functions in the 1946 edition was meticulously thorough. The basic structure had not changed greatly, but a number of important developments were achieved before the end of the summer of 1946 and Lord Woolton's assumption of the position of Chairman of the party organization.[70] By the summer of 1946 a Local Government Department and a Young Conservative Department had been established; Eric Adamson, as the man responsible for the development of the trade union councils, had embarked on his new rôle at Central

Office; and the publicity and press department had been reorganized and enlarged. At the time of the general election George Christ had combined the functions both of the Publicity Department and the Press Department. After the election he expressed the view that the development of the propaganda techniques which had come with the war would require Central Office to give special attention to this subject in the post-war years. He also felt that a liaison officer was required to co-ordinate the efforts of the parliamentary party with the party organization. He therefore proposed to concentrate his own attention on the job of liaison with the parliamentary party, and that an appointment should be made of an official whose function it would be to plan and co-ordinate short and long-term propaganda for the party. On 17 January, 1946, it was announced that W. E. Bemrose, formerly a press officer, would become the party's Chief Publicity Officer, and that Gerald O'Brien had been appointed a press officer.[71] On 19 January, *Newspaper World* reported that H. S. Woodham, formerly of Kemsley Newspapers, had joined the Central Office staff as a special writer. Finally arrangements had been made for a greater concentration of the party's Central Office staff in new headquarters at Abbey House. The announcement of the party's acquisition of new accommodation came towards the end of June 1946. The party did not begin using Abbey House until mid-August 1946. Abbey House housed the main body of the Central Office staff, but Palace Chambers, which had been the party's headquarters since 1921, continued to be used by the London and Home Counties Area organization. A number of new men had come into the organization to perform long-standing duties: C. J. M. Alport had joined Central Office as head of the (Political) Education Department; A. G. Mitchell had succeeded E. T. Rivers as Establishment Officer; and Capt A. E. Entwisle (formerly a Conservative agent in Yorkshire) had come in as Central Office Agent. Some of the personnel who had been missing for the general election had returned to their old jobs, and those who had served at Central Office during the campaign had been relieved of the double duty they had been performing.

* * *

The description of the Conservative Party organization during the first year in opposition is now complete, with the emphasis on the chief characteristics of Ralph Assheton's period as Chairman of the

Party Organization. During the first year following the general election many of the most important features of the party's reconstruction had been undertaken – especially developments in the structure of the National Union; but there had been not inconsiderable changes at Central Office as well. It speaks highly of Assheton's ability as a Chairman that so much of permanent utility to the party could have been undertaken at a time when some sections of the party were cramped by doubts and disillusion and others fretted in sheer impatience to get on with the task of regaining political power. But it was Assheton's fate to have to stand at the sidelines and watch the Conservative Party organization grow to full power under his successor, Lord Woolton. For Woolton's genius was to strike hard and fast at the one factor which restrained the organization from the full development of its potential – the party's need for money.

REFERENCES

[1] McKenzie, p. 180.

[2] McKenzie, p. 180.

[3] McCallum and Readman, p. 2. See pp. 2–4, for a general discussion of the electoral truce.

[4] McCallum and Readman, p. 4.

[5] Council Minute Book, I, pp. 352ff. Twice in 1943, and again in 1945, the party conference was held in conjunction with the Central Council meeting. There was no Council meeting or party conference in 1944.

[6] Council Minute Book, I, 30 March, 1939, p. 336.

[7] Council Minute Book, I, 29 June, 1939, p. 346.

[8] Council Minute Book, I, 4 April, 1940, p. 354.

[9] Council Minute Book, I, 4 April, 1940, p. 356.

[10] *Reports to Central Council*, 4 April, 1940, p. 8.

[11] Council Minute Book, I, p. 357.

[12] *Reports* 27 March, 1941, p. 8.

[13] *Reports* 27 March, 1941, p. 9.

[14] Council Minute Book, I, 2 October, 1941, p. 369.

[15] Council Minute Book, I, 7 October, 1943, p. 395.

[16] *Wartime Activities in the Constituencies: Need for Maintaining the Organization* (London, probably 1944).

[17] Council Minute Book, I, 20 and 21 May, 1943, p. 390.

[18] *Reports*, 14 and 15 March, 1943, p. 20.

[19] *Reports*, 14 and 15 March, 1943, p. 21.

[20] *Reports*, 14 and 15 March, 1943, p. 21.

[21] *Reports*, 20 and 21 March, 1943, pp. 14–15.

[22] *Reports*, 14 and 15 March, 1945, p. 18.

[23] *Reports*, 14 and 15 March, 1945, p. 19.

[24] At the meeting of the Central Council in 1946 Ralph Assheton announced that he had accepted the recommendations of the joint sub-committee and that the Board was in the course of formation under the chairmanship of Lord Llewellin. The full membership of the Board was announced on 14 June, 1946.

[25] *Reports*, 14 and 15 March, 1945, p. 19.

[26] *Reports*, 14 and 15 March, 1945, p. 22.

[27] *Reports*, 14 and 15 March, 1945, p. 22.

[28] *News of the World*, 28 July, 1945; *Western Mail*, 31 July, 1945; *Birmingham Post*, 31 July, 1945.

[29] *The Times*, 6 October, 1945.

[30] *The Times*, 6 October, 1945.

[31] Tom Driberg, *Beaverbrook: A Study in Power and Frustration* (London, 1956), p. 302. See *News Chronicle*, 6 October, 1945, for a similar report of the meeting.

[32] *Daily Telegraph*, 6 October, 1945.

[33] National Union Central Council Minute Book, 1945– (hereinafter called Council Minute Book, II), 28 November, 1945, p. 4.

[34] Council Minute Book, II, 28 November, 1945, p. 3.

[35] Council Minute Book, II, 28 November, 1945, p. 4.

[36] *Central Council Annual Meeting* [Agenda], Wednesday, 27 March, 1946, p. 14.

[37] Council Minute Book, II, 27 March, 1946, p. 8.

[38] Council Minute Book, II, 27 March, 1946, p. 7.

[39] Conference Minutes, 1946, pp. 25–6.

[40] *Central Council Annual Meeting* [Agenda], 8 and 9 March, 1951, p. 9.

[41] *The Party Organization* (London, March 1945), p. 6.

[42] *The Party Organization* (London, March 1946), p. 6.

[43] Later Lord Cilcellin.

[44] *Central Council Annual Meeting* [Agenda], 27 March, 1946, p. 14.

[45] Conference Minutes, 1946, p. 28.

[46] *Central Council Meeting* [Agenda], 28 November, 1945, pp. 11–12.

[47] Conference Minutes, 1946, p. 27.

[48] Conference Minutes, 1946, p. 28.

[49] Conference Minutes, 1946, p. 30.

[50] Council Minute Book, II, 28 November, 1945, pp. 1–2.

[51] *Central Council Annual Meeting* [Agenda], 27 March, 1946, p. 11.

[52] Conference Minutes, 1946, p. 32.

[53] L. S. Amery, *My Political Life*, III, pp. 21–2, for a discussion of the influence of the Research Department on the creation of the party's tariff policy.

[54] Members of the Parliamentary Secretariat did occasionally act as honorary secretaries for the party's functional committees, but the practice did not become widespread until after the amalgamation in 1948.

[55] *Political Education Handbook* (C.P.C., May 1951), p. 3. R. T. McKenzie stated that 'the stimulus which led to the setting up of the Conservative Political Centre was provided by R. A. Butler in February 1946 . . .', *Parties*, p. 283.

[56] *Education with a Purpose* (C.P.C., 1947), p. 5.

[57] *Education Handbook*, p. 3.

[58] Lord Woolton, *Memoirs* p. 331.

[59] Richard Bailey (ed.), *The Practice of Politics* (C.P.C., 1952), cover page.

[60] C. J. M. Alport [now Lord Alport], *Objective*, January 1949, p. 3.

[61] Conference Minutes, 1946, p. 32.

[62] Conference Minutes, 1946, p. 33.

[63] *The Junior Organization*, November 1945, and the resolution on the 'Junior Organization' in Council Minute Book, II, 28 November, 1945, p. 2.

[64] *Model Rules*, revised ed., January 1946, p. 2.

[65] *Central Council Annual Meeting* [Agenda], 27 March, 1946, p. 13.

[66] *The Party Organization*, March 1946, p. 26.

[67] Council Minute Book, II, 28 November, 1945, p. 2.

[68] Conference Minutes, 1946, p. 29.

[69] Conference Minutes, 1946, p. 29.

[70] For a reference to the improvement in the general spirit of Central Office see *Liverpool Daily Post*, 'New Order', 17 January, 1946.

[71] *World Press News*, 17 January, 1946.

CHAPTER IV

Lord Woolton and Party Reconstruction, 1946–51

SO CONVINCED was Lord Woolton that the election of a Labour Government in 1945 meant disaster for the economic life and personal freedom of Britain, that (according to his own account) without waiting for the final results, he joined the Conservative Party at twelve o'clock on the day of the defeat of the National Government.[1] Seldom, if ever, has there been a more fortunate conversion to the party. For within a year the former Minister of Food had been invited by Churchill to take over the chairmanship of the party organization, from which position he provided the Conservative Party with the vigorous and dynamic leadership which was in part responsible for the party's electoral revival.

Lord Woolton's appointment to the chairmanship of the party organization was announced on 1 July, 1946, but he did not take over at Central Office until September[2]. He brought to his new job not only a great talent for administration and inspiring confidence but also a great deal of authority. He had accepted Churchill's offer only after receiving assurance of a completely free hand in the running of the party organization. Armed with the full confidence of the Leader, Woolton was always able to act with speed and certainty. As a result he succeeded in implementing a number of measures which would otherwise have been bogged down in the party's ladder of administrative decision-making.

Lord Woolton's first close look at the Conservative Party was a shock. It was, he wrote, 'the most topsy-like arrangement that I had ever come across',[3] and 'there was the strongest possible temptation to come to a sound business conclusion and tell the party that the best thing to do with machinery of this nature was to scrap it and start again'.[4] But compelling reasons caused him to delay acting on his original inclination:

> The truth was [he later wrote] that whilst it seemed, on paper,

> almost ridiculous to call this an organization, what mattered was not machinery, but people, and like so many British institutions . . . this organization at the Central Office had in fact grown up around a lot of very hard working and faithful members of the party, and in its decentralization was fulfilling the primary function of any good political organization by its work in the constituencies.

Further:

> The constituency organizations, through their branches and the branches through their ward committees, had the makings of an instrument that could get in touch with the voter. Moreover, this form of organization gave the opportunity for local enthusiasm and pride of competence.[5]

Woolton therefore decided that no major decision affecting the party organization should be made until he had seen the organization at work at the Blackpool party conference in October 1946.

This appears to be the last time that he gave serious thought to a major reorganization of the party structure, for, although innovations were to be made during his term of office, there was to be nothing approximating the scale of reorganization considered in his first months as Chairman of the party organization. There are, perhaps, two main reasons for this development. First, Lord Woolton became convinced of the validity of the reservations he had held before he went to the conference. For one reason or another he decided at Blackpool that 'whilst [he] might be able to create a political machine that looked better, that would be more streamlined and less wasteful of human effort, [he] might, in practice, lose the interest and drive that comes from the feeling that success or failure depends on the individual efforts of large numbers of devoted supporters'. It may be cynical (but not altogether unreasonable) to suggest that the Blackpool experience was enough to provide Woolton with a realistic appreciation of the relative unimportance of the *formal* organization of the party, and the awareness that from his central position in the party structure he would have sufficient control over the informal agencies of effective decision-making to achieve the results desired, without disrupting, and thereby risking the antagonism of, the party's traditional interests.

Secondly, and more important, was the emphasis (keynoted in Churchill's speech at the mass meeting following the party conference in 1946) on gaining new party members and increasing party funds. Members and money rather than party reorganization were to be the real challenges for Woolton – challenges which, as will be seen, he was more than capable of meeting. But changes in the structure of the party organization did occur over the next five years. This chapter traces the evolution of the party organization and assesses developments in the light of the general importance of party reconstruction as a factor in the party's revival.

WOOLTON'S FIRST YEAR

It is not surprising that as a result of the brevity of his tenure of office, Lord Woolton's rôle at the Blackpool conference was mainly that of an observer. But the debate on a resolution dealing with party reorganization provided him with an opportunity to develop two important themes, both of which were to engage his interest in the years ahead – the necessity of fighting local government elections on a party basis, and the need for broader class representation of Conservative candidates at all levels.

Woolton was absolutely convinced that however such independence from political machinery in local government elections might be the ideal, it was not practical. Socialism, he observed, had its roots in local government, and if the Conservative Party was to reduce Labour's 'bureaucratic control' then it must concentrate on loosening its grip at the local level as well. Moreover, he was aware that the organization of a Conservative machine at the local government level would greatly assist organization for national elections; for by the careful development of the marked register party agents could improve their knowledge of the location of Conservative voters.[6]

For these reasons Woolton threw his full support behind the efforts of Herbert Brabin and his Local Government Department at Central Office and the Advisory Committee on Local Government. There was, it seems, rather widespread reluctance among some higher party officials to embark seriously on the programmes envisaged by these bodies for the development of Conservative local government politics. But Woolton's powerful support made it possible for them to overcome the objections that were constantly raised. Indeed, it was largely as a result of his interest that the annual conference on local government, inaugurated at the time of the 1947 party conference at Brighton, came to realization.

Reference has already been made to Churchill's speech at the party conference in October 1946 in which a strong appeal was made for more members and money. This speech was, in fact, the signal for the party's national membership campaign which was to extend from October until the end of December. The details of the campaign had been planned before Lord Woolton assumed office. Special campaign literature and posters were prepared by Central Office, and a special booklet in the Party Organization Series was distributed in August explaining how 'campaigners' corps' could be set up for the recruiting effort which Lord Woolton has called 'Operation Knocker', and described as 'the power that revolutionized the party'.

The basic concept of the plan was that every constituency association should be responsible for the organization of campaigners' corps in every ward or polling district or village as an integral part of its local organization. The fundamental unit in the organization was the 'block' – in heavily populated areas this might be a row of houses or flats and in scattered country districts perhaps a grouping of houses or hamlets – which was to be the responsibility of an individual voluntary worker, preferably one residing in the 'block'. A 'district warden' was usually in charge of all campaigners in a ward or polling district, but in unusually large (or well-covered) wards there was an intermediate division, the 'group', overseen by a 'group warden'.[7]

The main purpose of the corps during the membership campaign was, of course, to canvass these 'blocks' and to enrol new members for the association. But the organization was also designed to perform a number of other functions for national and local government elections both before and during the campaigns: to distribute literature, spread propaganda, deliver invitations to meetings and social functions, to recruit active workers and helpers of all kinds, and, perhaps most important, to collect information for the association's 'marked register'.

This programme in the constituencies was combined with mass rallies in each and a National Rally held in London shortly before Christmas. The first target of the campaign was the enrolment as subscribing members of the local associations of those electors who voted Conservative in the 1945 election; then non-Socialists who voted Labour, and finally, 'tepid Socialists'.[8] Despite all these efforts, the campaign was only a mild success. 'Party membership has increased satisfactorily,' the Central Council reported in October 1947, 'though there is still room for further improvement.'[9] In all there were some 300 constituencies involved in the campaign, as a result of which only 226,000 new members were enrolled.

With the exception of the recruiting campaign, there appear to have been few striking developments in the Conservative Party's organization between the party conference in October 1946 and the Central Meetings of 13 and 14 March, 1947; the report of the Executive Committee suggests that it was a period of gradual development of the institutions described in the previous chapter. Nor were there any innovations of great importance at the Central Council meeting in March 1947. Shortly after the Council meeting, however, Lord Woolton made an appeal to the constituency organizations to increase their incomes sharply.

One of Lord Woolton's major contributions to the Conservative Party was to encourage it to spend large sums of money. With the assurance of a businessman experienced in the handling of giant sales promotions, he set about to reshape and improve the party's machinery for fighting the propaganda battle with the Labour Party. One of his first acts – even before he had moved into Abbey House – was to appoint E. D. O'Brien as Director of Information Services at Central Office and to reorganize (once again) the information and publicity departments. Thereafter T. F. Lindsay was appointed to take charge of the Information Department; Colin Mann was appointed Public Relations Officer; Miss Elizabeth Sturges-Jones was appointed to a new position of Women's Press Officer ('to maintain contact with the women's press and to handle publicity for the women's activities of the party');[10] and John Profumo joined the Information Department as Broadcasting Liaison Officer. Plans were made for the 'Trust the People' Exhibition at Dorland Hall in June 1947, and public relations officers (called Area Information Officers) were appointed for each of the twelve areas. All this cost a great deal of money – an outlay which, it is said, the party at that time simply could not afford.

But the Chairman of the party organization believed that the party's traditional financial arrangements could be revitalized to provide greater income for the constituency associations themselves, to free the centre from the need to reimburse the perimeter, and even to allow for the collection of a central fund through donations from the constituencies. Lord Woolton's emphasis on the need for the improving of the party's income at both levels was based on an appreciation of the scale and cost of political warfare likely (or necessary) in the post-war period and an awareness that once the old practice of members and candidates paying for many of the costs of running constituencies and elections was completely abolished, constituency associations would have to learn to raise the whole of their income through more widespread and efficient efforts.

It will be recalled that the Conservative Party had tried, before the end of the war, to improve its financial machinery. Early in 1946 the Central Office published a booklet which reviewed the decisions made at the 1945 party conference and Central Council meeting and made an extremely strong appeal to all constituency associations to concentrate on the business of collecting funds. 'Too frequently in the past,' the booklet asserted, 'many who voted Conservative contributed nothing to the party . . .'.[11] It decried the drawing away of the best agents and organizers to safer seats where salaries and party revenue were assured, and reminded all constituency associations that it was their 'direct and unquestionable responsibility . . . to raise, or endeavour to raise, sufficient money to ensure the provision of ample educational and propaganda activities in its own constituency area, and also to collect fighting funds to cover election expenses at parliamentary and municipal elections'.[12]

A number of methods of fund-collecting that could be or were being attempted with success were suggested to constituency associations in the booklet *Constituency Finance*, and in a series of appendices circulated privately.[13] The standard method was the well-tried monthly or quarterly personal collection of small subscriptions by door-to-door canvassing. Constituencies were reminded that 'before the war the minimum subscription to many local associations was only a shilling a year' and that 'this tended to become a maximum from people who could afford to give very much more.' The booklet therefore recommended a new minimum of 6d. to one shilling a month.[14]

Two additional methods of collecting funds, when the personal approach was not feasible, were the 'book scheme' and the 'envelope scheme'. The latter method, the simpler of the two, involved 'the enrolment of subscribers who contract[ed] to subscribe a certain sum monthly or quarterly, the supply to the subscriber of a set of envelopes numbered and dated in which the subscription [was] enclosed, and the periodical collection of these envelopes by the collector'.[15] The scheme was designed mainly for the collection of small subscriptions and had the advantage of saving the time of both the subscriber and collector. The 'book scheme' was more subtle and aimed at developing a body of subscribers willing to contribute annually amounts ranging from ten shillings to five pounds or more. The success of the scheme depended on the idea that contributors of this sort like to know what others have given and do not want to give less themselves than their business or social position demands. A book listing the names of subscribers and the size of their donations was therefore circulated to these contributors along with a personal letter of appeal. A banker's order form was to accompany every book to encourage subscribers to pay in this way and to ensure a permanent subscription.[16]

This description of the methods of fund-raising outlined by the party literature early in 1946 will also serve as an illustration, with only minor changes in emphasis, of the machinery of constituency finance which obtained during the rest of the party's term of opposition. The machinery itself seems to have been sound enough but it lacked inspiration; what it needed was for some life to be breathed into it.

In many respects the function of the Central Office *vis-à-vis* constituencies is analogous to Bagehot's well-known description of the functions of the British monarchy,[17] but within these limitations the Central Office, under Woolton's leadership, set out to give some energetic encouragment. 'Finance bulletins' to assist constituencies in overcoming difficulties with generally-used methods of fund-raising and for suggesting new methods were circulated privately to constituency chairmen, honorary chairmen, candidates, prospective candidates, Area chairmen, Area honorary treasurers and Central Office agents. The first bulletin providing examples of the successful operation of fund-raising techniques – Hemel Hempstead's use of the book scheme, Hampstead's one-day bazaar, the Barnet Division's profitable fête and the Cambridgeshire Division's ball – sought to encourage other constituencies through some sort of 'demonstration effect'.[18] The second bulletin depended more on sheer exhortation. 'Before it is too late,' it warned, 'the Conservative Party has got to revise its ideas on the question of association incomes; it has got to realize that these incomes today are too little and that the contributors are too few.' 'We must try,' it further announced, 'by every means, in speeches, in the press, in our local publications and leaflets, and in our personal contacts with other people, to make it clear that the days of "too little and too few" are over.'[19]

Lord Woolton's first demand on the machinery of constituency finance – his request that all constituency associations should aim at a target of from £2,000 to £3,000, a year – appears to have left some constituency officers gasping, for it seems that 'only a handful of [the] associations were at any time achieving this target'.[20] Given the secrecy which traditionally surrounds the question of Conservative Party finance it is difficult to assess how successful constituencies were in meeting Lord Woolton's first major request. The report of the Central Council to the party conference in October 1947 stated merely that:

> The Chairman of the party organization has called on associations to aim at a target of £2,000 to £3,000 as their necessary income. While it is still beyond the reach of many associations, an increasing number are attaining to it, or are at least in sight of it.[21]

* * *

Lord Woolton's first year as Chairman of the party organization was one of limited achievement. The recruiting campaign was, measured by later campaigns at least, a failure, and the drive to improve the financial position of the party's constituency associations appeared to be labouring against the built-in inertia of previous decades. Except for the expansion of the publicity organs at Central Office there were few important developments in the party structure. By the time the Brighton conference was held in 1947 a Central Trade Union Advisory Committee had been established, replacing the older Central Labour Advisory Board, and, in response to a demand from certain teachers, a Conservative and Unionist

Teachers Association had been formed (in March 1947) 'to advise the party generally on matters relating to education and the teaching profession';[22] but the two main projects of the period – the recruiting campaign and the income appeal – were effected without any need to modify the existing machinery. Considerable progress was, however, made with the recruitment and training of party agents and organizers. With justifiable pride it was reported to the Brighton conference that:

> There are more certified agents and organizers employed by the party than at any time in its history. Since November 1945, 160 agents and 69 organizers have been recruited and trained and have obtained the certificate of the Examination Board. In addition there are about 70 men and women now in training and the supply of certificated workers should meet the demand.[23]

The constituency associations had hardly recovered from the shock of Lord Woolton's request for the raising of higher incomes when he confronted the party again, this time at the Brighton conference, with the demand for £1,000,000 for the party's central funds. Money had been spent liberally at Central Office in the first year of Lord Woolton's chairmanship – by his own admission the party was actually overspending five times its resources[24] – and some means had to be found quickly of filling the party's coffers. Woolton therefore decided on a national appeal. He was strongly advised that such an appeal must succeed; that another failure for a defeated party might mean disaster, and that for this reason the appeal should aim at a fairly modest target – say £250,000. Woolton favoured a more dramatic attempt – 'shock tactics' as he called it – to provide the party with 'the thrill of high endeavour'.[25] Lord Woolton's idea prevailed, and during the debate on the resolution stating 'that this conference considers that constituency associations should be asked to accept some responsibility for contributing to the central funds of the party',[26] he announced his request for £1,000,000, adding that he had obtained the 'support and approval' of the area chairmen for his attempt to secure 'the financial stability at the centre. . . .'

Woolton's bold plan was a master stroke. Not only was the full amount raised by the end of the year, but it also had the effect of greatly enhancing his reputation with the party in the country, raising the hopes of a slightly dispirited organization and providing it with a profound sense of accomplishment. The success of the appeal was a key point in the party's recovery, for, as Woolton recorded in his memoirs:

> It . . . was the beginning of a long trail of hard individual work done by the rank and file of the party, who not only gave their time to go canvassing, but trained themselves to do well. The party members throughout the country began to realize that it was not the large public meetings addressed by important people that would be the predominant factor in winning the election, but the advocacy of people who, combining personal friendliness and their approach to individuals with a sense of high national purpose . . . took these things to the houses of the voters.[27]

The effects of the successful national appeal for party funds carried over into the appeal begun in April 1948, for a million new party members. The national recruiting campaign in 1946 had added some 226,000 members to the party. At the end of 1947 party membership had reached a total of 1,200,000, and it was from this position that the party set out in April 1948, to fulfil Lord Woolton's request for another million by 30 June, 1948. This time the recruiting campaign was much more successful: 429 constituency associations participated in the effort which added 1,049,000 members to the party by the campaign deadline.[28] At the end of June 1948, the membership of the Conservative Party stood at 2,249,031.[29] (Thereafter party membership grew very slowly; by the time the party regained power in 1951 the membership had increased by less than 500,000.)

REPORTS AND REORGANIZATION: 1948–49

I

When the party conference in 1947 passed the resolution calling for the collection of central funds for the party in the constituencies, it was doing more than giving permission for Lord Woolton's Fighting Fund. As the first speaker in the debate pointed out, the resolution which he was putting forward was designed 'to take a long-term view, and to place . . . the financial structure of the party on a permanently satisfactory footing'.[30] The conference, in accepting the resolution, did not settle the details of the collection of such a central fund but accepted the broad principles and left the rest up to Lord Woolton. Woolton was not long in acting, and the Central Council was informed in March 1948 that a committee had been appointed to consider how effect might be given to the conference's long-term proposal.[31]

Lord Woolton shared his predecessor's concern over the extent to which the free selection of parliamentary candidates was being hindered by the insistence of some constituency associations on financial contributions (sometimes substantial ones[32]) from candidates or prospective candidates. Not only was he disturbed by the fact that the Conservative Party could not be regarded as classless if working men could not afford to stand as candidates, but also because he had noticed that 'the organization was weakest in those places where a wealthy candidate had made it unnecessary for the members to trouble to collect small subscriptions'.[33] For these reasons he decided to put the problem to the Executive Committee and asked it for a committee to advise on the question. In this action Lord Woolton was also following the lead given at the 1947 party conference. The Brighton Conference had passed a resolution which requested the Executive Committee 'to examine the possibility of reducing still further the maximum contribution which candidates may make towards election expenses, and the maximum subscriptions which M.P.s and candidates may pay to their constituency associations'.[34] The Executive Committee acted promptly on this resolution as well and reported to the Central Council meeting on 17 March, 1948, that it had also set up a sub-committee to look into the problem of the financial arrangements of candidates. It was further announced at this time that: 'on receipt of the report of the Sub-committee on Party Finance and the Financial Arrangements of Candidates, it was proposed to appoint a Special Committee to examine the whole organization of the party'.[35]

The results of these investigations were the famous *Interim and Final Reports of the Committee on Party Organization*,[36] reports which R. T. McKenzie has described as 'the most extensive review of the party organization which has been undertaken in this century'.[37] While this may well be true, their importance must not be over-estimated either in respect to their own effect on the party structure, or in relation to the other developments that have been described. However, the reports are of some real importance in their own right and must receive our careful consideration in all their aspects.

The sub-committee established to consider how constituency associations might be responsible for providing central funds for the party, the Committee on Party Finance, or Committee 'A' as it was also called, consisted of nine regular members, four co-opted members (two of whom were chairmen of the other sub-committees), a secretary, and a chairman, Henry Brooke.[38] According to its report, the committee used 'every means open to it for consulting the party collectively and individually'. Ten meetings were held between December 1947 and May 1948, at which oral evidence was provided by 12 witnesses including Area chairmen and treasurers, constituency chairmen and treasurers, officers of women's branches, Area agents, and constituency agents, the Treasurer of the Party and the General-Director of the Central Office. In addition, the report stated:

> A letter was sent in January 1948, to the chairmen of all 534 constituency associations in England and Wales, inviting them to submit any views they wished from their constituencies on the practical methods by which the Brighton resolution should be implemented and associations should accept responsibility for contributing to the Centre, whether by way of quota, capitation fee, percentage levy or any other method. One hundred and fifty replies were received.[39]

Suggestions were also called for from any member of the party through invitations inserted in two party publications, *Tory Challenge* and *The Newsletter*.

The Committee on Financial Arrangements of Candidates (Committee 'B') was rather smaller than Committee 'A', and met less frequently. In addition to the chairman, W. Robson Brown, there were seven regular members, two co-opted members and a secretary. Six of the nine members were past or prospective candidates. According to the report, the committee met five times between January and May 1948, and heard evidence, especially on the question of an annual subscription, 'from individuals whose experience [entitled] them to be regarded as experts on the financial problems of the actual or intending Member of Parliament'.[40]

There was also a third sub-committee, a Committee on the

Employment of Agents, set up immediately after the party conference in October 1947, which held its first meeting on the sixteenth of that month. The committee, established by the Executive Committee of the National Union (undoubtedly on Woolton's inspiration), was charged with the following terms of reference:

> To prepare a report on the status and prospects of agents within the party, the method of their appointment and the system of their employment; to make urgent recommendations in consultation with all interested parties, with a view to improvements and increasing the efficiency of the party.[41]

The committee, consisting of 11 regular members, four co-opted members, a secretary and a chairman, Arthur Colegate, met on nine occasions between 16 October, 1947, and 26 May, 1948, to consider problems related to the central employment of agents, their salaries, training, examination and accommodation.

The Executive Committee's intention to appoint a special committee to review the work of the sub-committees once their reports were completed was carried out in June 1948 with the appointment of a 14-member committee under the chairmanship of Sir David Maxwell Fyfe. After completing the job of studying the reports of the three sub-committees and suggesting methods for implementing their proposals, the committee was to go on with Lord Woolton's further request 'to examine the constitution of the National Union and the relationships between the constituencies, the provincial areas, the National Union and the party as a whole'.[42]

It was thought that the Maxwell Fyfe Committee ought to meet with the Executive Committee to submit its report at the last meeting of the Executive Committee before the party conference in October. Between the meeting called for this purpose on 2 September and the first meeting of the Maxwell Fyfe Committee on 25 June the Committee on Party Organization met twice. Without access to the individual reports of the sub-committees it is impossible to ascertain the extent to which proposals were amended or dropped entirely by the compositing process of the 'Special Committee'.[43] But, given the amount of time and energy spent by the Maxwell Fyfe Committee and the three sub-committees in studying the problems set before them, one might have expected a more impressive result. The so-called Interim Report which was produced by the Maxwell Fyfe

Committee in time for the party conference at Llandudno, contained very few *new* proposals of any great importance. It was, in many respects, a *post facto* formalization of measures that Lord Woolton had already proceeded with before the report was published.

Nowhere is this fact more obvious than in the case of the report of the Committee on Employment of Agents. The recommendations of the committee fell into three general categories: salaries and superannuation; training; and accommodation. The latter was dealt with in one paragraph: 'A number of constituency associations have recently bought houses for the occupation of their agents and we recommend that wherever the problem arises it should, if possible, be solved in this way.'[44] The recommendations on the nomination and training of candidates were almost as brief, and only slightly more novel. The Examination Board (composed of representatives of the National Union, the Agents and Central Office) were asked *to give full consideration* to proposals that the Central Office Agent or Personnel Officer of the Organization Department should approve candidates before they were nominated for training as agents; that the minimum age limit of 23 should be established for candidates taking the Agent's Final Examination; that the period of training should be extended; and finally, that 'as soon as conditions permit, a residential course, lasting for two weeks should be held immediately before the Agent's Final'.[45]

When the committee came to the subject of agents' and organizers' salaries it did no more than recommend that the minimum scales of salary and the scale of increment which Lord Woolton had instituted in November 1947 should be followed. The same is true of recommendations on the superannuation scheme. Certain amendments had already been made and approved by the Executive Committee and the Trustees and Management Committee of the Agents' Superannuation Fund, and Lord Woolton had already undertaken 'to provide from party funds the capital sum which was required to make the new scheme actuarially sound'.[46] The new arrangements had come into force on 1 January, 1948. The committee's report merely noted that a number of eligible agents were not members of the scheme, and urged all employing associations to give support to the scheme by agreeing to pay their share of the premium.

The report of the Committee on Financial Arrangements of

Candidates, although as brief as the former, had more point. 'We recognize,' the Interim Report stated, 'that the National Executive and the party intend that means should be found to remove financial obstacles which prevent suitable individuals from putting their names forward and constituency associations from selecting the best men and women available.'[47] It went on to recommend that, 'after the next general election or after any by-election anterior thereto', the following rules should apply:

> (1) The entire election expenses of Conservative candidates in every constituency shall be the responsibility of the constituency associations (including, in suitable cases, the candidate's personal expenses during the election not exceeding £100), and no subscription shall be made directly or indirectly by the candidate to the fund for the statutory election expenses.
>
> (2) It shall be the responsibility of each constituency association to make annual appropriations to an Election Fighting Fund to cover all election campaign expenses in the constituency.
>
> (3) Constituency associations shall be permitted to apply for grants from the party's central fund on strict proof that they have made every effort to raise sufficient funds to meet their election expenses. This fund should be replenished by a national appeal to the whole of the party. Candidates and associations included, to contribute according to their means before each general election.
>
> (4) With regard to election campaign payments, the Agent's fee shall be paid out of the funds placed at the disposal of the candidate by the association.
>
> (5) Candidates may, by arrangement with their constituency associations, make nominal subscriptions each year, but the subscriptions must in no case exceed £25; the annual subscription of Members of Parliament to their associations shall in no case exceed £50.
>
> (6) In no circumstances shall the question of an annual subscription be mentioned by any constituency selection committee to any candidate before he has been selected.
>
> (7) Notwithstanding the proviso with which these recommendations are preceded, these recommendations shall apply forthwith in any constituency where a new candidate is selected after 31 December, 1948.[48]

This section of the Interim Report ended by noting that the sub-committee had recommended that 'Conservative candidates for local elections should be as completely relieved as parliamentary candidates'. But the Maxwell Fyfe Committee chose to state only that it considered that 'the recommendation should receive very careful attention from the Local Government Committee of the Party'.[49]

Lord Woolton has recorded in his memoirs 'that the committee reported even more drastically than [he] dared to hope',[50] but it is difficult to appreciate the basis of his surprise. In the first place, the Special Committee was headed by a chairman, picked by Lord Woolton himself, whom he knew shared completely his views on the problem of financial limitations on candidates. Secondly, even if the chairman had not had Maxwell Fyfe's strong pre-disposition, the trend of opinion in the party from well before the end of the war would certainly have indicated that the formal reduction of all financial barriers to candidature for the party was imminent.[51]

Lord Woolton was, of course, delighted with the results of the committee's report. 'The change was revolutionary,' he wrote; 'and in my view did more than any single factor to save the Conservative Party.'[52] There is some natural reluctance to dispute the obviously genuine opinion of a man who was at the centre of the Conservative organization during the party's years of opposition; yet, if Lord Woolton meant by his remark that the party was saved because the freeing of candidates from financial burdens made possible the infusion of a new type of candidate – working-class candidates – whose appeal was therefore greater to the general public, there is room for doubt about the correctness of his conclusions.

As far as the 1950 general election was concerned – the election in which the bulk of the Conservative Party's recovery was realized – very few of the candidates were chosen after the recommendations of the Maxwell Fyfe Report came into effect; for, as Henry Brooke assured the conference in October 1948, 'this scheme [would] not operate in the vast majority of constituencies until after the next general election, because they [had] already chosen their candidates'.[53] Even at the general election the following year the effect of the report was minimal. In a great number of cases the candidates in 1951 were the same as those chosen for the 1950 election and would therefore have been selected by the constituency associations before the new ruling. Comparison of the class-occupation backgrounds of successful candidates in 1945, 1950, and 1951, suggests that there was very little change in the type of Conservative candidates chosen to contest seats in which the Conservative Party stood the slightest chance of winning.[54]

The real effect of the recommendations of the Committee on Financial Arrangements of Candidates was not so much upon the type of candidates chosen by the constituency associations, as upon the associations themselves. Denied the easy income traditionally provided by wealthy candidates, the backward, least efficient, constituency associations were now forced to improve their financial machinery in order to meet their election expenses. In the process more attention had to be paid to the routine functions of running a constituency association. In other words, the necessity of providing an election fund through the association's own efforts served to strengthen the organization of that association and remove from the party those pockets of inefficiency which had worried Lord Woolton before the report.

Finally, the report on party finance. The burden of Committee 'A's' report was to recommend – not surprisingly in view of the purpose for which it was established – that constituency associations should undertake to contribute, on a voluntary basis, to the general funds of the party. From this general conclusion flowed recommendations dealing with the need for greater information and consultation on finance within the party and the means of implementing the fund-raising.

The Maxwell Fyfe Committee agreed with the sub-committee that 'readiness to contribute . . . [would] only grow in proportion as the genuineness and urgency of the need [were] made plain', and concluded that 'the advantages of secrecy [were] outweighed by the disadvantages of failing to tell Conservative supporters frankly what bill they must foot . . .'.[55] It therefore recommended that the Treasurer of the Party 'should publish an annual financial statement – the exact form to be settled after consultation with the Chairman of the party organization, the officers of the National Union and the area treasurers'. The justification for such a revolutionary departure was the conviction that when the facts of Central Office income and expenditure were appreciated by constituency members the flow of funds from the constituencies would be more readily forthcoming.

Committee 'A' had discovered that there was a 'gap of some

£200,000 a year in present circumstances between the annual income of the party at the Centre and the sum which it ought to be able to spend . . .'.[56] To meet this 'gap' the Maxwell Fyfe Committee recommended that a 'quota system' must be established through which constituencies would contribute on a voluntary basis a certain amount determined 'according to local circumstances' but related to the general principle of the size of the constituency's Conservative vote.

The committee noted that, on the basis of the 1945 election results, it would be necessary to use a flat rate of 6d. for each Conservative vote to reach the desired £200,000. This figure, although it was the one reckoned necessary before the party's need could be met, was thought too high a demand at the beginning, and a basic figure of 3d. a Conservative vote was recommended at the outset. Later, this basic figure was to be modified by a complicated system of a 'ratio of Conservative vote to runner-up' designed to avoid over-assessing constituencies where Conservatives did poorly in 1945.

It is difficult to see how the Committee expected that the fully-operative system would yield anything approximating the stated gap of £200,000. When the modification formula was allowed to operate the rate for each Conservative vote might vary from as little as a half-penny (where the ratio of Conservative vote to that of the successful candidate was less than two in six) to a maximum of 6d. (in constituencies where the ratio of Conservative vote to runner-up was two to one).[57] Since a full 6d. for every Conservative vote was deemed necessary to fill the 'gap', it seems likely that the system as recommended would, even if every constituency co-operated, yield in practice no more than about £100,000. It may be that the size of the 'gap' was actually closer to £100,000 and that the higher figure was given in order to allow 'equalizing adjustments' to be made when the scheme was presented.

Nor is this the only surprising feature of the quota system. A very elaborate system of adjustable rates was provided for the calculation of a constituency's quota. The Area's contribution was then to be calculated by the addition of each of its constituency associations' quotas, allowing for some adjustment through consultation with the Treasurer of the party. Constituency chairmen and treasurers were then to meet with the Area treasurer to negotiate the size of the constituencies' contributions 'allowing for local circumstances', but under the general understanding that the Area's total quota would not fall below the figure reached by agreement between the Area Treasurer and the party's Treasurer. The quota was to be a very 'rough guide' indeed.

The Interim Report noted, but did not put forward as a specific recommendation, that 'the plan [would] allow for the basic figure to be reviewed from year to year, and [that] this duty should fall to the Treasurer of the party and the Area treasurers in conference...'.[58] However, the report did specifically recommend that 'no sanctions should be applied against an association that fails to reach its quota, except encouragement to do better next time'.

Finally, a number of recommendations were made the general purpose of which was to improve the channels of communication on financial matters both within and between constituencies. Perhaps the most spectacular of these suggestions was that the Chairman of the party organization should chair a meeting at the next party conference of chairmen and treasurers of constituency associations which would be addressed by the Treasurer of the party and at which the Chairman of the Central Board of Finance would be present. A 'general picture of party finance' would be presented and an opportunity afforded for discussion and questions. The report also recommended what amounted to an amendment of the Rules of the National Union – the addition of the constituency treasurers to membership of the Area councils.[59]

How important were the recommendations of the Committee on Party Finance? For all the report's pretence of careful argument, its central point – the establishment of the quota scheme – was a rather weak invention. Nor was the 'gap' which it was designed to meet a very challenging figure. The simple truth of the matter is that Lord Woolton had been spending more money than the Central Board of Finance could provide for the purpose. Money was needed from the constituencies, but since the constituencies could not be forced to provide the money that he needed, they had to be persuaded. Lord Woolton might have set about to get money from the constituencies by any number of means – he could have repeated his Woolton Fund appeal of the previous year. Instead he wisely had a 'democratic' committee established to achieve the same ends, which in the process set the idea of constituency contributions to a central fund on a formal, and therefore relatively permanent, footing. The compulsion behind the new method was no stronger than a personal appeal.

But the quota scheme was important at least in that it was applied and in that it did provide some permanency to the flow of funds from the constituencies to the centre where they were well utilized by Woolton's able propaganda machine. The same fate, unfortunately, did not await another important suggestion in the report. The key assumption of the report of the Sub-committee on Party Finance was, as we have seen, that the request for central funds from the constituencies must be accompanied by the provision of much greater financial information for the party rank-and-file, and this assumption was logically followed up by the recommendations of an annual financial report and a meeting at the time of the party conference of association treasurers to discuss financial problems with the party's leading finance personnel. Such a meeting was held at the time of the 1948 party conference, but the idea of an annual financial statement was nullified by the Final Report of the Committee on Party Organization.

The Interim Report is contained in some 21 pages; it makes 23 specific recommendations, seven or eight of which are of chief importance. Closer examination has revealed that some of these main recommendations were recapitulations of *de facto* party policy, and that another was not put into practice. The relevance of the individual recommendations as factors leading to the party's recovery have been discussed throughout. A broader view of the importance of the report must await the completion of the survey of the party reorganization in the entire period of opposition.

The report of the Maxwell Fyfe Committee was referred to earlier as the *so-called* Interim Report. Some explanation may be necessary. It will be recalled that the Committee on Party Organization was set up in June 1948 with two main responsibilities: to review the reports of the three sub-committees and to report how their proposals could best be implemented; and to carry out an examination of the whole party organization. Not unreasonably, in view of the enormity of the task, the terms of reference authorized the committee 'to present an interim report'. The committee and Lord Woolton were anxious that the recommendations of the three sub-committees – especially, one would think, the recommendations dealing with party finance – should be put to and considered by the next party conference. The committee therefore chose to use the proviso contained in the terms of reference to submit an interim report – based solely on the recommendations of the three sub-committees as reviewed by the Maxwell Fyfe Committee. This report was first reviewed by the Executive Committee who were unanimous in its support, then printed and distributed to the constituency associations for pre-conference consideration, and finally presented to the conference at Llandudno. There is some doubt, however, about the extensiveness of the pre-conference notification for some representatives at the conference complained that they had not received a copy of the report until 22 September, and others said that they were given access to the document only at the conference.[60]

The presentation of the report to the conference took the form of a resolution moved by Henry Brooke, Chairman of the Committee on Party Finance, requesting 'that the Interim Report . . . be considered'.[61] Lord Woolton had discussed with Brooke beforehand whether the committee ought to try to get the recommendations through at that time. Brooke was confident that he could do it. In a brilliantly persuasive speech he set out to review quickly the measures recommended by the report while at the same time countering the stock objections that he expected would be made by its critics. Despite the ambiguous resolution, there was no doubt that he was arguing for the *approval* – not *consideration*, whatever that might have meant – of the report. It is also clear that he was not above implying that the report which the conference was being asked to consider was only an interim report, and they would have another chance of debating the final report. At the outset of his remarks he argued:

> I am here this evening to move that the Interim Report of the Committee on Party Organization be now considered. This is an Interim Report. In it we say that there are further jobs for us to do. We want to get on with them and we hope to present a further report at the Central Council next March, and it may be that there will be other matters which will require a third report at next year's conference – I do not know. But this report is not our last word; it is our first. We have to go on to a special study how to increase further the efficiency of our party organization.

> . . . What we have here is an Interim Report that you will note is unanimous.[62]

The speech was briefly seconded by Mrs John Warde, a member of Brooke's sub-committee and the Maxwell Fyfe Committee, who emphasized the necessity of implementing the report in time to affect the coming election. In the general discussion which followed, those representatives who favoured reference back of the report did so, as Brooke later correctly noted, not on the basis of any profound objections to the recommendations themselves, but on the grounds that the inadequate pre-conference discussion in the constituencies placed an inordinate responsibility upon the representatives at the conference. Representatives had, they complained, no 'mandate' to take such action. The bulk of the anti-resolution speakers took this line and dwelt mainly on the recommendations of the Committee on Party Finance. Two speakers had minor complaints over the recommendations affecting agents, but these were not serious and were easily shown to be based on an incomplete knowledge of the facts. One speaker criticized the Executive Committee for accepting the principle of sanctions on constituency associations and wondered whether the rules affecting the selection of candidates would not prevent the party from putting up 'a really good mixed bag of the very best of all sorts, all ages and all incomes'.[63]

All but one of the speakers for the motion were members of one of the sub-committees involved in the report. Mr P. Livesey, a member of Henry Brooke's sub-committee, argued with compelling candour that 'there [was] no point in referring back these recommendations on party finance, because the report [made] it perfectly clear that there [was] a gap of £200,000 and there [was] no way of raising it except through the constituencies'.[64] The mailed fist had made one of its rare public appearances from out the velvet glove. But it was probably Miss Pat Hornsby-Smith's subtle appeal which was the most effective for the Executive's position. With gentle derision she reminded the representatives that it was their decision that had passed the resolution at the previous conference on which the report was based and it was their responsibility to see it through.

When, at the end of the debate, Henry Brooke took up his right to reply, he clinched victory with a move of extreme brilliance. After quickly dismissing the minor objections raised in the previous speeches, he came to his main point. With the exception of the plea for time to consult further, there had not been, he argued, 'a single major objection raised against the recommendations of the report, except certain objections from the Winchester constituency which as [he] sensed it, were not supported by the majority of opinion in the hall...'.[65] Then came the 'compromise'. 'I do not think,' he went on,

> that if we approved this tonight we should be taken as approving it in every detail. Obviously detail must be discussed further, and the first opportunity will arise at the meeting which Lord Woolton and the party Treasurer are going to address, of the chairman and treasurers on Friday, and I think that we should leave them scope for making minor adjustments if it so seems good to them.[66]

'But I do hope,' he said, drawing to the crux of his proposal, 'we shall get approval in principle . . .'. For, he went on, if the amendments to refer back the report were defeated, he would ask leave to move a new resolution calling for conference to approve the Interim Report in principle, 'on the understanding that no constituency was committed to the quota system until it had been directly consulted'.

Mirabile dictu, the amendments demanding reference back of the reports of the three sub-committees were all 'overwhelmingly' defeated, and the motion adopting the full report was declared accepted 'with a few dissentients'. The following morning the conference unanimously approved a resolution set out in the same terms used by Brooke the previous evening. How skilfully Brooke had guided the report through to acceptance! Without giving away a thing, he gained what could have been his only objective – the approval of the entire report in principle – merely at the price of the proviso that no constituency would be committed to the quota system until it had been directly consulted – a proviso which, if conference representatives had been more familiar with the contents of the Interim Report, they would have appreciated went no further than the provisions already clearly set out in the report.

It only remains to add that the Interim Report was a very special type of interim report. It was, in fact, interim and final report in one. When the conference accepted in principle the Interim Report of the Committee on Party Organization, it was the last time the reports on party finance, employment of agents, or the selection of candidates came within the purview of the mass party. It reveals an insight into Conservative Party tactics and logic that the Interim Report had no final report and the Final Report had no interim. Lightning, for the Conservative Party, seldom strikes twice.

II

Now we come to the much-talked-of Final Report of the Committee on Party Organization, the report which dealt with the constitution of the National Union and the relationships between constituencies, provincial areas, the National Union and the party as a whole. Despite its greater length – it runs to 37 pages – it demands no more space here than the Interim Report. In spite of its being based on a most intensive review of the party structure, the Final Report recommended very few important changes.

The Maxwell Fyfe Committee held 17 meetings to consider the problems placed before it concerning party organization. According to its account, it 'consulted and heard evidence from a great many officers, officials and members of the party at all levels'.[67] To assist its work, a questionnaire, accompanied by explanatory notes, was sent to all constituency associations. There are two matters worth noting in connection with the questionnaire. First, the response of the constituencies, although better than the reaction to the Committee on Party Finance's letter, was nevertheless remarkably poor. Replies were received from only 209 associations including the Central Offices of a number of divided boroughs. Secondly, with the exception of the questionnaire's very general fifth question – 'has your association any suggestion for improving the organization and arrangements of the party in any other respects?'[68] – the information sought by the committee was on quite narrow and specifically defined subjects. Constituency associations were asked, for example, whether the present system of constituency representation on and communication with the Area councils was satisfactory; whether they wanted any changes in representation at meetings of the Central Council and the party conference; and whether they had any views on the question of national membership. Indeed, when one compares the questionnaire with what must be considered the major recommendations of the report, it is difficult to escape the conclusion that these recommendations came less as a result of ideas expressed by constituency associations through the questionnaire than from opinions gathered informally from officials more highly placed in the party's organization.

It is unlikely that the committee's first recommendation – the establishment of a Consultative Committee on Party Finance – could have been inspired by suggestions from the constituency associations, since its purpose was directly to avoid the Interim Report's recommendation (which must have been welcomed by associations) to publish information on the party's financial situation. The Final Report recommended that the Consultative Committee should be constituted as follows: 'It should consist of the Treasurer of each Area (with the respective chairmen as alternates), one representative (with an alternate), of the Executive committee of . . . "The 1922 Committee", one representative of the Conservative and Unionist Peers, the Chairmen of the Executive Committee of the National Union, the Chairman of the party organization and the Treasurers of the party. The Committee should have power to co-opt not more than three persons whose experience and knowledge would make their membership desirable. The Chairman of the party organization should be *ex-officio* Chairman of this Committee and the Treasurers of the party should be deputy chairmen.'[69] It is instructive, in this respect, to compare the two sub-sections entitled 'The Need for Information' in the Interim Report (p. 15) and in the Final Report (p. 34) to see the extent to which the committee's enthusiasm for making information on the party's finance readily available to party supporters had waned. When arguing for the need for constituency associations to contribute to the central funds of the party the committee had been convinced, it will be recalled, that 'the advantages of secrecy are outweighed by the disadvantages of failing to tell Conservative supporters frankly what bill they must foot if they want the country properly governed', and had gone on from this premise to argue that 'the only effective basis from which to explain to Conservative supporters the main facts about party finance' was to publish an annual financial statement. The tune had changed, however, in the Final Report. Time, or pressure from the upper reaches of the party, had modified the committee's view:

> It follows naturally [the report stated] that [associations] will expect to have a closer knowledge of the administration of Headquarter's funds. The rank and file will also require to have a

> *reasonable assurance* that the money they raise is being wisely spent. This question inevitably arises – what machinery, *if any*, should be set up which will keep the party, as a whole, aware of the *broad facts* concerning party finance?[70]

The answer the committee produced effectively scrapped the suggestions made for the same purpose in the earlier report.

The Consultative Committee, as the Maxwell Fyfe Committee saw it, was not to be a budget or accounts committee – these functions would presumably remain with the party Treasurers – but rather it was to 'receive information', which in turn would be passed along with advice to the Treasurers of the party. There was to be no published financial statement, as recommended in the earlier report. 'Each Area, being represented by its treasurer or chairman [on the Consultative Committee], would be kept in touch [so the argument ran] with the financial position, would be aware in general of what was being done and what was required, and would have the opportunity of raising questions on any matters of party expenditure in which the area was interested or upon which it desired to make representations.'[71] The 'confidential channel' whereby financial information would be imparted to the constituencies, the report suggested, would then be from the Consultative Committee to the Area treasurers of constituency associations. The report added that 'although the Executive Committee of the National Union may be given a confidential report by the Consultative Committee . . . on the general financial position, such a report could not be published'.

At this point it is necessary to distinguish between the Final Report of the Committee on Party Organization as it was accepted by the Executive Committee on 20 May, 1949, and the report as it was finally passed with amendments by the Central Council on 15 July, 1949; for the question of the Consultative Committee on Party Finance is one of the few points where the two versions differ. The committee's unamended report had recommended, in addition to the establishment of the Consultative Committee, that 'a Subcommittee of the Consultative Committee . . . consisting of the party Treasurers and Area treasurers (with the respective Area chairmen as alternates) should replace the existing Central Board of Finance'.[72] But at the special Central Council meeting an amendment, moved on behalf of the Area treasurers, was passed negating the Executive's recommendation on this point.

> We recommend [the amendment stated] that the Central Board of Finance be reconstituted and consist of the party Treasurers, the Area treasurers with the respective Area chairmen as alternates, and up to a maximum of five co-opted members and that such Board have power to elect their own chairman from the whole body of members, co-opted or *ex-officio*.[73]

It is difficult to appreciate what, beyond innate conservatism, prompted the Area treasurers to press this alternative position. The Central Board of Finance would, as they demanded it, have the right (not specifically stated in the Maxwell Fyfe Committee's recommendation) of choosing its own chairman and of co-opting five members, but aside from these minor differences the Board, like the Sub-committee, would be formed of the party Treasurers and the area treasurers and would be *responsible to the Chairman of the party organization.* Whichever version had been accepted it could hardly be regarded as a major recommendation; so long as the responsibility for the party finance remained with the Leader of the party, minor modifications in the structure of the party's machinery to deal with party finance must be accounted of little importance.

The same applies generally to the new Consultative Committee on Party Finance. Judged in the light of its relevance as a contribution to the reorganization of the party – especially reorganization that might be expected to have some effect on the party's revival – the significance of its creation is minimal. The Committee's main importance is that its invention allowed the Maxwell Fyfe Committee to skirt around the problem it created for itself by recommendations in the earlier report, while at the same time providing a workable, if not very ambitious, method of integrating the machinery of party finance.

We now come to Chapter V of the Final Report and the recommendation to establish a new Advisory Committee on Policy. With a giant 'but' hanging ominously unsaid over the entire sentence this section of the report began by admitting that: 'A great deal of excellent work has undoubtedly been done by the Advisory Committee [on Policy and Political Education].'[74] 'We do, however, regard it as vital,' the report went on, 'that the powers of the Committee should be so defined [deliberately misleading word meaning "revised"] and that the party should have absolute confidence in it.' In the pretence of merely removing the responsibility for political education from the advisory committee, the report recommended 'that the Advisory Committee on Policy [*sic*] be reconstituted and should cease to be concerned with political education'.[75] What the Maxwell Fyfe Committee did in fact was to establish an entirely new committee – supposedly an advisory committee of the National Union, but in effect one directly responsible to the Leader of the party through its chairman and deputy-chairman and not to the National Union. Since the Advisory Committee on Policy and Political Education was in the strictest sense a committee of the National Union (with its chairman appointed by the National Union itself) the Maxwell Fyfe Report had the effect of removing from the domain of the National Union its one and only important advisory committee.

Changes were made in the membership of the new Policy Advisory Committee; there were also subtle changes in its powers. In addition to the chairman and deputy-chairman there were to be 14 members, half to consist of Peers and Members of Parliament, 'to be chosen by whatever means other than his personal choice the Leader consider[ed] appropriate' and 'half selected by the Executive Committee of the National Union from its own members',[76] and the co-option of up to four members. The report further recommended that Scottish and Welsh interests should be represented; that regard should be given to the geographical distribution of membership; and that the Committee should have the full resources of the Research Department at its disposal. The Final Report empowered the Advisory Committee to appoint from within its circle of membership any sub-committees considered necessary to deal with particular subjects, and also suggested the possibility, but did not specifically recommend, that discontented members of the Advisory Committee drawn from the Executive Committee could report their disagreement to the National Executive.

Only two specific rôles for the new Advisory Committee were recommended by the Maxwell Fyfe Report. The first – what the report called 'one of its main functions' – was 'to examine and either approve or disapprove documents submitted by [the] Sub-committees'. The second was that the committee should 'submit regular reports to the Leader'. What is so interesting about the first recommendation is that the original report submitted for the approval of the Executive Committee on 20 May, 1949, had recommended that the Advisory Committee should examine and either approve or disapprove *policy* documents submitted by the sub-committees; but the word 'policy' was deleted by amendment from paragraph seven of the chapter. It is difficult to imagine in the circumstances what type of document that was not a policy document would be passed on to the full advisory committee, but the implication of the recommendation may well have been that the consideration of party policy in the early stages of the policy process, which had been characteristic of the earlier Advisory Committee on Policy and Political Education, was henceforth to cease and that the function of the full committee would be merely to report on policy documents *submitted to it by the Leader of the party*. Whether this was the intention or not, it was not the practice, at least in the case of the preparation of *Britain, Strong and Free*.[77]

The reasons for the reconstitution of the Advisory Committee on Policy and Political Education are not hard to discover. The Maxwell Fyfe Report noted that 'what is needed is a committee so strong that the Executive of the National Union will have confidence both in its examination and in its approval or disapproval of all policy documents submitted to it which are designed to be published under the authority of the party'.[78] Referring to the strange ambiguity of this and the preceding sentence of the report, R. T. McKenzie has suggested that: '. . . one can only assume that it is intended to acknowledge, but not to refer too specifically to, a widespread uneasiness within the Executive Committee of the National Union about the activities of Mr Butler and his "back-room boys" . . .'.[79] Although theoretically the position of the Executive Committee was stronger under the former arrangements, the fact that in practice appointments to the Advisory Committee on Policy and Political Education were made on the personal invitation of Butler meant that the Executive Committee stood to gain in influence as a result of the new 'representative' composition of the Advisory Committee on Policy. Not only was the Executive Committee anxious to be brought into closer consultation on policy; the parliamentary party had also begun to feel the desire to be more closely linked with policymaking.

The changes which were made in the composition of the new Advisory Committee clearly reflect a concession to both points of view. Moreover, it may well be that Winston Churchill had in mind the question of policy creation when finally the party had been returned to power. It is not surprising then that he should have been anxious to have the control of policy formulation pulled tighter within his grip at a time when an election and even the party's return to power might be realistically contemplated.[80]

In order to complete the uniformity of the party's structure, with every Central Office body being balanced by a comparable unit of the National Union,[81] the Final Report recommended the establishment of an Advisory Committee on Political Education 'consisting of the chairmen of the Area Education Committees and nominees of the Executive Committee of the National Union, with power to co-opt'.[82] The report made no mention of the functions of the committee, but presumably it carried on the functions of the former Sub-committee on Political Education of the Advisory Committee on Policy and Political Education.

Aside from bringing the control of party policy-making more closely into the Leader's control, the abandonment of the Advisory Committee on Policy and Political Education and its 'reconstitution' as two separate committees was not of very great importance. The new sub-committees were not fully operative until 1950 – by the time of the party conference in October 1950, the Advisory Committee on Policy and the Advisory Committee on Political Education had both met twice[83] – and the great bulk of the policy statements developed during the party's period of opposition had been completed before the Maxwell Fyfe Report had had its effect. The final responsibility for the publication of any statements of policy, even in the hey-day of the Advisory Committee on Policy and Political Education, had still been Churchill's, and although the new arrangements may have acted to restrain to some extent Butler's independence in the examination of new policy proposals, it is unlikely that the change in the formal machinery of policy-making had any notable effect on the policy itself – at least in the short run.

The recommendations of the Report of the Committee on Party Organization dealing with the party conference and conference resolutions can be considered briefly. After a quick resumé of the advantages and disadvantages of a large party conference, the report went on to suggest three possible courses of future action. The conference could remain substantially the same size, and thereby oblige its being held alternatively in London and Blackpool. It could maintain the present representation and be held in different halls (possibly according to subject). Or, the constituency representation at the conference could be drastically cut from seven to two making possible the accommodation of some 2,300 representatives in a number of single halls in different centres throughout the country. The report estimated that the theoretical attendence under this arrangement would be 2,820, but that in practice allowance for the absence of a number of Peers, Members of Parliament, candidates, and agents would bring the figure closer to 2,300.[84] Although the committee's preference for the latter solution was scarcely concealed, it did not recommend this course of action to the conference. Rather it recommended that the 1950 party conference, mindful of the possibilities outlined, should discuss the question and make recommendations to the Executive Committee. 'If any alteration to the rules governing representation at the conference then became necessary, such alteration should be carried out at a subsequent meeting of the Central Council.'[85] No meeting was required for this purpose, however, since the party conference in 1950 rejected any plans for reducing the representation of the constituencies.[86]

The Maxwell Fyfe Committee also apparently looked into the activities of the Standing Advisory Committee on Parliamentary Candidates, but did not recommend any changes in its composition or functions. The report did draw attention to what it considered a regrettable tendency since 1945 – namely, that instead of drawing their candidates from a list of names already approved by the Standing Advisory Committee, many associations had developed the practice of adopting candidates and subsequently seeking their endorsement. On the basis of this observation the Maxwell Fyfe Committee made a recommendation, the exact form of which differs in the final version (because of a subsequent amendment at the Council meeting of 15 July, 1949) from the one approved by the Executive Committee.

The original recommendation of the Maxwell Fyfe Committee had read as follows:

We recommend that the party should revert as soon as possible

> to the principle of all candidates being approved by the Standing Advisory Committee before their names are submitted to constituency association selection committees. If this recommendation is approved, all constituency association selection committees will be provided on request with a list of approved candidates. A constituency selection committee is entitled to recommend someone not already on the list, but, in that case, it will be the duty of the association, before actual adoption, to see that the candidate receives the approval of the Standing Advisory Committee and so is recognized as an official Conservative prospective candidate.[87]

But an amendment moved on behalf of the Yorkshire Provincial Area had the effect of lessening, to some extent, the urgency and positiveness of the Maxwell Fyfe Committee's version.

> We recommend [the final version of the report was modified to state] that candidates should be approved by the Standing Advisory Committee before their names are submitted to constituency association selection committees. A constituency selection committee may, of course, recommend someone not already on the list, but in that case, the association should see that the candidate receives the approval of the Standing Advisory Committee and so is recognized as an official Conservative prospective candidate before adoption as prospective candidate takes place.[88]

What is perhaps the most important recommendation of the Final Report appears in Chapter XI, 'Miscellaneous Remarks and Recommendations'. It will be recalled that the Interim Report had considered the question of relieving local government candidates of election expenses but had contented itself merely with the comment that the recommendation should receive very careful attention from the Party's Local Government Committee. In the Final Report the Committee faced up to the problem more boldly. It recommended 'universal adoption by constituency associations of the basic principle that no one who [was] qualified on merit to give useful service in local government should be debarred or in any way hindered from adoption as a Conservative candidate through being unable to pay the whole or part of the election expense'.[89] The committee appreciated, however, that 'to rule that no contributions whatever towards election expenses were to be received from local government candidates would place an unnecessary financial burden on constituency associations, which many of them would be unable to bear'. The committee therefore recommended that 'the question of the extent or form of the assistance afforded to candidates . . . by constituency associations must . . . be a matter for decision by the associations themselves'.

The committee was not prepared to let associations get off too lightly with excuses that they lacked the funds necessary to absorb reductions in payments by the candidates, for the report went on further to recommend a means of providing for such election expenditures:

> Associations should adopt the practice of making public appeals for fighting funds for local government elections, and it should be a point of honour among local people to see that the candidates . . . are not called upon to give more generously of their money than ordinary, loyal members of the party who are not candidates would be prepared to do. If any association, even after making a public appeal, finds insuperable difficulty in financing an adequate campaign for the local government elections from its own resources, its wisest course will be to consult with the area treasurer. But this should seldom be necessary.[90]

Representatives at the Central Council meeting called to accept the report were not completely satisfied with this last recommendation as it stood in the committee's report, although the exact nature of the objections are not revealed by the minutes taken on that occasion.[91] At any rate, as a result of such objections, it was agreed to amend the paragraph quoted above by changing the opening sentence to read: 'Associations should, *where necessary*, adopt the practice of making appeals for fighting funds for local government elections', and to delete the words 'even after making a public appeal' later in the paragraph.[92] The effect of this amendment was to lessen to some extent the universality of application of the recommendation and thereby leave constituency associations free to work out the financing of local elections in their own way.

The Final Report of the Committee on Party Organization was approved by the Executive Committee on 20 May, 1949, and was then put to a special meeting of the Central Council on 15 July, 1949, for final consideration. Attendance at the meeting was somewhat smaller than at other Central Council meetings in the post-war period, there being 536 representatives at the morning session and 478 at the afternoon.[93] It may be that some representatives were aware (as indeed many party people seem now to be blissfully ignorant) that the Maxwell Fyfe Committee's report had little of any great importance to recommend.[94] Even the five or six most important recommendations in the report[95] – with the possible exception of the one dealing with candidates' expenses in local government elections – were hardly of striking significance in their overall effect on the party organization. The most important recommendations – the creation of the Consultative Committee on Party Finance and the new Advisory Committee on Policy – were likely to have sprung less from the survey of the wishes of the mass party than from the advice of officials in the upper hierarchy of the Conservative Party. Important questions such as the functions of the National Union, relations of the associations with the Area Office and the Central Office,[96] and the appointment of the Leader of the party were apparently surveyed, but the report made no recommendations involving any changes in these fundamental factors in the party organization – changes which, had even one of their number been recommended, might have made the Final Report worthy of the attention and praise which it has hitherto been accorded.

The special meeting of the Central Council was opened by a general presentation of the report by Sir David Maxwell Fyfe. The report was then open for discussion chapter by chapter. Amendments were taken as they came up, and each chapter was voted on separately. Consideration has already been given to three amendments to the original version of the report which were effected at this meeting – the only amendments which were in fact successful. There were a few other attempts to change the recommendations of the report, which one now briefly examined, which can be taken as samples (the only ones we have) of latent objections – albeit of a small minority – to the contents of the Final Report.

Chapters I and II, the 'Introduction' and 'The Present Organization of the Party', neither of which made any specific recommendations, were, not surprisingly, passed unanimously without any amendments being put forward. There was an amendment moved to Chapter III, which dealt with the election of the Leader of the party and the appointment of the Chairman of the party organization. The report had considered that 'the present method of electing the Leader [was] satisfactory in theory and in practice'[97] and did not recommend any modification. Alderman G. Wilding, on behalf of the Cambridge Borough Association, moved the following amendment to the chapter: 'That the Council is of the opinion that the body to elect the Leader of the party should include a representative elected directly from each constituency association.'[98] But such was not the opinion of the majority of the representatives present, and according to the minutes, 'after a short discussion the amendment was defeated by an overwhelming majority'.[99] Chapter IV, subject to the successful amendment reconstituting the Central Board of Finance, was also passed unanimously.

Chapter V, recommending the reconstitution of the Advisory Committee on Policy and Political Education, and for this reason perhaps the most controversial in the report, was passed after only a very short discussion. The same quick approval was given Chapter VI. But Chapters VII and VIII, especially the former which dealt with the Area organizations and the constituencies, were not accepted without objection.[100] Brig.-Gen. R. L. Ricketts, on behalf of the East Hampshire Association, moved with reference to Chapter VII that:

> In view of the great importance which this committee attaches to independence for Area organizations under the sole responsibility of their own elected officers and similar in principle to that of constituency associations, it recommends that Chapter VII be referred back to the Committee on Party Organization for redrafting in the sense above indicated, especially with reference to sections 3, 4, 6(5) and (11).[101]

A short discussion followed at the end of which a vote was taken. The amendment was defeated, again by an overwhelming majority. On the vote on the entire chapter, the dissentients fell in line behind the main stream of opinion, and the chapter was accorded unanimous approval.

But the Hampshire Association was not prevented from a further attempt, during consideration of Chapter VIII, at cutting away from the Areas some of the power which the Maxwell Fyfe Report had granted at the expense of the constituencies. In reporting on the relatively minor matter of the submission of resolutions to the party conference the Maxwell Fyfe Committee had recommended that:

> . . . it should be made known that, whereas constituency associations should retain the unfettered discretion to submit resolutions direct to the General Purposes Sub-committee, that Sub-committee would pay special regard to resolutions which had been shown in advance to the Area council or Area executive committee and had been reported by the Area to be clearly and unambiguously drafted in all respects, so as to give rise to effective debate. We suggest that Areas should regard it as one of their normal functions to help to ensure clear drafting of resolutions for the annual conference, and where necessary, to consult with constituency associations or their officers to that end.[102]

The amendment proposed to change the recommendation to read as follows:

> We recommend that it should be known that constituency associations should retain unfettered discretion to submit resolutions direct to the General Purposes Sub-committee and that all resolutions should be judged strictly on their merits and dealt with on equality irrespective of the channel through which they arrived.
>
> We suggest, however, that resolutions be sent through Areas, who, before forwarding them, should regard it as one of their normal functions to help to ensure clear drafting, and, where necessary, consult the constituency associations to that end.[103]

Unaccountably, the minutes of the meeting provided no clue as to the nature of the discussion or the size of the vote. We can only assume from the fact that the recommendation remained unchanged in the amended version of the report that this amendment was defeated.

Chapters X and XI were accepted unanimously once the amendments discussed earlier were accepted; Chapter XII, which summarized the Committee's recommendations affecting the Executive Committee, was accepted after Henry Brooke's motion to add the Chairman of the Central Board of Finance was adopted. The Central Council then considered the report as a whole as amended and approved it unanimously. The recommendations of the Maxwell Fyfe Committee – such as they were – were free to go into effect.

FURTHER CONSIDERATIONS AND FINAL TOUCHES

At the same time as the committees studying the party organization were meeting and reporting, the slow development of the children's organization of the party, the Young Britons, was taking place. In response to a resolution from the London Conservative Union, the Executive Committee had decided in 1947 to revive this organization 'wherever conditions were favourable', and it had been arranged by the Treasurer of the party to set aside annually a sum of money for the Young Britons Headquarters Organization.[104] The organization, which had been formed in 1925 'primarily to counteract the blasphemous and seditious doctrine of the Communists by extending the teaching of patriotism to boys and girls who were too young to join the Youth Movement . . .'[105] had collapsed at the outbreak of the war, although its chairman, Viscountess Davidson, continued to sit as a member of the Executive Committee. It was felt that the need for such training of children from nine to 15 was as great if not greater in the post-war period; thus the Executive's decision.

But the reorganization of the Young Britons appears to have gone on rather haltingly. The Executive Committee could report to the Central Council in March 1949 only that: 'A Central Secretary had been appointed and branches were being formed.'[106] Plans for the further development of the movement, interrupted by preparations for the general election in 1950, were attended to after constituency associations returned to normal after the election; but the picture emerges that the revival of the organization had not progressed very far by the time the Conservative Party was returned to power in October 1951.

Late in 1948 a move was made to improve the efficiency of the party's research operations with the amalgamation of the Parliamentary Secretariat and the Library and Information Department of the Central Office with the Research Department that had been operating under Butler's chairmanship at 24 Old Queen Street. The new Research Department was jointly controlled by three directors until July 1951: Percy Cohen, who had been in charge of research at

Central Office, was left in control of information and publications; David Clarke took charge of research and administration; and Harry Hopkinson was responsible for parliamentary affairs. In July 1951 Michael Fraser became Director of the Research Department thereby setting the seal to the fusion of the three previously separate sections.

While the Conservative Party was in opposition the Research Department performed the functions that the civil service normally perform for the Government. The research activities of the department's various sections (external affairs and defence, economic affairs, home affairs, and general political affairs) were co-ordinated with the party's parliamentary committees through Research Department officers who acted as secretaries to these parliamentary committees. In addition, the department was instrumental in the preparation of the party's main policy statements. At the same time it kept Conservative M.P.s and party workers informed by means of a steady stream of publications.

One major development in the party's political education programme is worth singling out here for brief notice. In the spring of 1948 the Conservative College of the North – Swinton College – was opened 'for the training of Conservatives and others in the problems of present-day politics and . . . as the staff college of the party'.[107] Residential courses were held for the training of both voluntary and professional party workers, and week-end schools and discussion groups were regularly held by various Conservative Party clubs, groups, and constituency associations. The idea caught on quickly, and the Executive Committee reported in 1949 that, between July 1948 and July 1949, 2,000 students had attended the college and that 42 courses had been held.

By July 1946 the Young Conservative Organization had already formed nearly 800 branches. With the assistance of the Y.C. organizers working through the Area Offices the membership of the organization grew considerably in the following years. By December 1949 the Young Conservatives had formed 2,375 branches with a total membership of 160,433. A little more than a year later, despite the loss of membership through the 'wastage' of those original members who had passed the age limit of 30, the Young Conservative movement had increased its net membership and had expanded the number of branches to 2,494.[108] (The problem of wastage clearly worried the leaders of the Y.C. movement, however, and an attempt was made at the Central Council meeting in 1952 to get acceptance of the stipulation that 'Young Conservative Branch Chairmen are automatically [made] Vice-Chairmen of their Senior Branches as occurs at the Divisional level'. The motion was 'overwhelmingly defeated'.[109])

Young Conservative branches in the constituencies were formally linked with the membership of the association, and the members of the party's youth movement often provided useful assistance with routine constituency obligations. In the 1949 local government elections about 300 Young Conservatives stood as candidates, some of that number being successful. In 1948 the first of the organization's National Rallies was held, and during the next summer was begun the first of the so-called 'Young Conservative Holiday Weeks'. Both occasions provided an opportunity to combine social and political activities in a manner which was characteristic of the movement as a whole.

The party's appeal to the trade unionist did not enjoy the success of the appeal to youth. This was partly due to the fundamental contradiction on which the Conservative Trade Union Council movement was based – the attempt to use a Conservative-sponsored movement as an instrument for combatting 'the party political domination of the trade unions' – and in part, it is only fair to say, to the view of the Central Office organizers that a large membership was of less importance than a maximum number of Councils operating effectively in each industrial area.

The purpose which informed the actions of the movement as long as Adamson was responsible for its organization (which covers nearly the entire period of this study) was the notion that the Conservative Party should attempt to build up the resistance of wage-earners to the political domination of the trade unions, to preserve the 'real functions of the trade unions' and to assist and encourage members to become better trade unionists *qua* trade unionists. He regarded it as of great importance that the movement should depend not upon recruitment but upon voluntary participation, that the councils of trade unionists which it was hoped would be formed should bebased largely on an industrial rather than a constituency focus, and, indeed, that there should be no formal links between the constituency association and the Conservative Trade Union Council.

Given the situation in 1946 when the Conservative Party in the House had attacked the repeal of the Trades Disputes Act and the party in the country was waging a propaganda battle encouraging contracting out, it seemed more reasonable to appoint organizers for the party's movement exclusively from among trade unionists. These organizers were paid by Central Office, were attached to the provincial Area, and worked under the guidance and discipline of the Central Office agent. Co-operation in the development of Conservative Trade Union Councils (whose name was changed in 1950 to Conservative Council of Trade Unionists to avoid the implication of a clash with the T.U.C.) at the Area level was in most cases generous, but the movement received little assistance from many constituency agents who tended to regard the establishment of a council as just one more drain on the association's slender financial resources. No initiative came from Scotland for assistance with the organization of Trade Union Councils there, and little progress was made generally in the agricultural areas of England and Wales. By October 1948 Central Office was employing 20 full-time and two part-time organizers; 168 councils had been formed; and together with about 200 factory groups, club groups, and Labour Advisory Committees the Conservative movement covered some 274 constituencies and had enrolled some 6,637 members.

Over the next few years the Labour Department's 'establishment' expanded, and by the end of 1951 30 full-time organizers were employed by Central Office. The expansion of membership was, however, slow. Before Adamson handed over responsibility for the organizational side of the movement in January 1951 he conducted a careful examination of the membership statistics of the organization. As a result of this he placed the membership of the movement in January 1951 at about 12,000, covering 319 constituencies and possessing 248 councils. Considering that, according to one departmental estimate, the operational value of that membership was only about 25 per cent, it is clear that the numerical importance of the Conservative trade union movement during the years of the party's opposition has sometimes been considerably inflated. Yet it may be that in particular areas and in particular industries individuals made a contribution to the Conservative cause – by distributing party propaganda or putting the Conservative case at the shop-floor level – which transcended the slight numerical significance of the movement as a whole.

* * *

Although a few amendments to the constitution of the Conservative Party were made as a result of the recommendations of the Maxwell Fyfe Reports, other, sometimes more important, changes were made at other times largely on the initiative of the Executive Committee of the National Union. On 17 March, 1949, the Central Council brought the rules of the National Union with reference to the party's joint-treasurers in line with the practice of the party since mid-1948, by acknowledging their existence in two simple amendments to Rules IX and XIII.[110] At the same time the representation of the honorary treasurer of the constituency association was specified at the party's annual conference by an amendment to Rule XVIII (2), and the rule governing the annual conference, XIX (5), was modified to require 'a report of the Central Council for the past year' instead of an annual report prepared in the name of the Executive Committee.[111]

At the Central Council meeting of 29 April, 1950, a motion was put forward by the Executive Committee calling for the addition of one elected representative appointed by each provincial Area and the chairman of the National Society of Conservative and Unionist Agents to the membership of the Executive Committee.[112] The amendment was approved unanimously. Following this an amendment was moved by Stanley Bell, on behalf of the North Western Area, the purpose of which was to increase the powers of the Executive Committee. The resolution which was eventually carried with 13 dissentients made the following addition to the terms of the 'membership rule':

> The approval of the Executive Committee in respect of the membership of any such association (i.e. one which subscribes annually to the National Union no less than two guineas) may be withdrawn at any time at the discretion of the Executive Committee whereupon such association shall immediately cease to be a member of the National Union.[113]

The powers and duties of the Executive Committee (under Rule XIV) were accordingly amended at the same time by the addition of a clause enabling the Executive Committee to carry out such responsibilities.

Further amendments to the rules of the National Union moved by the Executive Committee at the Central Council meeting on 8 March, 1951, were in many ways more extensive than those passed two years before as a result of the recommendations of the Maxwell Fyfe Report.[114] Four representatives of the London University (Graduates) Conservative and Unionist Association, as well as the Chairman and Political Secretary to the Chairman of the Unionist Party of Scotland, were added to the membership of the Central Council. Three additional representatives of the City of London Conservative and Unionist Association were added to the annual party conference. The composition of the Executive Committee was also affected by a number of minor revisions: the secretary of the Central Women's Advisory Committee and the Secretary of the Young Conservative and Unionist Central Committee were dropped from membership, as were the Whip of the Scottish Unionist Association and the Political Secretary to the Unionist Whip. In the place of the latter two members, the Chairman of the Unionist Party in Scotland and his Political Secretary (both of whom had been added to the Central Council) were brought into membership on the Executive Committee. At the same time, two representatives of the Association of Conservative Clubs were added to the Executive Committee.[115] The rules relating to the advisory committees were also amended, bringing Rules XV, XVI, and XVII under one head (Rule XVII) and standardizing the names of all the committees as 'National Advisory Committees'.[116]

However, the most important change made by the amendments was the addition of further powers to the Executive Committee and the transfer of some of that committee's powers to the smaller General Purposes Sub-committee. Before this meeting of the Central Council constituency associations in which disputes or differences had arisen and which had been referred to the provincial Areas without reaching a settlement satisfactory to all parties had been invited to call on the Central Office for arbitration. But on Lord Woolton's suggestion it was decided that the Executive Committee of the National Union should take over this responsibility, and an amendment to this effect, which was put to and passed by the Central Council on 8 March, 1951, provided the Executive Committee with the power

> . . . to give decisions or take such steps as it shall think fit to bring about a settlement of any dispute or difference submitted by the executive council of a constituency association . . . after the officers of the appropriate provincial Area shall have failed to bring about a settlement acceptable to all parties to the dispute or difference.[117]

Although the entire clause outlining the powers and duties of the Executive Committee required redrafting because of the amendment, the responsibilities of the Executive Committee otherwise remained substantially as they had been. It is interesting to note that the amendment specifically mentioned the Executive Committee's power 'to recommend annually to the Central Council for election a President, Chairman and three Vice-Chairmen of the National Union'.[118] The *Rules*, before this amendment, had granted the Committee only the power (which it retained) of electing its own chairman; but in practice the Executive Committee had been making such recommendations for some time. The task of electing the President of the National Union, according to the 1945 edition of *The Party Organization*,[119] had been the prerogative of the annual party conference, and nowhere was that right officially controverted until this amendment. But the practice had developed, largely as a result of the infrequency of party conferences during the war years, of electing the President along with the three other chief officers of the National Union at the meetings of the Central Council. The practice of the Council electing the President continued unchallenged even after the war had ended and regular party conferences had been resumed. At the same time the Executive Committee regularly moved the resolutions dealing with the appointment of the chief officers of the National Union.

Although the General Purposes Sub-committee had been in existence since 1933, there was no specific reference to the body in the *Rules* of the National Union until 1951. The 1945 edition of *The Party Organization* described its function as handling some of the formal work of the Executive Committee which it was delegated by that body, and so its duties remained, officially at least, until the amendments of 8 March, 1951. But the size of the Executive Committee, especially after the additions of the Maxwell Fyfe Report and the subsequent Council amendments, had become awkwardly large, and the desire to transfer more and more of the work of the Executive

Committee to it must have been irresistible. In 1946 there were 103 members of the Executive Committee; by 1949 the number had grown to 133; after the amendments of 1951 the Committee totalled approximately 150.

It is a feature of the later years of the Conservative Party's period of opposition, and particularly of the period after the 1950 election, that the General Purposes Sub-committee played an increasingly greater rôle in the functions of the National Union. Between the party conference in October 1946 and the Council meetings of March 1947, the Executive Committee met five times while the Sub-committee met once; within the same period in 1950–51 the Executive Committee met four times and the Sub-committee three. In the year ending June 1952 the trend had fully asserted itself – for within this period the Executive Committee had met six times and the Sub-committee had met seven times.

The more frequent use of the Sub-committee as an instrument of the Executive Committee was accompanied by an increase in the size of the Sub-committee; in 1946 the General Purposes Sub-committee consisted of 26 members; in 1948 there were 39 members, and by 1952 there were 57. And in March 1951 the climax came with the addition of certain powers hitherto exclusively held by the entire Executive Committee. The most important of the powers transferred to the smaller body were the right 'to perform all ordinary and emergency acts on behalf of the National Union, except those reserved by Rule XIV to the Executive Committee', and 'to consider reports of the National Advisory Committees, and to circulate them to members of the Executive Committee for information'.[120] While considerations of size may have been sufficient reason for the removal to the Sub-committee of certain of the more time-consuming duties of the Executive Committee, changes in the rôle of the General Purposes Sub-committee may also have been motivated, to some extent, by the desire of the party leaders to shift the key functions of the National Union to a smaller body in which the parliamentary leaders might represent a larger proportion of a smaller whole. The change is consistent with other modifications to the party's structure designed to bring the major functions of the party more closely under the Leader's control in anticipation of a return of the party to political power.

THE 'WOOLTON REVOLUTION': A JUDGEMENT

Much space has been devoted to an examination of the major developments in the structure of the Conservative Party organization in the period from 1945 to 1951. Consideration of developments within the wartime period and concentration on structural changes during the year preceding Lord Woolton's becoming Chairman of the Conservative Party Organization gave a useful perspective from which to judge developments in the later years of opposition. The facts as set out here clearly show that the 'Woolton Revolution' has been overdone; the famous party chairman did not, as Wilfred Fienburgh once put it with more verve than accuracy, '[strip] the political machine down to its ball-bearings and rebuild it as a New Model Tory Party'.[121] Indeed, it is a striking feature of the six years of Conservative opposition that the main developments represented less a *reorganization* of the party than an *elaboration* of the party's structure in response to new or renewed interest in areas hitherto unexploited by the party machine. 'Reorganization' tends to suggest that old structures and methods are overthrown and new ones put in their place. But if one compares the organization of the Conservative Party at the time of the general election of 1945 with the organization in October 1951, the notable fact is not the differences in the bodies common to both, but the proliferation of additional bodies within the party structure.

There are, however, at least six developments within the period under concern which may be considered noteworthy *reorganizations* of either party structure or method:

(1) the reconstitution of the Post-war Problems Central Committee as the Advisory Committee on Policy and Political Education and the further reconstitution of the latter body as the Advisory Committee on Policy and the Advisory Committee on Political Education;

(2) the rebuilding of the party's youth movement and the subsequent rapid development of the Young Conservatives;

(3) changes in the structure, powers, and duties of the Executive Committee and its General Purposes Sub-committee;

(4) the revival of the Conservative Research Department and its later co-ordination with the Parliamentary Secretariat and Central Office Library;

(5) the virtual removal of financial limitations on candidature for the Conservative Party;

(6) the creation of the Central Fund by a new quota system.

If it were thought necessary to select the most significant of these it would have to be admitted that only the development of the Young Conservatives, the revitalization of the Research Department and the creation of the Central Fund were of real importance as factors *directly* assisting the party's recovery of political power – the first two being well under way before Lord Woolton became party Chairman, the last coming during his tenure of office.

It is worth noting that both the traditional demands of the Conservative Party in defeat – for greater representation of the party membership on the National Union, and for more effective communication between the mass party and the party leadership – were met in the period concerned. But the process by which this was achieved seems, in retrospect at least, almost accidental. There were no great battles over the issues. There were no resounding victories for the 'pretenders'. The demands were satisfied slowly over the first three or four years of opposition by the gradual development of new facets of the party structure which in their turn were accorded a place in the National Union. This was the essence of the Conservative 'democratization' of the party between 1945 and 1949; it was the expansion of participation within the party organization while preserving intact the traditional structure of effective decision-making.[122]

But, of course, developments in the party organization during the period of opposition did more than merely meet the requirements of internal pressure; many of the innovations which I have described were designed to make a positive contribution towards the party's chances of recovering political power. In this respect the effects of the 'democratization' are perhaps the least calculable, and the least important. At the same time the development cannot be dismissed out of hand; for even if extension of representation at the party conference and at other levels of the party organization tended to create bodies often too unwieldy for effective consideration and debate of party matters, the psychological effect on the 'activists' thereby brought a step closer to the seat of party political power cannot have been negligible. More effective communication between the party leadership and the organs of the mass party was in fact achieved, and the addition of advisory bodies at the local and Area levels along with the rapid expansion of the Young Conservatives created a large body of party workers who, largely under Lord Woolton's inspiration, were willing and able to make prodigious efforts on the party's behalf both at and between elections.[123]

Recent election studies have made us wary of giving too much weight to the efforts of constituency associations, remarkable though they may have been. A party's efforts (especially at times of general elections) at the local level are not as important as might otherwise have been thought. Indeed, these days, and the efforts of the Conservative Party in opposition are in a large measure responsible for it, a party's efforts at the national level through its national campaigns are much more important. Here the Conservative Party reconstruction assumes most significance in respect to its electoral revival. Here was brought to bear the full impact of the Conservative Political Centre with its political education training-courses, the Young Conservatives with their proselytizing zeal, the Research Department and Advisory Committee on Policy and Political Education with their newly developed and well-publicized policy statements, and, of very great importance, the propaganda machine of the Central Office capably directed by the Chairman of the party organization, Lord Woolton.

So much, and no more, can reasonably be said at this point on the relevance of the party reconstruction for the recovery of electoral fortunes. A final assessment of the structural changes between 1945 and 1951 must await consideration of two further possible explanations of the party's revival: the reformation of party policy, and the activities of the parliamentary opposition.

REFERENCES

[1] Conference Minutes, 1946, pp. 10–11.

[2] 'Crossbencher' in *Sunday Express*, 15 September, 1946.

[3] Woolton, p. 331.

[4] Woolton, p. 332.

[5] Woolton, p 333.

[6] Woolton, pp. 340–1.

[7] *Campaigners' Corps*, August 1946.

[8] *Membership Campaign* (C.C.O., 1946), p. 2.

[9] *68th Annual Conference: Verbatim Report of the Proceedings together with the text of Mr. Churchill's Speech* (London, 1947), p. 20 (hereinafter to be referred to as *Conference Report, 1947*). At the time of the Council Report, 'the latest available figures show[ed] a subscribing membership of 1,161,643 in England and Wales . . .'.

[10] *Conference Report, 1947*.

[11] *Constituency Finance* (London, 1946), p. 4.

[12] *Constituency Finance* (London, 1946), p. 3.

[13] *Constituency Finance Appendices 'A' to 'D'* (London, 1946), for private circulation only.

[14] *Constituency Finance* [booklet], 1946, p. 12. The revised edition of this booklet (April 1950), p. 16, referred to the minimum subscription as follows: '. . . nowadays there is a tendency to fix a higher sum, ranging from 2s. 6d. to 6s. The general feeling within the party is that, while it would be a mistake to dictate to constituency associations on this matter, there should be a genuine and widespread effort to increase the minimum to the equivalent of at least *6d. a month*.' In this respect the party was no more ambitious than in March 1946.

[15] *Appendix 'D'*, 'Envelope Scheme', p. 3.

[16] *Appendix 'B'*, 'The Book Scheme', and *Constituency Finance*, revised edition, April 1950, pp. 13–15. For details of election fund-raising schemes see: *Constituency Finance* (February 1946), p. 8.

[17] Cf. Blondel, p. 109.

[18] *How to Raise Funds*, Finance Bulletin No. 1 (London, 1947) [for private circulation only], pp. 4–15.

[19] *How to Raise Funds*, p. 3.

[20] *How to Raise Funds*, Finance Bulletin No. 2, p. 3.

[21] *Conference Report, 1947*, p. 20. On the difficulty of getting at the figures of Conservative Party finance see: Frank C. Newman, 'Money and Election Law in Britain', *Western Political Quarterly* (September 1957), p. 597.

[22] *Conference Report, 1947*. The annual report of the Executive Committee to the 1948 party conference noted that the Association's Central Committee had been accorded the status of an advisory committee of the National Union. See *Conference Report, 1948*, p. 15.

[23] *Conference Report, 1947*, p. 20. In May 1947 there were only approximately 150 full-time Labour Party agents in the country. Nicholas, p. 28.

[24] *Conference Report, 1948*, p. 77.

[26] Woolton, p. 336.

[26] *Conference Report, 1947*, p. 76.

[27] Woolton, p. 337. For details of the fund-raising techniques used see: F. C. Newman, 'Election Law', *op. cit.*, pp. 597–8, and 'Letter to Constituency Chairmen (England and Wales) from Lord Woolton, 15 October, 1947'. See also: *This Vital Year*, 64th Annual Report to the Members of the Political Council (of the Constitutional Club), January 1950, pp. 7–8, for details of grants from the 'political funds' towards local government election campaigns and in par-

ticular of the £10,000 grant towards the party's expenses at the 1950 general election.

[28] For details of the plan of the campaign see *Tory Challenge*, I (March 1948), p. 5.

[29] *Conference Report, 1948*, p. 45.

[30] *Conference Report, 1947*, p. 78.

[31] *Central Council Annual Meeting* [Agenda], 'Report of the Executive Committee', 17 and 18 March, 1948, p. 13.

[32] *Conference Report, 1948*, p. 36. See also above Chapter II.

[33] Woolton, p. 345.

[34] *Conference Report, 1947*, p. 28.

[35] *Central Council Annual Meeting* [Agenda], 17 and 18 March, 1948, p. 14. A third sub-committee of the Executive Committee was also formed as a result of a resolution at the 1947 party conference, the purpose of which was 'to study publications and other available information about Communist, Fascist, and other subversive organizations, to report on their political aims and to recommend methods of combatting them'. But the activities and report of this sub-committee are not relevant in this context. For its report see *Conference Report, 1948*, p. 17.

[36] *Interim and Final Reports of the Committee on Party Organization, 1948 and 1949* (London, 1949). Unless otherwise indicated all references to the reports will be to this edition which contains the Final Report as amended and approved by the Central Council in July 1949.

[37] McKenzie, p. 183.

[38] *Interim and Final Reports*, p. 15.

[39] *Interim and Final Reports*, p. 15.

[40] *Interim and Final Reports*, p. 3.

[41] *Interim and Final Reports*, p. 5.

[42] *Interim and Final Reports*, p. 3.

[43] According to P. Livesey, a member of the Committee on Party Finance, the sub-committee recommended double the quotas which were actually requested by the Maxwell Fyfe Committee's report. *Conference Report, 1948*, p. 41. One leading member of the Special Committee cannot now recall any other amendments to the sub-committee's recommendations.

[44] *Interim and Final Reports*, p. 10.

[45] *Interim and Final Reports*, p. 9.

[46] *Conference Report, 1948*, p. 15.

[47] *Interim and Final Reports*, p. 13.

[48] *Interim and Final Reports*, pp. 13–14.

[49] *Interim and Final Reports*, p. 14. See also *Conference Report. 1948*, p. 36.

[50] Woolton, p. 345.

[51] See the resolutions passed at Central Council meetings favourable to the idea of reducing financial barriers: Council Minute Book, I, 2 October, 1941, p. 367; 21 and 22 May, 1943, p. 390; Council Minute Book, II, 27 March, 1946, p. 8.

[52] Woolton, p. 346.

[53] *Conference Report, 1948*, p. 36.

[54] The Times, *House of Commons*, for 1945, 1950, and 1951; S. B. Chrimes

(ed.), *The General Election in Glasgow, February, 1950* (Glasgow, 1950), p. 38; and Nicholas, pp. 43, 44 and 48. Cf. David Butler, *1951 Election*, p. 36: 'The extent to which the Conservative Party was overhauled after its *debacle* in 1945 may be seen from the fact that 56 per cent of all its candidates made their debut in 1950 or 1951, compared to 43 per cent of Labour candidates.'

[55] *Interim and Final Reports*, p. 15.

[56] *Interim and Final Reports*, p. 16.

[57] *Interim and Final Reports*, pp. 18–19.

[58] *Interim and Final Reports*, p. 20.

[59] *Interim and Final Reports*, p. 23.

[60] *Conference Report, 1948*, pp. 38–40. *The Times* (27 September, 1948) carried details of the report.

[61] *Conference Report, 1948*, p. 35.

[62] *Conference Report, 1948*, p. 35.

[63] *Conference Report, 1948*, p. 42.

[64] *Conference Report, 1948*, p. 40.

[65] *Conference Report, 1948*, p. 44.

[66] *Conference Report, 1948*, p. 44.

[67] *Interim and Final Reports*, p. 26.

[68] *Interim and Final Reports*, p. 27.

[69] *Interim and Final Reports*, p. 34.

[70] *Interim and Final Reports*, p. 34.

[71] *Interim and Final Reports*, p. 35.

[72] *Final Report of the Committee on Party Organization* [approved by the Executive Committee, 20 May, 1949] (London, 1949), p. 12.

[73] Council Minute Book, II, 15 July, 1949, p. 2, and *Interim and Final Reports*, p. 34.

[74] *Interim and Final Reports*, p. 37.

[75] *Interim and Final Reports*, p. 38.

[76] *Interim and Final Reports*, p. 38.

[77] See below, pp. 204–7

[78] *Interim and Final Reports*, pp. 37–8.

[79] McKenzie, p. 212. Cf. *Sunday Times*, 'Conservatives Review Party Machinery', 6 March, 1949.

[80] *Interim and Final Reports*, p. 38, for the Maxwell Fyfe Report's reference to policy arrangements once the party was returned to power.

[81] McKenzie, pp. 288 ff., for a description and analysis of the realities lying beneath the report's naïve conception of the 'linked departments'.

[82] *Interim and Final Reports*, p. 40.

[83] *Conference Report, 1950*, pp. 14 and 17.

[84] *Conference Report, 1950*, p. 48.

[85] *Conference Report, 1950*, p. 49.

[86] *Conference Report, 1950*, pp. 72 ff.

[87] *Final Report*, p. 32.

[88] *Interim and Final Reports*, p. 54

[89] *Interim and Final Reports*, p. 57.

[90] *Final Report*, p. 35.

[91] Council Minute Book, II, 15 July, 1949, pp. 1–4.

[92] Council Minute Book, II, 15 July, 1949, p. 3 [my italics]. See also *Interim and Final Reports*, p. 57.

[93] Council Minute Book, II, 15 July, 1949, p. 1. Attendances at other post-war Council meetings were as follows: November 1945, 1,266; 27 March, 1946, 658; 13 March, 1947, 574; 17 March, 1948, 726; 17 March, 1949, 702. The figures in each case are for the morning session which is always the best attended.

[94] Contemporary reactions to the publication of the Final Report are interesting. *The Times*, 'Conservative Party Organization', 20 June, 1949, noted that 'no drastic changes are recommended' in a report 'concerned mainly with details'. The *Manchester Guardian*, on the other hand, found the report '. . . quite an impressive document'. Several reports emphasized the 'reconstitution' of the Advisory Committee on Policy and Political Education, the *Economist* noting that the reference to the work of the committee was 'hardly over-cordial'; but none of the reports noted the change-about on the question of a financial statement.

[95] A further, but less important, recommendation of the report was the addition of parliamentary representation on the Executive Committee. *Interim and Final Reports*, pp. 38–9.

[96] It might be noted, however, that the party conference in 1948 had debated the question of subjecting Central Office to the control of the National Union and that very little support indeed had been shown for the suggestion. *Conference Report, 1948*, pp. 121–3.

[97] *Interim and Final Reports*, p. 33.

[98] Council Minute Book, II, 15 July, 1949, p. 1.

[99] Council Minute Book, II, 15 July, 1949, p. 2.

[100] The report's recommendations dealing with the area-constituency relationship were all minor ones. See *Interim and Final Reports*, pp. 43–6.

[101] Council Minute Book, II, 15 July, 1949, p. 2.

[102] *Interim and Final Reports*, pp. 49–50.

[103] Council Minute Book, II, 15 July, 1949, p. 3.

[104] *Conference Report, 1947*, p. 15.

[105] *The Young Britons Organization* (May, 1949), p. 1.

[106] *Central Council Annual Meeting* [Agenda], 17 and 18 March, 1949, p. 17.

[107] *Conference Report, 1948*, p. 18.

[108] *Report of the Executive Committee to the Central Council*, 17 and 18 March, 1949, p. 14, and 8 and 9 March, 1951, p. 12.

[109] Council Minute Book, II, March 1952, p. 7.

[110] Council Minute Book, II, 17 and 18 March, 1949, p. 1. See also *The Rules and Standing Orders of the National Union* (London, 1949), pp. 5 and 8. Some confusion might arise from the fact that the numbers of the rules as quoted in this chapter refer to those in the version of *Rules of the National Union* published after the 15 July meeting of the Central Council which includes all the amendments made up until that time. The numbers of these rules differ in some cases from those referred to in the minutes of the Council meetings, but since the rules, rather than the minutes, are the more generally available source, it was

thought best to make all references standardized with the printed version. See *Conference Report, 1948*, p. 14, for reference to the appointment of Lord De L'Isle and Dudley to be Joint Treasurer of the party along with C. Holland-Martin.

[111] *Rules* (1949), pp. 11 and 12.

[112] Council Minute Book, II, 29 April, 1950, p. 1.

[113] Council Minute Book, II, 29 April, 1950, p. 2.

[114] Council Minute Book, II, 15 July, 1949, pp. 4–5.

[115] Council Minute Book, II, 8 and 9 March, 1951, pp. 1–3.

[116] *The Rules and Standing Orders of the National Union* (London, 1951), p. 11.

[117] Council Minute Book, II, 8 and 9 March, 1951, p. 2.

[118] Council Minute Book, II, 8 and 9 March, 1951, p. 2.

[119] *Party Organization* (1945), p. 5.

[120] Council Minute Book, II, 8 and 9 March, 1951, p. 3. See also *Rules* (1951), p. 11.

[121] W. Fienburgh, 'The Tory Machine', *New Statesman and Nation*, XLIII (31 May, 1952), p. 636.

[122] As a result of a resolution passed at the 1957 Central Council meeting a committee was established 'to examine the structure of the party organization with the aim of cutting out non-essential committees and in general streamlining the party organization . . .'. At the Central Council meeting the following year the Deputy Chairman of the Party Organization, Oliver Poole, informed the Council that he had received the report and that the committee had found that 'the general structure of the party organization did not require any fundamental re-organization'. Council Minute Book, II, 1957, p. 6, and 1958, p. 1.

[123] See Roy Vicker, *How An Election Was Won* (New York, 1962), p. 169, for praise of the rôle of the Young Conservatives as canvassers. See also L. D. Epstein, 'Politics of British Conservatism', *American Political Science Review*, XLVIII (March 1954), p. 40.

CHAPTER V

Policy Reformulation: The First Phase

THE point has already emerged that, almost immediately after the results of the 1945 election were known, many Conservatives, especially those most critical of the policy displayed in the campaign, began to demand a 'reformulation' of Conservative principles and policy. In May 1947 *The Industrial Charter* was published, to be followed by a series of further policy statements culminating in the party's election programmes for 1950 and 1951. The success of this process of policy reformulation has been widely acclaimed by leading members of the Conservative Party and is still frequently referred to by political correspondents as a major achievement of the Conservative Party during its years of opposition. At all events, the years from 1945 to 1951 are of great importance for the student of modern Conservatism for they contain the first flowerings of what has been called the 'New Conservatism'.

However, our concern is wider than mere description and analysis of the content of the policy restatements of the period; the *process* by which the policy was formulated – the policy-making process within the Conservative Party – is of equal interest. A fuller historical study of the policy-process within the Conservative Party has already been made by Dr Saloma, and it will be clear to those familiar with his views that my observations corroborate his. In terms of his theoretical framework the concern of this study with the policy-making process is almost entirely with the 'microcosmic' – with the interrelationships of power and interest within the political party itself and not so much with the wider political environment.[1]

What policy emerges from a political party is, of course, closely related to the question of who is involved in its determination. The six years of Conservative opposition provide an excellent case study of this interrelationship. There are a number of major policy decisions, each the product of a slightly different process, which can be readily studied, and the process of policy-making is more susceptible to closer observation when policy emerges as a result of the extra-parliamentary deliberation of an Opposition than when it comes down from the closed doors of cabinet and higher civil service.

To accept official Conservative descriptions of the policy-making process at face value is to explain away nearly all quality of the dynamic: the party constitution accords what appear to be very close to dictatorial powers to the Leader of the party in the matter of policy-making. But it is necessary to look beyond the Leader, to focus on an inner core who dominate the official and unofficial 'consultative-determinative' organs involved in the decision-making process. Here lies the main interest. There is, however, a third level of description of the Conservative policy-making process lying outside the 'formal' (strictly constitutional) and the 'real' (unofficial, practical) which cannot escape notice. It is what might be called the 'democratic-ceremonial' policy process. In many ways this level – the place of party conference and mass-party influence in general – is the most complex and fascinating, for at times it participates in the 'real' policy process by virtue of its being utilized (or manipulated) by a part or all of the inner policy-determining core or elite.

In an important sense too the 'formal' policy process *is* the 'real'. Great power is concentrated in the hands of the Leader of the Conservative Party. In addition to the power which falls to a potential prime minister (provided perhaps that potential is not a too unlikely prospect) the party constitution assures the Leader very considerable practical control of the party: the Conservative Leader, when in opposition, chooses his own shadow cabinet; has the ultimate responsibility for the formulation of party policy and the election programme; is not bound by conference resolutions; and controls, by what is virtually his personal machine, the main instruments of propaganda, research, and finance. Yet, as R. T. McKenzie has convincingly argued,[2] such powers, and especially the responsibility for formulating party policy, cannot be absolute; his position is more precarious and vulnerable than is suggested by the formal constitution, for he holds the position of Leader only so long as he enjoys the consent of his followers. A Leader of the Conservative Party cannot long retain power if he has lost the support of 'solid opinion' within his parliamentary party especially if at the same time his views on policy are rejected by the activists in the mass party.

In practice, then, the Leader of the Conservative Party does not have dictatorial power over the formation of party policy. Normally policy is worked out as a compromise of the views of the Leader, his closest advisers, weighty opinion within the party generally, and, in so far as it may be considered necessary or possible, with the consideration of the general wishes of the mass party. But the Leader's constitutional pre-eminence in the matter of policy-making does nevertheless establish the framework within which the policy-process operates. There was in the period from 1945 to 1951 very little questioning of the legitimacy of the process in which the Leader holds the final responsibility for policy. Even though policy might in fact be formulated at the level of the consultative-determinative core, and despite the fact that the Leader's own contribution to the policy might often be negligible, it was still the Leader's consent that was necessary before party policy could see the light of day. Publication of party policy statements required (as they still do) the Leader's consent. The Leader, in this case Churchill, had to agree to set his name to the party's official statements of policy and principles.

Obtaining the support of the Leader of the party for specific policy statements was no mere formality. Indeed, within the first two years of opposition, the question of whether or not policy statements should be produced and published was one of the most divisive problems the party had to face. How the policy statements were formulated and how Churchill ultimately came round to supporting their publication are therefore objects for close consideration in this chapter.

POLICY RESTATEMENT OR NO POLICY RESTATEMENT . . .

If the party organization was to remain the traditional scapegoat of electoral defeat, criticism of Conservative policy ran a close second. Almost as soon as the results were announced the cry went up, both inside and outside the parliamentary party, for a restatement of Conservative policies and principles. H. G. Nicholas has noted that 'Here . . . was not the familiar pattern of division between party leaders who want a free hand and the rank-and-file seeking a formula for their control. The disagreement in the party ran vertically; at each level were to be found advocates of either side.'[3] The cry was not immediately answered by Winston Churchill, and in his resistance to an immediate restatement of party policy he was supported (sometimes rather vaguely) by some members of his shadow cabinet. It seems fair to say that Churchill's objection and that of like-minded colleagues to a restatement of party policy was based less on deep-seated principle than on a difference of opinion over appropriate tactics. To Churchill's mind the production of detailed statements of party policy was 'to give a hostage to fortune'.[4] Accustomed to the idea that policy emerged as the acts of the governing party (which the Conservatives had been for some time), Churchill was not, at least for a time, disposed to listen to the argument put forward by Butler and other advocates of the 'policy-statement-now position' that being in opposition had changed all that. Some proof had to be given from time to time, they argued, that the Conservative Party was still alive and conscious of social and economic realities: if parliamentary activity would consist largely in responding to Labour initiative, some method must be found of capturing the initiative for its own views. This latter view was supported by many of those Conservatives who had been active, either through the Tory Reform Committee or the Post-war Problems Committee, in policy formulation before the election. The Post-war Problems Committee[5] had been reconstituted as the Advisory Committee on Policy and Political Education under the chairmanship of R. A. Butler, who quickly became the figurehead (and in many ways the prime mover) of those who wanted to re-formulate policy. After the election the Tory Reform Committee did not disband, but continued to hold dinner meetings at which certain aspects of Conservative policy were discussed. But there was not the concerted group action which had characterized its existence before July 1945. One prominent member of the Committee was prepared (after 1945) to sit below the gangway and act as a 'spur' to Government and Opposition alike, but the majority of the members of the Committee rejected this approach. Some members of the Tory Reform Committee became associated with Peter Thorneycroft's Design for Freedom Movement, working on the fringes of the Conservative Party seeking a common liberal policy to appeal to both Conservatives and Liberals. Others, notably Quintin Hogg, Hugh Molson, and David Gammans, found a niche within the consultative-determinative core. Associated as they were with criticism of Conservative policies before the election and committed also to the view that Conservatism must constantly adapt to maintain its vitality, it was not surprising that the Tory Reformers played a part both in the formulation of new party policy and in sustaining the pressure within the parliamentary party and in the mass party that was eventually to secure formal acceptance (and publication) of the Conservative Party's policy restatements.

The lines were pretty clearly drawn, then, between the two views of the appropriate response of the Conservative Party to the new situation in which it found itself, and the scene is set for the 'battle' for a restatement of policy.

* * *

The entire question of policy restatement was very much in the air during the months between the end of July and the meeting of the Central Council on 28 November, 1945. Letters written by Conservative supporters in the country appeared in *The Times* and the *Daily Telegraph* criticizing Conservative policy and demanding a progressive alternative to Socialism, proposing a federation of anti-Socialist parties, suggesting a new party name to avoid the present association with defeat – for example, 'Conservative Democrat', 'Progressive Conservative', 'National Democrats' – or rejecting the idea of changing the party's name[6] – all of them concerned with the central problem of finding a way of putting the party back on the high road to power.

Criticism of Conservative policy was taken up by Quintin Hogg in his *Daily Mail* column,[7] by Colin Coote in the *Daily Telegraph*,[8] and by an editorial in the *Yorkshire Post*.[9] The theme of nearly all these – the theme which became the cliché employed by most supporters of a policy restatement – was that the party could not count on the 'swing of the pendulum' to return them to power and that, unless the Conservative Party could present a more progressive policy the pendulum might, indeed, swing further to the left.[10] A former Unionist M.P. writing in the *Observer* in November 1945 advised: 'The more modern-minded members of the . . . party should be encouraged to form ginger groups, unorthodox, exploratory, and not tied down. Once again an 'F.E.' is needed to save them from internal attack.'[11]

The need for policy reformulation was also recognized by the meeting of defeated Conservative M.P.s held in London on 5 October, 1945, and the first formal support for the idea was shown by the submission to the Central Council meeting on 28 November, 1945, of a resolution calling for a new industrial policy (one that was not merely one of *laissez faire* but which envisaged direct action by the state to encourage industry and increase the national income) and a restatement of party policy in general 'to meet present-day conditions'.[12] These resolutions were conveniently not reached at the meeting, but the sentiments which they expressed continued to be put forward in the new year.

Support for policy reformulation came from many quarters. Lord Hinchingbrooke believed that 'public disillusionment with the Conservative Party [was] occasioned by the party's unwillingness to reform in any profound sense at all', and he complained that 'the Conservative Party alone had no proposals to capture the public imagination . . .'. To remedy the situation he favoured a reformulation of party policy; but he warned that: 'It is a mistake to imagine that the party to achieve success must go all the way to meet the electorate, for if so, it will find itself on Socialist ground and become despised and rejected for deserting its principles.'[13] Harold Macmillan also sided with the policy reformulators. But during the first months of 1946 he seemed to go out of his way to present the cautious objections characteristic of Winston Churchill's and Anthony Eden's position at the time. Eden's position on the question was never made very explicit; most of the time he seems to have been well on the fence. In a speech at Kingston-upon-Hull on 1 March, 1946, he said: 'Let me say at once that anyone who expects the Conservative Party to produce an industrial policy that can be summed up in one word or even one phrase will be disappointed'.[14] No one was asking for an industrial policy in one word or phrase. His remark may be taken as a vaguer repetition of Churchill's assurance that Conservative policy would not be a catch-word or a gimmick, and also a recognition that a policy statement on the subject might be necessary. New policy was all right, Macmillan told an annual meeting of Glasgow Unionists in February 1946, but he hoped that this did not mean a prospectus.[15] Three months later, in London, he toyed again with the antithesis between new policy and an election programme,[16] but he finally declared himself on the side of the policy reformulation. 'Beyond broad principles [he said] I would not go. At this moment I would concentrate on a policy not a programme. The details can be worked out when you are in office....'[17] Before very long, however, Macmillan became fully committed to a specific restatement of party policy on industry. Indeed, he was soon appointed to a committee to help formulate such a policy. Support for policy reformulation also came from L. S. Amery in an official party publication. He wrote: 'There can be no permanent revival of Conservatism without a positive alternative policy to the policy of the Socialist Left. . . . Disraeli's principles . . . contain, by implication, all the elements of Conservative policy. But they call for a clear and comprehensive restatement in the light of present-day conditions.'[18]

Pressure for policy reformulation continued to build up within the mass party, although as is revealed by the treatment of the motion calling for 'a definite programme' which was submitted to the Central Council meeting on 27 March, 1946, there was still some confusion in many minds as to what was really required – a restatement of principles, policy, or programme. At all events the agenda resolution was ultimately passed in a much weaker form stating merely 'that it is greatly to be desired that Conservative principles should be restated as a basis for future policy'.[19]

The Scottish Unionists at their conference the following month revealed themselves much more explicitly committed to a definite restatement of party policy. One resolution put forward for debate viewed 'with grave concern the fact that since the general election the Unionist Party have put forward no constructive programme as an alternative to the hard and fast policy of the Socialist Party'. The resolution also expressed the feeling that the party was relying solely on criticism of the Government, that this was not enough, and that 'a clearly defined policy acceptable and understandable to the man in the street should be issued from Central Headquarters'.[20] The conference on 29 April accepted the substance of this resolution in combination with three other resolutions on the subject of party policy; it rejected the notion that the pendulum was enough and demanded a constructive party policy.

This demand was echoed by a resolution passed, by 51 votes to 28, at a conference of the Northern Provincial Area in June calling on Central Office to undertake 'the early preparation and announcement of a policy programme'.[21] The conference chairman, counselling caution, reminded the representatives that 'a good deal of pressure [was] being brought to bear on the party Headquarters to formulate a policy of a definite nature' and informed them that the question of policy restatement would be considered at a meeting of the Executive Committee of the National Union in July, at which Churchill would speak.

It is not known whether Churchill gave much satisfaction on the question of policy restatement at this meeting. The report of the Executive Committee to the party conference later that year mentioned only that 'the Leader of the party . . . gave a review of the political situation'.[22] What is likely, if he referred to the matter at all, is that he repeated the line of argument which he had taken in earlier references to the subject: namely, that the party had 'a carefully thought-out and comprehensive Declaration of Policy' at the last election,[23] and that the Four-Year Plan which was 'a great new policy' had still not passed into law.[24] To this defence of his position he added (in different words from time to time but to the same effect, and with scarcely concealed derision) that the Conservative Party was not a party which believed 'that there is a sudden sweeping "cure-all" for human ills, which we would sell like a patent medicine to all who are willing to gulp it down. . . . We place our faith in the firm and upright character of the British people . . .'.[25]

No statement made by Churchill after the Executive Committee meeting in July gave any indication, moreover, that his concession to policy reformulation had gone beyond the observation (at the Edinburgh meeting of Scottish Unionists) that the Four-Year Plan and the Declaration of Policy should be added to 'from time to time as circumstances change'.[26] 'Liberty with security; stability combined with progress; the maintenance of religion, the Crown, and Parliamentary Government . . .' (for so Churchill defined the party's policy at Edinburgh) were all general principles with which no Conservative could quarrel. But many continued to hope, as the party conference of October 1946 approached, that the Leader of the party could be brought round to a more specific and distinguishing expression of where the party stood.

There was certainly no want of trying at the Blackpool Conference. The first shots in the campaign to achieve a restatement of party policy were fired in the opening minutes of the first day's proceedings. John Hay, the Young Conservative whose presence had disturbed the calm waters of an earlier Central Council meeting, took the floor at the conference to move the reference back of the report of the Central Council on the grounds that it contained insufficient information on what had happened to the resolutions passed at the last conference. He also protested that while eight motions had been submitted calling for a statement of policy, they had been placed among the Additional Resolutions at the end of the agenda.[27] Major Proby, the Chairman, sensing well the mood of the conference, promised that he would arrange to select one of the resolutions on the statement of policy for discussion before the end of the conference. With this the objections to the report were removed.

The debate on the question of a policy statement came on the second day of the conference on the following motion:

> That this conference is of the opinion that the Conservative Party, in order to counter the misleading and insidious propaganda of the Socialist Party, should, without further delay, prepare and issue a statement, in a concise form easily understood by the electorate, setting forth the policy for which the Conservative Party stands, and simultaneously a statement giving in fuller detail the principles and programme of the party.[28]

Mr Robson Brown, who moved the resolution, said that 'it was their task to prove to the "floating" neutral voter that the Conservative Party could provide a certain answer to Socialist totalitarianism and nineteenth-century liberalism'.[29] He was supported by A. F. G. Rippon, Cyril Osborne, Capt Crookshank, and Quintin Hogg, the latter repeating the argument he had put with vigour on many earlier occasions: that they must refute the Government supporters' lie that the Conservative Party had no alternative to *laissez faire*. Nigel Fisher opposed the resolution arguing 'that it was too early to provide a detailed programme',[30] but articulated opposition in the main was weak and at the end of a rather short debate the motion was carried by a 'large majority'.[31]

Looking back on the 1946 party conference from what he considered to be a much better one in 1947, Aubrey Jones expressed the belief that:

> Last year's conference at Blackpool contained less substance than this year's at Brighton. There was, on that earlier occasion, much facile revolt and much aimless candour, a cry that the party should march somewhere, though few could suggest where.[32]

While it may well be true that the mass party's demands for a policy restatement gave little clue as to the content desired, the discussion did have the effect of convincing many leading Conservatives – including Anthony Eden and Oliver Stanley who reported to the party Leader on the evening before his speech to the mass meeting of the party – that Churchill would have to satisfy the demand for the production of a policy statement. This point they put to Churchill long into the night, finally extracting from him the promise of a statement on policy and the announcement of such a statement at the mass meeting the next day. Rumours that a policy statement was to be announced made the rounds, and the excited meeting gave the Leader an overwhelming ovation.

It would be wrong to say that Churchill ignored the request altogether, for he did admit '[sympathy] with the desire that we should restate not only the principles which actuate our party, but the policy to which these principles give rise',[33] and he did, almost as an afterthought, refer in a very general way to certain aspects of a Conservative policy – namely profit-sharing schemes, a 'property-owning democracy', 'partnership in industry', and a limitation on monopoly abuses – which would, indeed, form a major part of later policy statements. But he continued to state his earlier objections to 'cure-alls', 'panaceas' and 'patent medicines' in uncompromising terms. 'Our main objectives are,' Churchill intoned, with surely a twinkle in his eye:

> To uphold the Christian religion and to resist attack upon it;
>
> To defend our monarchical parliamentary constitutions;
>
> To provide adequate security against external aggression and safety for our sea-borne trade;
>
> To uphold law and order and impartial justice administered by courts free from interference or pressure on the part of the executive;
>
> To regain a sound finance and strict supervision of national income and expenditure;
>
> To defend and develop our Empire trade without which Britain would perish;
>
> To promote all measures to improve the health and sound conditions of the people;
>
> To support as a general rule free enterprise and initiative against State trading and nationalization of industries.[34]

The Conservatives cheered and returned to their homes! But the point was not lost on the editorial writer of the *Scotsman* (a paper sympathetic to the Tory cause):

> ... it may perhaps be said that the 'eight points of policy' mentioned by Mr Churchill and the economic ideas which he borrowed largely from Mr Eden do not constitute a sufficient answer to the Blackpool conference's demand for specific proposals. The 'eight points', for instance, would describe Conservative economic policy at any time in the past 30 to 40 years, if not further back than that.[35]

If the Blackpool conference revealed that mass party opinion may occasionally bring pressure to bear on the Conservative Party leadership, Winston Churchill also ably demonstrated the ability of charismatic leadership to vitiate these same 'democratic' pressures. On this occasion Churchill drew upon reserves of eloquence (and the deference with which Conservatives almost always treat the utterances of their leaders) to frustrate the wishes of those most desirous of a restatement of party policy. But he did not overplay his hand. Whether because of the display of unity on this question within the mass party, or (more telling) because of the mounting desire of his shadow cabinet and parliamentary party, soon after the party conference Churchill established the formal machinery – an Industrial Policy Committee – to prepare the first specific policy statement, a statement ultimately published as *The Industrial Charter*.

Lord Woolton's *Memoirs* contain the following remarks on the decision to produce a policy restatement: 'It is always dangerous in politics to be committed to detail in any programme. But I concluded it was at least as dangerous to be so vague that the nation could think that the Conservatism that we were expounding would be no different from the Conservatism of the thirties. We therefore decided to take the risk of defining in terms the policies we would encourage the nation to undertake.'[36] The ambiguity of these sentences (strengthened by the tendency of political correspondents to exaggerate the influence of Lord Woolton in policy matters) might suggest an influence on the final decision to produce a policy statement which was, it seems, well beyond its real importance.

'SELLING' THE INDUSTRIAL CHARTER

The first paragraph of *The Industrial Charter* – giving a fillip to Conservative party democracy – stated that the declaration had been 'drawn up by a Committee appointed as a result of a resolution moved at the Blackpool Conference'.[37] Although the Industrial Policy Committee *was* set up after the party conference in October 1946, there can be no doubt that a great deal of thinking about the charter had already been done long before the conference resolution.

The machinery which was established soon after the election defeat for the purpose of assisting in the formulation, discussion, and dissemination of party policy has been described in an earlier chapter. With the Advisory Committee on Policy and Political Education, the Research Department, and the Conservative Political Centre linked with the shadow cabinet through the person of R. A. Butler (a man committed to the view that the election had been lost because 'a positive alternative was not put . . . with sufficient fervour'[38]) it seemed inevitable that a reconstruction of the bases of Conservative policy would soon begin – with or without formal encouragement. Indeed, according to Butler, Churchill gave early encouragement to such endeavours. In a speech to a political conference at Halstead Butler announced that the Leader of the party had agreed to the appointment of a committee 'to go into the question of the party's future policy, and to organize the party on democratic and modern lines'.[39] Although a *News of the World* correspondent the next month reported hearing that Butler was 'guiding a series of Conservative Party Committees engaged in the task of drafting what will amount to a restatement of policy',[40] nothing more was heard of the committee or of its efforts to organize the party on democratic lines. That Butler continued to guide the reformulation of party policy, however, there can be no doubt. Nor is there much doubt that, in the early stages of the thinking about *The Industrial Charter* at least, the Advisory Committee on Policy and Political Education played a significant rôle. Butler's enthusiasm may have got the better of him, however, when he described the Advisory Committee on Policy and Political Education as 'the body responsible for the research into and the development of party policy'.[41]

The Advisory Committee as reconstituted by the Maxwell Fyfe Report is a considerably different creature from the original Advisory Committee on Policy and Political Education as set up by the Central Council in November 1945. The Advisory Committee today is a representative body – representative that is of various sectional interests within the party – too large for the task of actually formulating party policy. In any case its powers do not seem to extend to this purpose. The Advisory Committee which met under Butler's chairmanship before the Maxwell Fyfe Report was a far more informal gathering: members of the committee were not in fact appointed by the Executive Committee (as set out in the founding resolution) but were asked to join by Butler and later approved by the Executive Committee. It was also a more deliberately intellectual, 'radical' committee than today's, composed of people who accepted Butler's invitation because they had an interest in, or some direct contribution to make to, the evolving party policy. At this time the Advisory Committee considered drafts of the policy statements not only at the end (just before they went to the Leader for his final approval), but also at the beginning of the policy-making process.

Some spade-work for the later *Industrial Charter* was begun, well before the Blackpool conference, under Butler's direction at the Conservative Research Department. In his report to the 1946 party conference he stated that one of its immediate tasks was the undertaking of 'an analysis of the industrial situation as a basis for the revision of our industrial policy in the light of modern conditions'.[42] Indeed the notion of producing industrial 'charters' was suggested months before the party conference by both Butler[43] and Macmillan[44] and several of the main concepts of the later document had been committed to print by the end of the summer of 1946. *Co-partnership*, a publication published anonymously by the C.P.C. in 1946, written by Geoffrey Block of the Conservative Research Department, anticipated references to the subject of profit-sharing as they appeared in *The Industrial Charter*.[45] Moreover, although *Co-partnership* 'had scrupulously refrained from encroaching on policy questions'[46] retroactively it was virtually accorded the position of a formal policy statement by *The Industrial Charter* when that document, skirting lightly the entire question of profit-sharing, stated that 'we have set out our views on this subject more fully in [*Co-partnership*] . . .'.[47]

But perhaps the most crucial evidence of pre-conference consideration of some of the main details of the charter (and also of the particular impact of Butler's views on Conservative Party policy), is provided by a comparison of *Fundamental Issues* (a publication based on a speech by the Chairman of the Research Department at a conference on political education on 30 March, 1946) and the wording of the charter itself. In this speech Butler developed a number of suggestions – for industrial 'codes of good practice' to be approved by Parliament,[48] joint-production committees,[49] and a tribunal to try abuses of restrictive practices and alleged monopolies[50] – all of which formed an important part of *The Industrial Charter*.

Ralph Harris, commenting on the policy-making process for the industrial charter, has stated that Butler's Advisory Committee on Policy and Political Education was 'not empowered to produce the restatement of industrial policy which the party conference demanded in 1946 and that Mr Churchill therefore appointed a special Industrial Policy Committee to work on this question . . .'.[51] While he is quite right in stating that 'without the consent of the Leader no such statement could be published', it does not necessarily follow that Churchill *had* to appoint a special committee to legitimize the policy-making process. The Leader could as easily have consented to a draft prepared for his consideration by the Advisory Committee, the Research Department, or even Butler alone for that matter. It seems more reasonable to assume that the main purpose in establishing a special committee to take the ultimate responsibility for the draft of party policy was to allow the parliamentary party to be brought more fully into the consultative-determinative process, to facilitate the transmission of views between back-bench and policy-makers, and, most important, to ensure a greater authority to the final document than would have been accorded to a statement produced by the relatively untried Research Department and Advisory Committee.

Chaired by Mr Butler, the Industrial Policy Committee – composed of four other front bench spokesmen – Harold Macmillan, Sir David Maxwell Fyfe, Oliver Stanley, and Oliver Lyttelton[52] – and four back-bench members – Heathcote Amory,[53] David Eccles, Sir Peter Bennett, and Col J. R. H. Hutchison – met several times in Butler's office at the Research Department or at the House of Commons to thrash out the details of the policy statement. The Committee was served by three secretaries: David Clarke from the Research Department (later a joint Director), and two assistants, Reginald Maudling from the then Parliamentary Secretariat and Michael Fraser from the Research Department. Butler who had been working nearly every morning at the Research Department in the company of his now famous 'back-room boys' had already developed a number of ideas which were embodied in *The Industrial Charter*,[54] and from his position at the very apex of the consultative-determinative core he unquestionably exerted a major personal influence on the content and expression of the policy document. But his was by no means the only influence at work. He had to work 'in tactful co-operation with other influential and aspiring members of the party'; and his associates were, as Francis Boyd has put it, 'not the kind of men who would stand feebly aside while Butler worked his magic'.[55] Macmillan (who, as we have noted, warmed rapidly to the notion of producing a positive statement of party policy) in particular played a considerable rôle in the writing of the charter.

The opinion of leading Conservative industrialists and some Conservative trade unionists was also consulted in the policy formulation. Meetings organized in nine large industrial centres throughout the country were attended by small groups of Industrial Policy Committee members accompanied by one or other of the secretaries. Such criticism as there was of the charter's proposals at these meetings did not take the form of some of the later criticism of the document – namely, that there was insufficient emphasis on the rôle of private enterprise – but rather concentrated on the point – very similar to that made by Churchill and some of the older members of the parliamentary party – that such a policy statement should not be made at all. Some of those consulted were also concerned with the difficulty of making a general policy statement dealing with industry as a whole which would be properly applicable to specific industries – a criticism which appears to be reflected in the restraint of the published charter.[56]

The final draft for submission to Churchill was worked out by the Industrial Policy Committee, again with Butler's hand clearly revealed in the wording. It has been suggested that Churchill did not bother to read it.[57] But the flurry of rewriting and the general atmosphere of tension surrounding the activities of the Research Department and particularly Mr Butler during the Easter recess in 1947 suggests that 'the old man' had some alterations in mind. It is generally believed that Churchill's reaction to the industrial policy statement was, as Ralph Harris, one of Butler's biographers, has put it, 'not instantly enthusiastic'.[58] Whether this can rightly be attributed, as Harris believes, to the Conservative leader's preoccupation with criticism of the Labour Party's domestic policy and 'the dark shadows of the world scene' is a moot point. In any case the final decision to publish the charter was left hanging for some time. In the meantime the Central Council meeting on 14 March, 1947, reiterated 'the urgent need for the publication of a realistic statement of policy . . .'.[59] Churchill told the party conference in October of that year that 'it was officially approved by me at what we call a Consultative Committee, six months ago',[60] but Ralph Harris tells a different version of the Leader's ultimate authorization:

> It appears that Mr Butler was left uncertain what the Leader's verdict would be until one day when Churchill gave a dinner party for his senior colleagues. Up to the last moment no one was sure what decision, if any, their host would announce. Then Butler found himself invited to take the place of honour at the table, on Churchill's right. Even so he was not prepared for the generous terms in which 'the old man' commended his work on party policy to the gathering.[61]

One way or another Churchill's consent was obtained for the publication of the party's statement of industrial policy. On 11 May, 1947, some details of the charter were 'leaked' by the *Sunday Express* and the *Observer*. Later that same day Butler presided at a press conference held to introduce the public formally to the new party policy. What was the new policy line he revealed?

Some people still talk of *The Industrial Charter* as a 'radical document'; others (unenthusiastic at the time of its publication) recall rather smugly that their warning that it would never be implemented has, largely, come true. One leading Conservative involved in its formulation now regards the document with less enthusiasm – in retrospect it appears to him that, like Labour thought at the time, it was too concerned with the problem of the thirties – unemployment – and not sufficiently with the problem of the fifties – inflation. Another, formally associated with the policy-making core, continues to regard its publication as a courageous act – a bold assertion of 'freedom' when the consensus of opinion favoured the dominant rôle of the state. All seem agreed, however, that it was the most important and influential of the post-war policy statements. It was, as another policy-formulator has put it, a 'tone-setting document which went far beyond industrial relations to set out the whole system within which other Conservative policy would operate'. As such its content must be viewed – not from our present vantage point of more than ten years of Conservative-managed capitalism in a mixed economy – but as the first extensive official statement after the war of the Conservative Party's position *vis-à-vis* the social and economic order emerging under the Labour Government.

'Too much emphasis on the "enterprise can do it" theme,' we were told, 'would not have hit the mood in 1947.' What was required was a demonstration of Conservative determination to preserve employment and the social services, to maintain central control of the operation of the economy while at the same time introducing more characteristically Conservative measures to expand individual initiative, reclaim a prominent rôle for private enterprise, and generally moderate what were considered the harsher features of Labour's central planning.

This *The Industrial Charter* achieved by combining a traditional emphasis on the rôle of private enterprise with the retention (although in a milder form) of many aspects of centralized control as instituted under the Labour Government. The charter set out at the beginning in terms to which surely only the most doctrinaire economic-liberal could object the party's commitment to the directing rôle of the state in a fundamentally private enterprise economy:

> Our abiding objective is to free industry from unnecessary controls and restrictions. We wish to substitute for the present paralysis . . . a system of free enterprise, which is on terms with authority, and which reconciles the need for central direction with the encouragement of individual effort.[62]

Its acceptance of a directing rôle for the state carried with it acquiescence in a number of policies – if not the most distinctive – which were being pursued by the Labour Government: the cheap money policy (which Conservatives promised to follow 'with restraint' [p. 14]); support for the Coalition White Paper on employment (on which 'in some respects [they] would go further' [p. 16]); controls (which they would do away with as soon as possible [p. 14]); and the principles of unbalanced budgeting [p. 16]). On the crucial notion of the directing rôle of the state, however, the contrast with the Labour position was clear-cut.

The Labour Party, the charter accused, instead of fighting the production battle had pursued the class war and had 'confused the real meaning of central planning'. Conservative planning and the incentives which the party was prepared to offer if believed would increase national production by 5 per cent. By central planning the Conservatives meant 'strong central guidance' in a 'tactical' sense. Part of this scheme would involve a national budget (or 'plan'[63]) which would be worked out between the Government and both sides of industry, but the implementation of the plan would be left to 'the enterprise and public spirit of industry'. The boldness of the Conservative Party's planning image is suggested by the reference in the charter to the establishment of 'wage-fixing machinery', although in fact the idea amounted to little more than the expression of hope that if the Minister of Labour kept both sides of industry informed about the general economic situation 'wage levels [might] be kept in proper relationship to productivity and wage rates between different industries [could] be harmonized'.[64]

The increase in national production anticipated under Conservative rule depended, as we have seen, on the assumption that further incentives should be extended to encourage private initiative. The existing level of taxation the Conservatives regarded as beyond the limits which the citizen was prepared to allow in time of peace. Conservatives therefore favoured the reduction of taxation (made possible, they argued, by the reduction of government expenditure), further relief of taxation on earned income, a simplification of P.A.Y.E., the consideration of further allowances to industry to allow for the ploughing back of profits for re-equipment, and the enlargement of the area within which small savings would be exempt from income tax.[65]

The Industrial Charter was also critical of restrictive practices on both sides of industry. It proposed with respect to the trade unions and the repealed Trades Disputes Act in particular, to abolish the closed shop, to restore contracting-in and to disallow a connection between civil servants' trade unions and political parties.[66] The charter also promised to enlarge the competitiveness of British business by combatting 'employers' monopolies and restrictive practices'. It proposed to establish a statutory commission to investigate allegations of restraint of trade and to make recommendations to the Government. The document envisaged that in most cases the 'floodlight of publicity' would be sufficient sanction to achieve modification of the offending practice, but it contemplated legislative action (possibly the imposition of maximum prices) in recalcitrant cases.[67]

The Conservative statement of industrial policy was also noteworthy for its references to the party's attitude to nationalization. Having set out its opposition to nationalization as a principle, it went on to accept the nationalization of coal, the railways, and the Bank of England, to propose the denationalization of road transport and to establish the party's firm opposition to the nationalization of iron and steel.[68] The acceptance of the 'scrambled egg' which could not be 'unscrambled' as regards coal and rail transport did not mean that the Conservatives accepted all features of the *status quo*: the charter warned that the Conservative Party would 'review the scope of the nationalized industries', 'submit them to the test of the highest standards of commercial efficiency', assure 'adequate decentralization with special regard to Scotland and Wales', ensure fair competition between nationalized industry and private firms, and 'strengthen the safeguards of the consumer against these monopolies'.[69]

The third and final section of *The Industrial Charter* dealt with the so-called 'Workers' Charter'. It consisted of a series of suggestions – arising from the party's stated intention 'to humanize, not to nationalize' – for the creation of security, incentive, and status for industrial workers. The charter proposed legislation to establish the practice of granting to the employee the right to receive a statement 'setting out the terms on which he is engaged and the way in which he may be dismissed';[70] but many of the other proposals amounted to little more than the expression of the pious hope that enlightened management would choose to adopt the ideas:[71] it was not thought that the charter could be made the subject of an Act of Parliament, but the charter did propose that Parliament should approve general statements of policy which would give employer and employee alike a clear indication of the nation's wishes. As an ultimate sanction, the charter suggested that 'contracts put out to tender by public authorities' should be withheld from those firms which, 'after a reasonable period [had] elapsed', had still not conformed to the general standards.[72]

What was the reaction of the British press to this new statement of Conservative policy? The London newspapers were divided. The *Daily Mail* and *Daily Telegraph* were enthusiastic in their support; the *Daily Express* was far less certain. It liked the references to imperial preference and admitted that there were 'many excellent proposals', but roundly condemned the document for its emphasis on state interference. In many respects Conservative industrial policy was, the leader complained, 'simply another version of the old planned economy of the Socialists'.[73] The *Evening Standard*,[74] on the other hand, took a milder line, welcoming the charter for its acceptance of Imperial faith. In characteristic style the *Daily Mirror* announced that 'the Tory Party had decided to go forward with the people'; but then warned its readers not to trust the Conservative Party.[75] The *News Chronicle* was very critical, finding the charter 'too obviously prompted by the desire to attract the Liberal vote'.[76]

Newspaper reaction in the provinces was far more favourable to the new policy. Indeed, a survey of the editorials of nearly 40 British dailies covering the bulk of the British public revealed that (in addition to those already mentioned) only three took a critical line towards *The Industrial Charter* – the *Glasgow Citizen*, *Glasgow Evening Times*, and the (Nottingham) *Evening Star*. The *Yorkshire Post* greeted the new policy with marked enthusiasm, calling it 'A Better Plan for Every Man'.[77] Even the *Manchester Guardian* found it 'as political documents go . . . fairly honest and courageous',[78] but it also called attention to an 'imperfect harmony' between the charter's position on controls and Lord Woolton's 'invective' on the same subject.

The charter's reception by the weekly journals and Sunday newspapers was rather more mixed. The *Observer* believed it was on the right lines but questioned whether it went far enough.[79] The *Economist* was also rather luke-warm; while noting that the charter was a 'pleasant surprise', it felt obliged to add that general elections were 'an inquest on the Government's policy, not a vote on a "mandate" for the Opposition'.[80] The *Spectator* found the charter 'a document of considerable interest and importance . . . [possessing] one outstanding merit, that it remove[d] the last excuse for labelling the Conservative Party as at present constituted as reactionary'.[81] The *New Statesman and Nation*, *Reynolds News*, and *Tribune* were, predictably, hostile to the new industrial policy statement, the latter adding for good measure the forecast that 'before the year is out the Butler Charter will split the Tory Party as it has not been divided for half a century'.[82]

Such evidence as existed of a potential split in the Conservative Party (in addition to the efforts of the Beaverbrook press) was provided by the bitter opposition to *The Industrial Charter* by three right-wing publications of limited circulation – The *Recorder*, *Truth*, and the *City Press*.[83] The *Recorder* was extremely critical of the new Conservative policy statement, and deeply regretted its indifference to the rights of property and the value of capitalism.[84] *Truth* took much the same line, expressing its disappointment with the 'fantastic series of compromises'.[85] With the aid of the *City Press* these two publications continued to assert most of the anti-charter sentiment from a non-party source throughout the summer and up to the party conference in October.[86]

* * *

The party conference in 1946 had demanded a statement of party policy. Such a statement was produced by what we have termed the consultative-determinative core. This policy statement was accorded 'formal' status through ratification by the Leader of the party. Neither the parliamentary party (as a group) nor the mass party had played any real part in the policy-determining process. It is sometimes claimed that the so-called 'Two-Way Movement of Ideas' played a rôle in the policy determination of *The Industrial Charter* and other charters. This view is, I believe, fundamentally incorrect. The Two-Way Movement of Ideas *did*, however, have a particular importance in the policy-process very broadly defined – an importance which will be analysed later in this and the following chapter.

Criticism of *The Industrial Charter* in a few small right-wing journals (even with the support of the Beaverbrook press) would have been of little account had it not touched a responsive chord in some sections of the parliamentary party and the mass party. It may be worth recalling that not all those who favoured a restatement of party policy at the 1946 party conference had shown enthusiasm for some of the 'progressive' aspects of the final product. Councillor John R. Bevins (now the Postmaster General), who moved reference back of the Report of the Advisory Committee on Policy and Political Education, had done so on the grounds that 'it was weak, vacillating and compromising, particularly in its reference to the nationalization of British industry'.[87] Robson Brown, who had moved the original resolution at Blackpool calling for a statement of party policy, had demanded that 'they should take an uncompromising stand against nationalization, and it should be made clear that *they propose to denationalize all nationalized industries*'.[88] Nor was the entire parliamentary party behind the new statement of industrial policy. Immediately after its publication a correspondent for the *Birmingham Post* reported:

> Most Conservative M.P.s with whom I have discussed *The Industrial Charter* expressed preliminary approval of its contents, though some reserve second thoughts on more detailed study. A small minority regard the report with some misgivings and particularly the disposition, as they see it, of the Butler Committee to accept as irrevocable so many Socialist measures.[89]

When, on 22 May, nearly two weeks after the publication of the charter, a meeting of Conservative M.P.s 'generally endorsed the industrial policy of the party as outlined in the pamphlet recently issued pending the next party conference',[90] it was clear that the battle to ensconce *The Industrial Charter* as the keystone of Conservative post-war policy was, at least in the eyes of its bitterest opponents, not yet over.[91]

The attack from the right, concentrating on the hope of obliterating or radically amending *The Industrial Charter* at the October party conference, was conducted on two fronts: first, by attempting to call into question the way in which Conservative policy had been formulated and publicized prior to conference approval; and secondly, by trying to create the impression that rejection of the document was very widespread within the party.

'Crossbencher' combined both attacks in an article in the *Sunday Express*:

> Conservative leaders [he wrote] are trying to sell their 'Industrial Charter' to the public. What right have they to do this when it

> has not been endorsed by the party? Production of the document was badly timed; it should have appeared shortly before the annual conference next October . . . when its acceptance or otherwise could have been tested.[92]

He added the assertion that the Young Conservatives disapproved of the charter. *Truth* soon afterwards published a letter from A. F. N. Rowan-Robinson, chairman of the Watford Y.C.s, expressing agreement with an earlier letter critical of *The Industrial Charter* 'as being, in effect, a mild form of Socialism'. But, he continued:

> The publication of the Charter did not indicate that the Central Office has become the property of crypto-Socialists. The charter is the recommendation of one small group of Conservatives and the views they express have yet to be endorsed by the party and officially accepted as part of its policy.[93]

This theme *Truth* took up again in its next issue in reply to Harold Macmillan's criticism[94] of 'Crossbencher's' article:

> Mr Harold Macmillan takes too much for granted. Because a few eminent Conservative politicians concocted a pamphlet termed *The Industrial Charter* Mr Macmillan blandly assumes that this eclectic document, which draws so freely on Fabian and other Left-wing sources, automatically becomes the policy of the Conservative Party.
>
> *The Industrial Charter* has not yet been accepted by the Conservative Party, and there is a strong possibility of its being at least substantially modified next October.[95]

A front-page story in the *City Press* the same day described the Conservative Party as 'split from top to bottom' over *The Industrial Charter*, producing, presumably as evidence of the split, the news that: 'The chairman of one of the Young Conservative organizations . . . [was] so disturbed about *The Industrial Charter* that he [had] resigned.'[96]

After this burst of opposition to *The Industrial Charter* the right wing's campaign lost impetus. Try as it might to suggest a split in the Tory Party,[97] only Sir Waldron Smithers and Sir Herbert Williams were produced as being fully committed to the cause. A number of Conservative M.P.s continued to have doubts about the party's ability to implement the charter, and a few others continued to doubt whether the party should ever try; but only Dr Kenneth Pickthorn[98] and Lord Hinchingbrooke made public their disagreement with the charter, and even the latter, whose criticism was far-reaching, did not align himself with the not-so-gentle knights. Dr Pickthorn was not opposed to the charter root-and-branch, but he did believe that 'if we stick to the words without amendment, we have promised more than we can be certain of performing'. He urged his local association not to 'allow [itself] to be bullied by the use of such words as "reactionary"'; they should 'make [their] views plain to the central authorities through the local papers.' Lord Hinchingbrooke's attack on *The Industrial Charter*, timed to appear before the party conference in October, is perhaps the most comprehensive criticism of his party's policy-making process in opposition.[99] The gist of his argument was that while Conservatives would accept the idea of leadership when the party was the Government, in opposition a different principle ought to prevail. 'The duty of democratic party leadership in opposition,' he wrote, 'is not to hand down tablets of stone from high altitudes but to listen to the noise and the dogma from underneath and turn it to good account.' His appeal for more democracy in policy-making seems to have been a clear attempt to encourage those in the mass party who shared his displeasure with some aspects of the charter to put their case vigorously at the forthcoming conference.[100]

In retrospect, at least, the efforts of the right against *The Industrial Charter* appear something of a damp squib; the counter-attack which came from the supporters of the charter was, by comparison, powerful, protracted, and extremely well-executed. When it emerged that the testing time of *The Industrial Charter* would be the party conference at Brighton, no effort was spared to assure the mass party's commitment to the new statement of industrial policy. There were three general features of the pro-charter campaign: the first, and most crucial, was a well-conducted programme of political education among the constituency associations; secondly, there was, almost as soon as the charter was published, a tendency to underplay it as a firm statement of party policy; thirdly (and this is linked closely with the former) the mass party was encouraged to think that there existed the possibility of considerable modification of the charter through its 'democratic influence'.

Whether deliberately or unwittingly, the *Daily Telegraph*'s political correspondent was preparing the ground for the official line even before the charter was published. 'The survey [a reference to *The Industrial Charter* to be published in about two weeks],' he wrote, 'is in the form of a report to Mr Churchill as Leader of the party, and does not automatically become party policy. It is aimed, rather, to provide a basis for discussion in arriving at policy.'[101] On the day after the publication of the charter the *Liverpool Daily Post* assured its readers that:

> Mr Churchill and Lord Woolton do not regard the text of the industrial policy statement as entirely inviolable. Publication has committed the party to it of course, but local associations are invited to suggest amendments if they wish, or further proposals for discussion at the next annual conference.[102]

Later that same week Anthony Eden told his audience at Cardiff that: 'This charter is a statement of industrial policy, but it is not, of course, a detailed party programme.'[103] It was not always possible to maintain consistency on this point. The *Liverpool Daily Post*, a few days later, quoted a speech by Lord Woolton in which the following comment on the charter was made: '. . . it would need very little adjustment for its application whenever [we] came into power. We foresee a crisis and indicate the measures that must be taken.'[104]

The main burden of public speaking in favour of the charter and responsibility for attacking the right for its rejection of the policy statement fell on the shoulders of Harold Macmillan. The fostering – and curbing – of 'party democracy' during the Conservative Party's period of opposition was almost exclusively the task of R. A. Butler. It is a fascinating study in the subtleties of language (and politics) to trace the means by which, throughout this period, he cultivated, nurtured, pruned, and occasionally dug under the flowers of intra-party democracy blooming within the Conservative Party.

In an article in the *Daily Telegraph* a week after the charter's publication, Butler coaxed the seeds of democratic policy-making:

> The report [i.e. *The Industrial Charter*] has been issued at a moment which is particularly opportune for our branches. Now is the time in which resolutions can be prepared and sent in for discussion at the Brighton Conference of the party. . . .

> The Charter will also be discussed by numerous discussion groups set up by our education organization under the system known as the 'two-way movement of ideas'. The democratic method of framing suggestions on ultimate party policy is in full operation within the Conservative Party.[105]

A few days later Macmillan, speaking at the Constitutional Club in favour of the charter, claimed that it had received a 'wonderful welcome': 'The Socialists are afraid of it; Lord Beaverbrook dislikes it; and the Liberals say it is too liberal to be fair. What more could one want? Was ever a child born under such a lucky star?'[106]

The suggestion in the Beaverbrook press that the party had no right to issue the charter until the party conference had accepted it irked the supporters of the charter into a strong counter-attack. In a speech, which the *Observer*'s political correspondent noted must have had the backing of Conservative Headquarters,[107] Macmillan levelled his fire at 'all the forces of reaction' – the *Daily Herald*, Lord Beaverbrook, and 'Sir Waldron Smithers and Co.' – who were 'united in saying that the charter was not Tory policy'. 'What they really mean,' he said, 'is that they wish it were not Tory policy.'

> He [Lord Beaverbrook] accuses me [Mr Macmillan continued] of having seduced the Conservative Party into a progressive statement of policy. I would gladly accept the blame for this, if it were blame. But in fact there has been no seduction. *The Industrial Charter* is merely a restatement in the light of modern conditions of the fundamental and lasting principles of our party.[108]

On the same day as Macmillan was speaking, further evidence of the charter's support within the party was being assembled: at a conference of about 200 Conservative and Liberal National prospective candidates in London a motion 'welcoming wholeheartedly the policy set out in *The Industrial Charter*' was carried unanimously.[109]

For about two months – from mid-May to mid-July, a period in which many constituency associations held their annual meetings – the case for *The Industrial Charter* was put vigorously by prospective candidates and Conservative M.P.s throughout the country. This – what Lord Hinchingbrooke called – 'propagation' of the charter was assisted by the Speakers Department at Central Office (particularly through talks to Conservative women's groups in the constituencies) and by the individual efforts of committed M.P.s writing to (or for) their local newspapers.

It is as a major component of this political education campaign associated with *The Industrial Charter* that the 'Two-Way Movement of Ideas' can best be appreciated. Whether it was a deliberate continuation of the idea or not, the 'two-way movement' which operated through the C.P.C. after the war had a forerunner in the 'Looking Ahead Circles' organized in 1943 to assist the Central Committee on Post-War Reconstruction.[110] The purpose of the two institutions was to establish a two-way flow of ideas about policy between the consultative-determinative core and discussion groups within the mass party. To this end, during and after 1946 under the leadership of the Conservative Political Centre, discussion groups voluntarily organized within the constituencies were invited to express their views on topics indicated by the C.P.C. *Policy Papers*, setting out the subjects to be discussed and the time-period of the particular 'phase', were issued accompanied by the sources that could be used in the study of the topics, to be followed by a series of pamphlets specially prepared for the particular phase. These pamphlets, called the *What Do You Think?* series, written by leading figures in the parliamentary party – often those people playing a leading part in the particular policy committee associated with the policy statement being produced – and assisted by members of the Conservative Research Department, outlined a general argument on the specific subject and detailed specific questions around which the group-discussion leaders could frame their reports. At a specified time the reports of the discussion groups were forwarded to the Area Education Committees, and were thence forwarded to the C.P.C. These reports were then, according to Mr Butler, analysed by the Research Department, and the results of this analysis were forwarded to the Advisory Committee on Policy and Political Education.[111] General reports of the discussions were later published by the C.P.C. – Richard Bailey of the C.P.C. acting as editor – in the form of *What We Think* reports.

During the first phase of the movement – i.e. the one which was in progress at the time of the formulation and publication of *The Industrial Charter* – more than 150 groups (about 2,000 people) participated; more than 200 reports were submitted, of which 46 were forwarded to the Research Department. One would have thought that the great bulk of the reports produced during the first five phases (the only phases for which full information is available) would be accounted for by the efforts of a relatively small group of activists participating faithfully in each stage of the two-way movement. Many groups did, during each phase, produce more than one report, but a study of the participation over the five phases does not confirm this hypothesis. Of those groups participating in phase one, 43 did so again in phase two; 32 in phase three; 10 in phase four and 12 in phase five. Of those groups which began in phase two, 38 repeated in phase three, 25 in phase four and 7 in phase five. One group – from Sheffield, Attercliffe – produced no less than 11 reports in the first five phases; but only the groups from Newport Monmouthshire, Chelsea, and Tiverton participated in every phase.

What was the relationship of this phase to the policy-process and to the formulation of *The Industrial Charter* in particular? The short answer is 'very little'! The Two-Way Movement of Ideas was in fact productive of very few original ideas which could be or were embodied in party policy statements. But this fact could hardly have been a disappointment to the organizers of the movement. For, as is revealed by a study of the timing of the discussion phases and the period of formulation of the policy statements, discussion by the mass party was – with one or two exceptions – designed to *follow* the publication of party policy statements formulated by the consultative-determinative core. More than that, policy discussion by way of the Two-Way Movement of Ideas was scheduled to precede conference consideration of previously published policy. The discussion pamphlets of the *What Do You Think?* series can, then, be seen as an adjunct of the campaign of political education in which the policy formulators attempted to bring the mass party more closely into touch with the details of evolving Conservative policy, thereby facilitating its smooth acceptance at party conferences. The great importance of the movement as an educational force and its relative unimportance as an autonomous source of policy was acknowledged by the 'editor' of the report of the second phase of the movement: '. . . we realize that in the majority of cases we are doing no more than confirming views on policy which have already been put out from your end'. And further: 'The scheme is . . . an important element in the education of the party and indeed in the enlightenment of the electorate as a whole.' But in *Policy Paper 5*, more substantial claims were made for the influence of the movement: 'Here is an opportunity for those Conservatives who want to think things out for themselves to do so in a clear and purposeful way. That's not all – here's a chance to become a real partner in shaping the party's policy for the future.'

The relationship of the Two-Way Movement and *The Industrial Charter* is very illuminating. Only two of the five topics on which discussion groups were encouraged to forward their opinions in the first phase were connected with the content of *The Industrial Charter* – trade unions and profits. The *What Do You Think?* pamphlet dealing with trade unions was not published until February 1947. The other, on profits, was published as early as August 1946, but only four groups considered it and none of these reports was forwarded to the Research Department. In any case, since the phase did not end until after the charter had been written, the views on neither topic could have been forwarded to the policy-makers in time to affect their deliberations.

The real emphasis on *The Industrial Charter* came in phase two – the study period from September to December 1947. Three of the five topics specified for this phase – *The Industrial Charter*, the 'Worker's Charter', and taxation – were concerned with the details of the previously published industrial policy statement. Discussion within the groups was revolved around three pamphlets in the *What Do You Think?* series written by R. A. Butler, Heathcote Amory, and Oliver Stanley (all members of the committee responsible for *The Industrial Charter*) and published in September 1947 (a few weeks before the party conference).

However much the result may be credited to the effectiveness of the political education campaign there can be no doubt that the 'Rout of the Right' to which journalists have since (more colourfully than accurately) referred was virtually completed by the end of 1947. On 15 September, 1947, the *Yorkshire Post* confidently predicted, on the basis of the evidence of motions sent in by the constituency associations for the annual conference, that *The Industrial Charter* would have a 'good reception':

> Critics have been outspoken enough in the privacy of their pubs; but none has been willing or able to persuade his local association

> to sponsor a straightforward motion opposing the charter. There are a few motions which criticize special points, but these accept the charter as a whole. This makes it all but certain that the document will be approved by a big majority.[112]

The editor of the *Recorder* was also ready to admit that the cause of the right had been lost. 'Yes,' he told his readers in late September, 'the charter will be accepted at the Conference. That is because all the branches are hypnotized by central authority and accept anything that looks official.'[113]

But the 'central authorities' did not relax. For good measure, Butler took to the pages of the September issue of *Tory Challenge*, a party publication intended mainly for an activist readership, to put the final case for the acceptance of the charter at the party conference. His article was a rather obvious attempt to encourage the conference's initiative in expressing views on the charter, and, at the same time, to ensure its acceptance intact.

> I do not believe [he wrote] that the National Union desires to bind and tie our Leader by card vote in the 'high Socialist manner'. But it is through the expression of views on all aspects of our affairs that delegates can make sure that the framing of the final policy is on lines entirely sympathetic to their own.[114]

Butler then reminded his readers that *The Industrial Charter* had 'the approval of the Private Members Committee and the Candidates Conference' and that Churchill had described it 'as a broad statement of policy, to which those who are opposed to the spread of rigid Socialism can now rally'. As if this were not enough, the Chairman of the Research Department felt constrained to add: 'Some of the Opposition Press desire to see our party split on the question of industrial policy.'[115]

The ultimate acceptance of *The Industrial Charter* by the party conference had about it the air of inevitability one associates with a brilliantly executed chess win: pawns were moved; knights attacked; and always the pro-charter players pressed the advantage. The first bold move came with Peter Thorneycroft's contribution to the debate on the first resolution of the conference, one dealing with the economic crisis. Sir Herbert Williams and Mrs Lorne Sayers had introduced and seconded the General Purposes Sub-committee's resolution calling for a new Parliament and pledging the conference:

> to promote a national and practical policy without regard to special interest, which will unite the forces on which the survival of Britain depends and turn our resources to the vital tasks of industrial and agricultural production and moral revival.[116]

To this Thorneycroft urged the addition of the following words:

> and which is designed to follow the line of Industrial, Domestic, and Foreign Policy laid down by the Leader of the Conservative Party since the last conference and to which the conference pledges its full approval and support.[117]

'The purpose of this addendum,' he explained, '[was] to show in unequivocal terms that we approve the policy which has been put up by Mr Winston Churchill,' but it was also, incidentally, a means through which he could bring up the subject of *The Industrial Charter*. Conference should discuss the charter, he argued, but having done so it should 'come to a clear conclusion upon the matter'. Then, almost in passing, he threw out a remark which was absolutely crucial in the light of his addendum: *The Industrial Charter*, he held, 'was launched by Mr Churchill and it has been defended on countless platforms by Mr Anthony Eden'.[118] The amendment was seconded by Hugh Molson and accepted by the original speakers. The amended resolution was carried unanimously.

Since – to reconstruct the effect of Thorneycroft's intervention – the party conference had 'pledged its full approval and support' to policy laid down by the Leader of the party since the previous conference, and since *The Industrial Charter* was part of the Leader's policy, it might have seemed that nothing more needed to be said about the document. The logic of events, however, required that the resolution on the conference agenda dealing specifically with the charter should be duly debated. Nevertheless, the charter supporters had achieved a valuable insurance policy.

The resolution on the subject of the industrial policy statement chosen for discussion was one submitted on behalf of the Hendon North Conservative Association. The resolution – 'welcoming *The Industrial Charter* as a basis for discussion of the general principles of Conservative economic policy' and 'recommending that the Committee which prepared it should be kept in being in order that the charter can be kept fully up to date so that the party may be able, at short notice, to publish an industrial programme based on the charter'[119] – was a variation of a motion passed at the annual meeting of the Hendon North association during the summer.[120] It had been moved then by the constituency's prospective candidate, Charles Orr-Ewing, and it was he who introduced the resolution to the party conference in October.

Despite the loose talk about 'the duty of delegates . . . to make constructive suggestions as to the course of future progress' and their 'practical opportunity to voice their views on *The Industrial Charter*',[121] the debate on the conference resolution – like the debate at most Conservative Party conferences – gave little or no opportunity for this at all. The debate itself was remarkably short considering the importance of the topic, and the arguments which were presented fell into either of two simple categories – for, or against, the charter as it stood.

Orr-Ewing's speech in support of the motion was – very much to his credit – a straightforward, rather uncompromising justification of *The Industrial Charter*'s acceptance of central planning and certain specific aspects of nationalization.[122] His seconder's speech – slightly more emotional in tone – stressed the point that the charter had been produced in response to the 1946 conference's resolution. Then, all too obviously,[123] the floor was given to Reginald Maudling (an officer in the Conservative Research Department and a secretary of the Industrial Policy Committee) who proceeded to move an amendment to the resolution.

> I think it is a pity [he said] that this resolution, worded as it is, was chosen for discussion today because in its present form it effectively prevents the conference from recording an opinion in favour of the charter. If you vote against this motion as it is at present you will kill the charter dead. If you vote for this motion without amendment you condemn it to a lingering death.[124]

The connection with Thorneycroft's earlier encouragement to 'come to a clear conclusion upon the matter' is obvious.

In place of the phrase 'welcoming . . . as a basis for discussion' Maudling proposed to substitute the words 'welcoming . . . as a clear statement of the general principles of Conservative economic policy'. The purpose of his intervention was, as he put it, to make it clear that the document was a charter of Conservative economic policy on the basis of which the party would produce an industrial programme for the next election.

The case against the resolution was put most strongly by Sir Waldron Smithers.[125]

> I have five minutes [he said] in which to convince you that the existence of the Conservative Party, therefore of Britain, depends on the rejection of *The Industrial Charter* (cries of dissent). There can be no compromise with Socialism or Communism. You must not let the Conservative Party become infected with the Socialist bug. The Conservative Party must stick to its principles or perish.[126]

After a recitation of the three Disraelian principles of Conservatism and an attack on the charter as 'milk-and-water socialism' he urged the conference 'not [to be] afraid of the Central Office or the platform. Vote according to your conscience. By rejecting this charter you can save the Conservative Party and save England.'[127]

Sir Waldron's speech was met, at several points, by dissenting cries from the body of the hall, and his virtual isolation was emphasized by the immediate rejection of his position on the charter by the chairman of his own constituency association. Anthony Nutting, then threw the full weight of the Young Conservative movement behind the move to achieve a 'clear-cut decision' on the charter. Frank Burrow's support for Sir Waldron's rejection of the charter came too late to stem the tide. Sir John Marling suggested an amendment to Maudling's form of words to ensure that the charter's wording would suffer no amendment,[128] and it merely remained for Butler, as the last speaker in the debate, to welcome wholeheartedly the constructive amendments to the motion that had been suggested. The chairman then announced that the mover and seconder had accepted Maudling's amendment and that Maudling was prepared to accept Sir John's suggestions.[129] The resolution 'welcoming *The Industrial Charter* as a clear statement of the general principles of Conservative economic policy' was put to the conference for its approval and passed with only three dissenting votes.

We have already noted that the force of the attack against the charter had lost much of its strength by the time the party conference was held; but the mustering of a mere three votes against it at the end of the debate must have been surprising to even the most committed of the charter's supporters. The report on the second phase of the Two-Way Movement reveals that – even after the charter was accepted so overwhelmingly at the party conference in October – some participants in the discussion groups were still quite critical of certain details.[130] Maurice Edelman has expressed the opinion that 'at least half the conference was emotionally more in harmony with its wide-ranging extremists than with the paternal Conservatism of Macmillan, Eden, Thorneycroft and Butler',[131] and there is certainly much evidence from the later stages of the Brighton conference to suggest that Edelman had not wandered by mistake into the Labour Party's annual conference.[132] And yet the 'progressive' *Industrial Charter* was endorsed virtually to a man. Why?

Part of the answer was, as has been stressed, the effectiveness of the campaign of political education of the party activists which followed its publication. (It will be recalled that, before the end of the war, Conservative conferences had often been susceptible to persuasion from progressive quarters.) But perhaps as important was the extremism with which the case against the charter was conducted. Some Conservative M.P.s had doubts about the value of *The Industrial Charter*, but none appeared willing to link himself with the position adopted by Sir Waldron Smithers and Sir Herbert Williams. A specific attack on the details of *The Industrial Charter* before and at the party conference – one which centred on the vagueness of the charter's suggestions for implementation – might well have produced a better response among members of the parliamentary party and, in consequence, might have bolstered the confidence of the charter's detractors in the mass party. Sir Waldron's frontal attack on the whole notion of governmental control, smacking of an extreme *laissez faire* attitude associated with the pre-war period, proved entirely out of keeping with the spirit of the times, and resulted in his virtual isolation.[133]

REFERENCES

[1] Saloma, Chapter I. I am also indebted to Dr Saloma for the use of a manuscript containing a longer draft of this chapter, 'A Theoretical Framework for Analysis', although his approach is reflected less in the exposition than the general organization of our material.

[2] McKenzie, Chapter III.

[3] Nicholas 'The Formulation of Party Policy', *Parliamentary Affairs*, V (1951–52), p. 145.

[4] Cf. Lord Salisbury's advice to Balfour in 1906, Kenneth Young, *Arthur James Balfour* (London, 1963), p. 259.

[5] See above pp. 70–1.

[6] *The Times* (London), 1945, 3 August, 28 September, 1 October; *Daily Telegraph* (London), 1945, 5 October, 3, 8, 12, and 16 November.

[7] Quintin Hogg, 'Too Many Micawbers in the Tory Party', *Daily Mail*, 11 September, 1945; see also *Daily Mail*, 25 September, 1945, and 4 November, 1945.

[8] Colin R. Coote, 'Conservatives and Their Policy', *Daily Telegraph*, 3 October, 1945.

[9] *Yorkshire Post*, 'Conservatives and the Future', 9 November, 1945.

[10] Quintin Hogg, *Daily Mail*, 11 September, 1945; Harold Macmillan, 'Strength Through – What?', *Oxford Mail*, 26 January, 1946; Lord Hinchingbrooke, 'The Course of Conservative Politics', *Quarterly Review*, January 1946, pp. 61–2; Victor Raikes, 'The Outlook for the Conservative Party', *New English Review*, XIII (November, 1946), pp. 478–9.

[11] *Observer*, 'Unionism up to Date', 25 November, 1945.

[12] Council Minute Book, II, 28 November, 1945, pp. 6–7.

[13] Hinchingbrooke, *Review*, January 1946, p. 62.

[14] Anthony Eden, *Conservative Policies and Objectives* (C.C.O., 1946), p. 4. See also Eden's remarks at the Blackpool Conference in 1946 cited in *The Times*, 4 October, 1946.

[15] *Glasgow Herald*, 23 February, 1946.

[16] Harold Macmillan, *The Conservative Approach to Modern Politics* (C.C.O., 1946), p. 6.

[17] Macmillan, p. 11.

[18] L. S. Amery, *The Conservative Future* (C.C.O., 1946), p. 5.

[19] Council Minute Book, II, 27 March, 1946, p. 6. Cf. *Central Council Annual Meeting* [Agenda], 27 March, 1946, p. 9.

[20] *Glasgow Herald*, 18 April, 1946.

[21] *Sunday Times*, 'Policy Call by Conservatives', 23 June, 1946.

[22] Conference Minutes, 1946, p. 26.

[23] *The Day Will Come* (C.C.O., 1946) [Reprint of Churchill's speech to the Scottish Unionist Association conference at Edinburgh, 29 April, 1946], p. 12.

[24] *A True People's Party* (C.C.O., 1945) [Reprint of a speech by Churchill to the Central Council meeting 28, November, 1945], p. 10. Cf. *The Day Will Come*, p. 12.

[25] *The Day Will Come*, p. 10. See also *A True People's Party*, pp. 10–11.

[26] *The Day Will Come*, p. 12.

[27] Conference Minutes, 1946, p. 2.

[28] Cited in *Conference Report, 1947*, p. 24.

[29] *The Times*, 5 October, 1946.

[30] *The Times*, 5 October, 1946.

[31] *Conference Report, 1947*, p. 24.

[32] Aubrey Jones, p. 221.

[33] *The Times*, 7 October, 1946.

[34] *The Times*, 7 October, 1946.

[35] *Scotsman*, 7 October, 1946.

[36] Woolton p. 347.

[37] *The Industrial Charter* (C.C.O., May 1947), p. 3.

[38] R. A. Butler, *Fundamental Issues* [A Statement on the Future Work of the Conservative Education Movement] (C.P.C., 1946), p. 2.

[39] *Halstead Gazette*, 'Conservatives Organize', 28 September 1945.

[40] *News of the World*, 14 October, 1945.

[41] R. A. Butler, *Observer*, 'The Two-Way Flow of Ideas', 23 March, 1947.

[42] Conference Minutes, 1946, p. 32.

[43] R. A. Butler, *Observer*, 'Charters for Democracy', 5 April, 1946.

[44] *Beckenham Journal*, 27 July, 1946 [report of an address by Macmillan to a party meeting, 19 July, 1946].

[45] Cf. *Co-partnership* (C.P.C., 1946) and *Industrial Charter*, pp. 33–4. For the first three years of the existence of the C.P.C. all its publications were in fact written for it by members of the Conservative Research Department. The 'Topics for Today' series was written by the Research Department; *The House of Lords* (C. P. C., 1947) was written by Peter Goldman, then a member of the Research Department.

[46] Harris, p. 103.

[47] *Industrial Charter*, p. 33.

[48] *Fundamental Issues*, pp. 9–10; cf. *Industrial Charter*, pp. 28–29. It seems clear that Butler originally envisaged the *passing by Parliament* of certain codes of industrial practice (*Issues*, p. 9); and in his article in the *Observer* (5 April, 1946), he spoke of drafting with Parliament's aid 'a code of conditions which would guide authority'. In the charter itself the notion of compulsory codes passed by Parliament is rejected (as a Socialist disease) (*Industrial Charter*, p. 28), preferring example plus pressure (by withholding large contracts of public authorities) as means of realizing the observance of the proposed codes.

[49] Cf. *Issues*, p. 12, and *Industrial Charter*, p. 33.

[50] Cf. *Issues*, p. 10, and *Industrial Charter*, pp. 23–4. Note other similarities of idea or turn of phrase in the two documents: cf. *Issues*, p. 2, and *Industrial Charter*, p. 3; *Issues*, pp. 7–8, *Industrial Charter*, p. 4; *Issues*, p. 13, and *Industrial Charter*, pp. 31–2.

[51] Harris, p. 103. See also *Conference Report, 1947*, p. 119.

[52] Now Lord Chandos.

[53] Now Lord Amory. Contemporary reports of the composition of the Committee occasionally confused L. S. Amery with Heathcote Amory. Amory entered the House in the general election of 1945.

[54] Harris, p. 103, noted the 'suspicious alacrity' with which 'a cut-and-dried series of remarkably detailed proposals were embodied in the form of a charter for industry'.

[55] Francis Boyd, *Richard Austen Butler* (London, 1956), p. 91.

[56] *Industrial Charter*, p. 34, and especially p. 28: 'The conditions of industrial life are too varied to be brought within the cramping grip of legislation.' See also *Industrial Charter*, p. 19, 'Industrial Taxation', for a reference to the views of 'Working Party Reports'.

[57] R. H. S. Crossman's 'The Ideologist of Inequality', in Kingsley Martin and Vicky, *New Statesman Portraits* (London, 1957), p. 68.

[58] Harris, p. 104. See also p. 106.

[59] Council Minute Book, II, 13–14 March, 1947, p. 3.

[60] *Conference Report, 1947*, p. 119.

[61] Harris, p. 107.

[62] *Industrial Charter*, p. 3.

[63] *Industrial Charter*, p. 11.

[64] *Industrial Charter*, p. 11.

[65] *Industrial Charter*, pp. 18–19.

[66] *Industrial Charter*, p. 22.

[67] *Industrial Charter*, pp. 23–4.

[68] *Industrial Charter*, pp. 24–6.

[69] *Industrial Charter*, p. 26.

[70] *Industrial Charter*, p. 29.

[71] *Industrial Charter*, pp. 20–37.

[72] *Industrial Charter*, p. 29.

[73] *Daily Express*, 'Under Which Flag,' 12 May, 1947.

[74] *Evening Standard*, 'Change of Heart', 12 May, 1947.

[75] *Daily Mirror*, 12 May, 1947.

[76] *News Chronicle*, 'Tory Policy', 12 May, 1947.

[77] *Yorkshire Post*, 'A Better Plan for Every Man', 12 May, 1947.

[78] *Manchester Guardian*, 'The New Toryism', 12 May, 1947.

[79] *Observer*, 'Charter', 18 May, 1947.

[80] *Economist*, 'Tory Reformation?', 17 May, 1947.

[81] *Spectator*, 'Tory Programme', 16 May, 1947.

[82] *Tribune*, 'The Tories are Split', 16 May, 1947.

[83] The *National Review* was a further, if not quite so persistent, critic of *The Industrial Charter* on the right-wing of the Conservative Party. See Arthur Page, 'Conservative Laodiceans', *National Review*, CXXIX (September 1947), p. 207.

[84] *Recorder*, 'Has Anyone Heard of Capitalism?', 17 May, 1947.

[85] *Truth*, 'The Recipe as Before', 16 May, 1947.

[86] *Truth*, 23 and 30 May, 1947; 20 June, 1947; *Recorder*, 16 and 30 August, 6, 13 and 27 September, 1947; *City Press*, 'British Economic Policy Causes Anxiety', 20 June, 1947.

[87] Conference Minutes, 1946, p. 2.

[88] *The Times*, 5 October, 1946.

[89] *Birmingham Post*, 'London Letter', 13 May, 1946.

[90] *Daily Telegraph*, 23 May, 1947.

[91] *Observer*, 'Tory Headquarters versus Beaverbrook', 15 June, 1947.

[92] *Sunday Express*, 'Crossbencher', 8 June, 1947.

[93] *Truth*, 13 June, 1947.

[94] *Observer*, 'Tory attack on "Forces of Reaction" ', 15 June, 1947.

[95] *Truth*, 20 June, 1947.

[96] *City Press*, 20 June, 1947.

[97] *Recorder*, 'The Milk-and-Water Charter', 30 August, 1947, while admitting that 'about 10 to 1 Conservatives writing to us about *The Industrial Charter* agree with it' still stated that '[it] will split the party unless it is abandoned'.

[98] *St Helens and District Reporter*, 'M.P. Discusses the Industrial Charter', 1 July, 1947.

[99] See below, p. 178, for other criticism of the policy-making process.

[100] Hinchingbrooke, *Review*, October 1947, pp. 492–3. For his criticism of *The Industrial Charter* in particular see pp. 493–7. The essence of his objection to the charter seems to have been that it was 'not sufficiently weighted on the side of individual initiative', p. 497.

[101] *Daily Telegraph*, 'Conservative Report on Industry Soon', 28 April, 1947.

[102] *Liverpool Daily Post*, 12 May, 1947.

[103] *The Times*, 'Mr Eden on the Charter', 19 May, 1947.

[104] *Liverpool Daily Post*, 16 May, 1947.

[105] R. A. Butler, *Daily Telegraph*, 'The Industrial Charter Has Made a Good Start', 19 May, 1947. Lord Woolton writing in the party journal, *The Onlooker*, in the same month described party policy-making as follows: 'Resolutions passed by the National Union are sent to [the Leader] for his information and guidance, but no resolution, however emphatic, binds him on questions of policy. In short, the party Leader is expected to formulate policy.'

[106] *Daily Telegraph*, 'Socialists Fear Charter', 22 May, 1947.

[107] *Observer*, 'Tory Headquarters Versus Beaverbrook', 15 June, 1947.

[108] *Observer*, 'Tory Attack on "Forces of Reaction" ', 15 June, 1947.

[109] *Sunday Express*, 'Tory Plan Welcomed', 15 June, 1947; *Daily Graphic*, 16 June, 1947.

[110] '*Looking Ahead Circles' and How to Form Them*, [early 1943]; and *Looking Ahead*, [early 1943], both published by the Post-war Problems Reconstruction Committee.

[111] R. A. Butler, 'The Two-Way Flow of Ideas', *Observer*, 23 March, 1947. In practice only the best reports were forwarded from the C.P.C. to the Research Department.

[112] *Yorkshire Post*, 'The Industrial Charter', 15 September, 1947.

[113] *Recorder*, 'The Editor's View', 27 September, 1947.

[114] R. A. Butler, 'Prelude to the Brighton Conference', *Tory Challenge* (C.C.O., September 1947), p. 1.

[115] R. A. Butler, *Tory Challenge*, p. 1. Cf. *Manchester Guardian*, 'Conservatives and Industry', 23 September, 1947.

[116] *Conference Report 1947*, p. 26.

[117] *Conference Report 1947*. p. 26. See also p. 37.

[118] *Conference Report 1947*, p. 37. In times like these strict accuracy counts for less than emotive impact.

[119] *Conference Report 1947*, p. 26.

[120] *Hendon Times*, 'Industrial Charter', 6 June, 1947.

[121] R. A. Butler, *Tory Challenge*, p. 1.

[122] *Conference Report*, *1947*, p. 47.

[123] Harris, p. 108.

[124] *Conference Report*, *1947*, p. 48.

[125] The only other spokesman against the motion was Frank Burrow (Lancaster). Considering the size of the vote against the motion the opponents of the charter were well represented in the debate.

[126] *Conference Report*, *1947*, p. 49.

[127] *Conference Report*, *1947*, p. 50.

[128] *Conference Report*, *1947*, p. 51.

[129] *Conference Report*, *1947*, p. 54.

[130] *What We Think* (Second Phase Report), pp. 6–9.

[131] Maurice Edelman, 'A Day with the Tories', *New Statesman and Nation*, 11 October, 1947, p. 284.

[132] *Conference Report*, *1947*, for the debates on the 'Charter of Liberties', pp. 60–1, and 'subversive activities', pp. 95 ff.

[133] Aubrey Jones, p. 221.

CHAPTER VI

Policy Reformulation: The Second Phase

ONCE Churchill had consented to the publication of *The Industrial Charter* the way was clear for Butler to press on with his determination to restate Conservative policy on a broad front. He was supported in this aim by the enthusiasm for further statements of party policy shown at the Brighton party conference. Resolutions were passed calling for 'the immediate production of a Charter for British Farms',[1] 'a policy for furthering the Empire's economic and political unity',[2] and 'a policy for Wales to the fulfilment of which Welsh people [might] look forward with real hope'.[3] Within the next year and a half such policy statements were duly published as *The Agricultural Charter*, *Imperial Policy*, and *The Conservative Policy for Wales and Monmouthshire*, and Conservatives were fortified by further statements of policy on women's affairs[4] and Scotland.[5]

These documents hardly warrant the attention we have previously given to *The Industrial Charter*. And yet they are not without significance. A survey of the process by which they were formulated and later considered by the mass party adds further to appreciation of the variations through which the Conservative policy-making process in opposition proceeded. A glance at the main features of their contents should also fill in a few details of the emerging 'New Conservatism'.

ROUNDING OUT CONSERVATIVE POLICY

I

The process by which *The Agricultural Charter* reached the state of a published document and then, months later, was accorded the blessings of the party conference was similar to that for *The Industrial Charter* – except, it should be added, that the birth of the industrial policy was altogether a far more traumatic affair. Again Churchill set up a special committee to handle the formulation of the documents, again Butler chaired it. The committee consisting of three members of the party's Agricultural Committee, Capt Harry Crookshank, Sir Thomas Dugdale, and Anthony Hurd, was assisted by Michael Fraser (who had just served as one of the secretaries for the Industrial Policy Committee). Whereas *The Industrial Charter* had its origins in a draft prepared beforehand for the Industrial Policy Committee by the Research Department, it appears that the process was reversed in the case of *The Agricultural Charter*. Members of the party's agricultural committee (including R. H. Turton, Major Christopher York, William Snadden and John Baker White) apparently helped to play a rôle in the drafting of the agricultural policy document in the early stages, even before the conference resolution in October 1947.[6] The general views of this committee– and according to Butler, at the party conference in 1948, the Committee of Peers in the House of Lords as well[7] – were then forwarded to the Research Department, where details were added. Presumably the Advisory Committee on Policy and Political Education had a look at the document at some stage, but specific references to its rôle – in contrast here to the prominent part played in the production of *The Industrial Charter* – are totally lacking. A Central Office press release referred to the production of the charter by the committee 'in consultation with over 200 experts in England and Wales and in Scotland'.[8] The final drafting of the document by Butler was confirmed by the special shadow cabinet committee and forwarded to the Leader of the party for approval. *The Agricultural Charter* was published on 25 June, 1948.

Press reaction to the policy statement on agriculture was, on the whole, less favourable than it had been for *The Industrial Charter*.[9] But it was the reaction of the farming papers which was crucial. The following extract from a report on farm newspaper reaction written by a Central Office official gives a fair summary of their response:

> From reading the attached press cuttings it would appear that *The Agricultural Charter* has not received a wildly enthusiastic reception from the farming papers. In fact, the *Dairy Farmer* is slightly hostile. The general line taken is that there is not a great deal of difference between the Labour and Conservative agricultural policies, and this is a matter for self-congratulation by the farmers as it provides a certainty of continuation of the

> present policy of guaranteed prices, etc. The chief point which is commented on favourably is the unequivocal guarantee of prices as opposed to the somewhat dubious one in the Agriculture Act.[10]

Central Office may have been a little disappointed that the papers did not show more enthusiasm for the 'Agricultural Workers' Charter', but they could hardly have been surprised or annoyed that the tendency was to find little difference between Conservative and Labour agricultural policy in general. There was much to commend in *Truth*'s observation that Conservatives could not be accused of stealing their charter from the Labour Party since the Labour Party had taken its agricultural policy largely from the Conservatives in the first place.[11] Considering the conditions under which British agriculture was operating and the fact that the farming community (a privileged interest with the Conservative Party at any time) was generally satisfied with the main lines of Labour's agricultural policy, it would have been very surprising indeed if Conservative policy had diverged greatly from Labour's. In fact, *Dairy Farmer*, in July 1948, noted that at the press conference to introduce *The Agricultural Charter*, Butler was unable to point to any radical differences between the charter and Government policy. *The Agricultural Charter* is an excellent example of a crucial characteristic of British Conservatism – of the way the Conservative Party will take over the main lines of policy laid down by the left and shape the details of that policy to conform to its own particular principles and biases.

The key notion of the Conservative statement of agricultural policy was the acceptance – nay, the improvement – of the system of guaranteed prices provided for by Clause I of Labour's 1947 Agriculture Act. The present wording of the Act, the charter claimed, was too evasive. The Conservatives promised: '[to] give the British farmer real confidence in the future by guaranteeing prices and markets for all the food that he can produce, in accordance with the rules of good husbandry, up to our overall target'.[12] The document claimed, reasonably enough, that it was impossible to specify this overall target. In addition they would 'include oats in the schedule of commodities for which guaranteed prices are provided' and guarantee the price of wool. The charter also promised to increase the level of agricultural production compared to

1938–39 by 50 per cent ('given fair prices and stable markets and adequate priority for capital development'[13] and depending on the availability of food stuffs). When returned to power the Conservatives would (perhaps) reintroduce sliding tariffs seasonally adjusted to protect British horticulture, and encourage efficient marketing and distribution of horticultural produce. Subsidies for animal foodstuffs would also be removed, once the guaranteed price system was in operation.

'It is the duty of the Government,' the charter stated, 'to set out the long-term aims for agriculture, to ensure the stability without which the farmers cannot achieve these aims, and to use its machinery and powers to promote efficiency.'[14] In promoting efficiency the charter visualized the taking over and – to the Conservative mind – improving of the machinery largely set out by Labour legislation. While accepting the system of appointing County Committees instituted since the war, the charter proposed to make certain important changes in the way the committee system worked: the permanent staff of civil servants assisting the committees would be reduced; the amount of pool labour would also be reduced 'and the Machinery Service as far as possible replaced by commercial enterprise on a co-operative or private basis'.[15] It is also proposed to 'free the N.A.A.S. [The National Agricultural Advisory Service] from bureaucracy',[16] expand agricultural research facilities and make available greater credit facilities for farmers. The charter also, accepted the main lines of the Government's 1945 Forestry Act, but proposed to make the Minister of Agriculture and the Secretary of State for Scotland (instead of the Board of Trade) responsible for price fixing and issuing felling licences, accepted the statutory regulation of minimum wages and agreed to continue the present powers of the Wages Boards, and promised to extend the provision of loans to smallholders who rent their holding from private landowners as part of the encouragement of a 'property-owning democracy'.

This review of the content of *The Agricultural Charter* has deliberately emphasized Conservative acquiescence in many aspects of Labour policy. But this is not the entire story.[17] A glance at the charter's proposals dealing with marketing arrangements illustrates the limit beyond which Conservative accommodation would not go.

The system under which the Ministry of Food controlled both the prices and supply of food in a post-war situation, the Conservatives considered 'not conducive to efficient marketing'. They proposed to abolish many of the existing powers of the Ministry of Food when food rationing ended and to restore private enterprise in the international trade of foodstuffs. They rejected completely the Commodity Commission proposed by the Lucas Committee; instead of government commission-controlled distribution and processing the charter favoured 'producers' co-operation both through voluntary organizations and through statutory marketing boards'. These marketing boards would be relieved of the responsibility of fixing prices and regulating sales: their main tasks would be to improve distribution (to be handled privately) by providing better marketing information and storage and processing facilities. Rather than central regulation from the beginning, the Conservative approach was to favour *ad hoc* investigation 'where there [was] a *prima facie* case that distribution [was] below the required standard'.[18]

The presentation of the party's statement of agricultural policy to the public and more particularly to the party activists had some characteristics similar to the handling of the previous charter. Again Butler encouraged the mass party to take a part in shaping the party's ultimate policy: '[*The Agricultural Charter*] was issued now,' he said at the press conference, 'so that the proposals could be studied and discussed with a view to the adoption of a definite policy at the party's annual conference in October'.[19] In the charter itself it was stated that: 'we have not aimed at producing a final party programme'; but in a preface to the pamphlet *What Do You Think . . . About the Agricultural Charter* it was said that 'the charter had laid down the lines of policy which the party will follow when it regains power'. Again the full scale Two-Way Movement of Ideas discussion of *The Agricultural Charter* was set up to follow the publication of the document, while the *What Do You Think?* discussion pamphlet on the charter (written by Sir Thomas Dugdale) was to be published in September 1948 to precede the party conference debate. Again the party's published document was 'warmly welcomed' by the party conference.[20]

But there were a few differences too. In the first place the policy-making process for *The Agricultural Charter* did actually allow for a certain limited influence from the Two-Way Movement of Ideas.

The first phase of the movement had included a discussion topic dealing with agriculture, and this phase in fact coincided with the policy formulation going on within the party's back-bench agricultural committee. *Policy Paper 5* informed the participants in the movement that:

> . . . selected reports of those groups which studied agriculture in the first phase are being made available to the committee which is engaged in drawing up the charter for that industry. Thus the Two-Way Movement of Ideas is really working and a new link between private members of the party and those who are responsible for drawing up its policy is being created. Our experiment has begun to work.[21]

Having established this difference between the process for *The Industrial Charter* and *The Agricultural Charter*, it is nevertheless important to note that a comparison of the original *What Do You Think?* pamphlet, setting out the specific discussion questions, with the report of the first phase of the movement and *The Agricultural Charter* itself reveals that, as was nearly always the case, the contribution of the discussion groups to the content of the new charter was very minor indeed.

Secondly, although the right-wing press reacted to *The Agricultural Charter* in much the same way as it had earlier responded to *The Industrial Charter*, there was nothing approaching the same feeling against the second charter within the mass party and the parliamentary party that had followed the publication of the industrial policy statement.[22] There was also not the same concerted campaign of political education from Central Office to assure the charter's safe passage at conference.[23]

Thirdly, although there was only one dissentient vote on the resolution welcoming the charter as a statement of party policy, there was a tendency on the part of speakers in the debate to take Butler's earlier vagaries seriously and actually to suggest future modifications to the published document.[24] Butler listened from the platform to criticism of the paucity of the charter's references to hill-farming and fertilizers, to a proposal for a properly constituted judicial tribunal to hear appeals against dispossession under the 1947 Agriculture Act,[25] to expressions of disappointment with the charter's bloodless references to the 'Agricultural Workers' Charter', and to several appeals to the policy formulators to incorporate the suggestions of the conference and the Two-Way Movement dealing with agriculture that was only then beginning to operate. When he rose to sum up the debate he made it clear that the 'definite policy' to be adopted by the party conference to which he was giving his support was the already published *Agricultural Charter*; but he did give the assurance that: '. . . the points raised in the debate [would] be considered with a view to incorporation in the final party policy when it is produced for the next election'.[26] And, indeed, his promise was in part made good, for there is clear evidence in the party's synoptic policy statement, *The Right Road for Britain*, published in July 1949, of the influence of suggestions on the subject of hill-farming which were made at the party conference in 1948.[27]

The one person who voted against the charter, R. Statham, Chairman of the Newcastle-under-Lyme Conservative Association, later wrote an article in *Tory Challenge* criticizing the manner in which the document had been foisted upon the conference. 'My first objection to *The Agricultural Charter* was,' he wrote, 'its method of presentation. For we, as representatives of the party, were asked to confirm a document that had already been sold to the public as the party policy.' 'If this had been rejected,' he continued, 'what would have been the position of the party? Just a laughing stock.' Mr Statham also objected to certain features of the contents of the charter and claimed that from his survey many would have voted against who did in fact abstain. His parting shot in the article expressed the hope that '. . . when our Imperial Charter is published . . . we shall first be given the ordinary democratic right as representatives of discussing it before it is sold to the public.'[28]

II

As a statement of party policy, *The Agricultural Charter* failed to make the impact of *The Industrial Charter*. The policy statements which followed made even less. *The Industrial Charter* had already laid down in as specific terms as the party felt willing or able to state the main lines of the party's social, economic, and (in a few lines) even imperial policy if and when it was returned to power. *The Agricultural Charter* had clarified the party's agricultural policy. To go much further into details – on, say, the oft-mentioned plans for the reorganization of the nationalized industries or for a housing policy – might have risked the dangers of over-saturating both public and party activists alike and, more important, might perhaps have provided the Labour Party (as Conservatives now claim Labour's detailed policy statements have provided them) with useful ammunition.[29] The course chosen – and quite the wisest one in the circumstances – was to keep up the image of a party deeply involved in rethinking the basis of its policy while in practice turning out largely innocuous general statements of policy – blending criticisms of the Labour Party with the occasional positive promise – on subjects sure to mollify sectional or regional interests within the party and electorate as a whole.

One indication of the minor importance of the specialized statements of party policy which followed the publication of *The Agricultural Charter* was that Butler took less direct responsibility for their production. *The Conservative Policy for Wales and Monmouthshire*,[30] was written almost entirely by Enoch Powell, an officer at the Conservative Research Department and slipped rather unobtrusively on to the political scene on St David's Day, 1949. Its main proposal – the creation of a Cabinet Minister with special responsibility for Wales – had been mooted in 1948 by Butler, and the party conference that year had registered its agreement with the suggestion.[31] The remaining proposals in this brief document – published in English and Welsh – were largely a rag-bag of ideas drawn from the industrial and agricultural charters judiciously mixed with concessions to the Welsh national spirit. There was no Two-Way Movement of Ideas set up to accompany its production, or to follow its publication. And Butler had seen to it at the 1948 party conference that there would be no need to present the policy statement at the next annual conference for approval.

> We have ready [he said, at the conclusion of the brief debate at the Llandudno Conference in 1948] if the conference approves this resolution today – I hope unanimously – a full statement of our attitude to Welsh problems, which we can set about publishing immediately. I therefore hope that you and the Conference will come to this unanimous decision, and we shall take that as a sign that you would like us to publish . . . the outline of our views upon these most vital matters.[32]

The 'report' on women's affairs, like the policy statement on Wales, took a long time to materialize; moreover, its development was not nearly as smooth. As early as 30 August, 1948, the *Yorkshire Post* referred to the formulation of a 'Women's Charter' by a Committee[33] under the chairmanship of Malcolm McCorquodale, a member of the shadow cabinet. The membership of the committee, according to its report 'remain[s] anonymous', but the names of the following women were associated with the document: Lady Tweedsmuir; Lady Davidson; Mrs Dorothy Russell (a Conservative candidate for Leicester); Miss Marjorie Maxse; and Mrs T. A. Emmet. The Committee's secretary was Miss Helen Low. The committee, the *Yorkshire Post* account continued, 'have been working steadily, receiving and sifting evidence, and have met at least once a week since the spring, except for an August holiday break. But they will not have the charter ready for the autumn Party Conference in October as was first hoped'.[34] The question of a policy for women was, however, brought up at the 1948 party conference. A resolution was moved in the following terms:

> That this conference warmly welcomes the work of the Women's Charter Committee and asks that, in view of the continual misrepresentation of our intentions, opportunity be taken to restate in their Report the general principles of the party's policy for the care of children and adolescents, the sick and the aged, and in regard to the status of women, home-owning, nutrition and the fundamental importance of satisfactory home life.[35]

Only one man (in addition to McCorquodale who summed up the debate) participated in the debate, and he supported the notion of the proposed charter. The bulk of the speeches – fittingly – fell to the women. Surprisingly, perhaps, the majority of the women speakers were antagonistic to the idea of publishing a charter and to the resolution itself. The line adopted by most opponents of the resolution – a line put very effectively by Miss Eileen Holden and particularly Miss Frances Vale (a member of the Young Conservative Central Committee) – was that 'the charter habit was psychologically unsound': that it could end up in a mere 'vote-catching stunt'; that it would be unwise to set women's problems as a thing apart; and that they should be integrated with general policy statements.[36] McCorquodale attempted a manly defence of his committee's intentions, assured the conference that the remarks made would be taken to heart, and begged conference for approval 'to go forward and finish our report'. Whether or not conference was put off a little by his comment that '*when* the report is published, [critics would find] a great deal of what they have actually said here had been considered'[37] we cannot say, but the Llandudno conference acted as few Conservative conferences before or since have acted, and defeated the conference resolution!

The Committee appears to have been only slightly perturbed by the decision; for in late October it was announced that, despite the conference vote, the committee was going ahead with its plans. It would, however, Mrs T. A. Emmet announced, welcome suggestions for a new name for the document.

In March 1949 the formula had been found, and the committee's efforts were published under the title *A True Balance*. The document was formally presented at the 22nd Conservative and Unionist Women's Annual Conference on 19 May, 1949, and given 'enthusiastic approval'.[38] But this was the end of it. The report was not, as McCorquodale had rather innocently suggested, before the axe fell at the 1948 party conference, 'available for consideration by the Great Conference . . . next autumn'.[39]

III

The Brighton Conference in 1947 had demanded a statement of imperial policy. The 1948 party conference came and went – accompanied by a full-scale demonstration of Conservative commitment to the Imperial Cause and an urgent re-affirmation of its earlier expressed request – with only the assurance by Col Oliver Stanley that 'work is far advanced'.[40] Its gestation period equalled the elephant's. Then finally, on 24 June, 1949, the long-awaited statement – *Imperial Policy* – was published.

'The groundwork for the statement,' the *Yorkshire Post* reported, 'was prepared by a Committee consisting of Lord Tweedsmuir, Mr Lennox Boyd, Mr Gammans, Brigadier Low and Mr Dodds-Parker, all experts in this field.'[41] Lord Tweedsmuir was described by several papers as presiding over the committee, and many others connected Oliver Stanley with the guidance of the drafting of the text and Churchill or Butler with the editing.

It was the longest of the policy statements yet produced: well turned-out and bearing more than a few traces of the flourish associated with the High Churchillian Style. And yet, considering the amount of time spent on it, there was nothing very original in it. The old notion of an 'Empire economic partnership' was put forward once again bolstered by vague suggestions for 'adequate machinery for economic consultation' and 'a system of Imperial Priorities for the investment of money, capital goods and trade'.[42] Imperial preference would be preserved. Old ideas were refurbished in the form of the suggestion for a Commonwealth Tribunal to act as an advisory panel to which disputes between Commonwealth countries could be referred in cases where they could not be resolved by other methods and the proposals for a British Empire and Commonwealth Defence Council of an advisory nature and a 'Commonwealth Combined Staff'.[43]

But *Imperial Policy* was not entirely a copy of old Tory rhetoric: it had about it, as the *News Chronicle* remarked, 'the marks of the "new liberalism" ' – at least 'the roll of Imperial drums [was] notably absent'.[44] With this policy statement the Conservative Party showed a clear acceptance of the constitutional development of the post-war Commonwealth as it was shaping under the Labour Government, and affirmed as its 'objective' the guiding of colonial peoples along the road to self-government – but still, be it noted, 'within the framework of the British Empire'.[45]

The *Imperial Policy* statement was accepted unanimously by the 1949 party conference without any accompanying Two-Way Movement of Ideas. Two aspects of the subject matter of the document were, however, topics of discussion within earlier phases of the movement. During the first phase (1946–47) participants had been invited to send in their opinions on 'The Commonwealth and Empire', and during the fifth phase 'Western Union' was discussed. Although the report of the first phase would certainly have been available for the eyes of the consultative–determinative core in framing the final document, it is unlikely – judging from the quality of the report[46] – that it was of much use. On most questions the replies followed closely the lead laid down by Lord Cranborne in his *What Do You Think?* pamphlet. The discussion on the subject of Western Union ended on 31 May, 1949, and reports from the groups would not have reached the policy-formulators before publication of the policy statement. In any case opinion on the subject was very divided – although 'almost without exception', according to the report, the participants supported it 'as an ideal'[47] – and it was perhaps as well that the policy document contented itself with the generalities of two brief paragraphs.[48]

With the publication of *Imperial Policy* Conservative restatement of specific areas of policy was virtually completed. (The party's specialized policy statement on Scotland was not published until November 1949. The document, entitled *Scottish Control of Scottish Affairs*, was prepared by a committee of Scottish M.P.s and Peers under the chairmanship of James Stuart, and assisted by Iain Macleod (Research Department Officer) who acted as secretary. The main point of the document was, as the title implies, the proposition of greater devolution of responsibility to Scotland, especially for the nationalized industries. A brief summary of the document can be found in *This is the Road*, a Conservative Central Office document published in 1950.) The task remained of pulling together the specialized statements and rounding them out into a comprehensive document which would deal – at least in passing – with subjects not yet covered and, then, of producing from this a positive programme for presentation in the election campaign.

DRAWING POLICY TOGETHER

I

Although, once *The Agricultural Charter* had been published, the chairmanship of committees producing the less important policy statements passed into other hands, Butler by no means withdrew from his crucial position at the apex of Conservative policy reformulation. The Research Department at which he still spent much of his time continued to produce drafts of Conservative policy in a number of subjects not intended for immediate publication, and Butler maintained a watch over the documents being prepared for publication. More important, however, he began in late 1948 to supervise the production of a comprehensive statement of party policy.

By this time the parliamentary party was taking a keener interest in the policy-making process. Two-Way Movements, self-appointed advisory committees, and the consultation of experts throughout the country may have been acceptable when charter-making was a novelty and when the results were regarded as merely general statements of the party's attitude to specific problems. Now the proposed policy restatement assumed in the crisis atmosphere of 1949 the flavour and importance of an election document. It has been suggested earlier that the 'reconstitution' of the Advisory Committee on Policy and Political Education reflected the desire to achieve two main ends: to bring the parliamentary party more formally within the policy-making process, and to assure that, as the election approached, the policy-process was more tightly centred upon the Leader of the party. Minor changes in the policy-making process for the full policy statement – what was to be called the *Right Road for Britain* – confirm this assertion.

A sub-committee of the shadow cabinet was again formed to take the chief responsibility for the policy statement. This time Anthony Eden, who had not played a significant rôle in the policy-making process to date, took the chair. David Clarke and Harry Hopkinson (joint directors of the Research Department along with Percy Cohen) acted as secretaries to the committee. Butler was, of course, a member of the sub-committee, and his position as chairman of the Research Department – where the preparation of further policy had been going on for some time – assured his continued prominence in the proceedings. Clarke was, under Butler's direction, given the main burden of co-ordinating previously published material with the newly-produced ideas and preparing a first draft of the new document. Meanwhile, members of the shadow cabinet contributed their own memoranda on party policy. At the same time Butler appointed Oliver Poole to act as his 'right-hand man' to keep in touch with 'the people that mattered on the party's back-benches' and enlist their support, to acquaint them with what was going on at the Research Department and, generally, to make the parliamentary party feel a part of the policy-making process.

But the 1922 Committee had for some time been taking an interest in the formulation of party policy. A sub-committee of the Executive Committee of the 1922 Committee consisting of David Eccles, Guy Lloyd, and Robin Turton had been charged with the task of preparing a statement of party principles in the light of which party committees would be encouraged to frame their specific policy statements. Each prepared separately a draft of the statement and an agreed draft was put to the committee as a whole. Their product – a ten-point statement of 'Principles of Policy' – was an undistinguished recitation of clichés, timeless in their irrelevancy to the particular problems then facing Britain. 'Man's first duty is to serve God, and not the State'; 'The aim of the community should be to secure that as many as possible own their own homes and their own land'; 'Britain and the Commonwealth Empire have a joint responsibility to prevent the world from being dominated by fear, and to give the world the same liberty that we enjoy,'[49] were three 'principles' typical of the quality and originality of the others!

Written communication of opinion between the 1922 Committee and the Leader of the party is apparently rare, but on 27 February, 1949, Sir Arnold Gridley, Chairman of the 1922 Committee, sent to Churchill a letter in which was included 'in condensed form the suggestions [on policy] put forward by members of the 1922 Executive Committee'.[50] These 'suggestions' were presumably supposed to be drawn from the sub-committee's draft, but in changing the ten 'Principles of Policy' to 'Nine Points of Conservative Policy' the original was thoroughly lost in the process. Sir Arnold's version of the committee's document – a clear improvement – made recommendations on a number of specific topics, and perhaps only the recommendation to 'maintain existing social services subject to requiring private payment for any services which can be shown to be elaborate or unnecessary'[51] would have embarrassed Butler and his policy formulators had it been transferred immediately to published party policy. Otherwise, the 'Nine Points' seemed to fit in well with 'official' policy.

Sir Arnold's letter to Churchill coincided with renewed pressure from the mass party and the parliamentary party to get on with the publication of a full restatement of party policy. For some time disappointment with the party's failure to win any seats from Labour in the by-elections had brought criticism of its policy – among other things.[52] The victory of the Labour Party in the Hammersmith South by-election on 24 February, 1949 – a by-election which the Conservatives clearly expected to win – upset the party as nothing before had done.[53] Part of the criticism by Conservative M.P.s, it is true, centred on the poor showing the party had been making in the House, but, as usual, party policy did not escape their critical glare. To this was added a chorus of criticism from a generally Conservative-disposed press. The *Scotsman* warned that the party must frame alternative policies without stunts: the chief lesson for the Tories was, it believed, that the party must have a positive policy.[54] The *Sunday Times* expressed the view that: 'It is plain that the constructive policies of the Opposition as expounded on the platform and by the Opposition in the House of Commons have so far had little effect.'[55] The *Daily Telegraph*, even, noted that: 'The party has not succeeded in translating its policy and intentions into terms which are acceptable or even intelligible to large numbers of the electorate.'[56] The *Telegraph*'s political correspondent in an article entitled 'Hammersmith Causes Conservative Unrest', on 26 February, stated that: 'It has become apparent that such statements as *The Industrial* and *Agricultural Charters* have not been fully appreciated in the country.' A few days earlier an editorial in the *Birmingham Post* (21 February, 1949) had complained that *The Industrial Charter* had not been well publicized or properly explained.

Hugh Massingham, the *Observer*'s political correspondent, and surely the shrewdest and best informed of the students of the political scene at the time, forecast that the 'ultimate effect of the Hammersmith by-election may be a new statement of policy'. He recognized the dangers inherent in the party's continued failure at by-elections – the possibility that the extreme right wing, although still very small, might be able to make political capital from a connection between the 'dangerous' *Industrial Charter* and the party's inability to recover the electoral initiative – but his general impression was that 'Hammersmith had strengthened Mr Butler's position'. Butler, he wrote, 'has always been in favour of a new policy statement and is now much more likely to have his way than before'.[57]

The *Daily Telegraph*'s political correspondent also thought a demand likely from the parliamentary party for an immediate restatement of party policy. Sir Arnold Gridley's letter to Churchill on 27 February had referred to a meeting on Thursday, 10 March, at which the back-benchers hoped to have the opportunity of discussing with the Leader the policy suggestions he was forwarding on behalf of the 1922 Committee. The 'unrest' in the party brought about by the Hammersmith result led the *Telegraph*'s correspondent to believe that the subject of party policy would come up at the 1922

Committee's meeting on 3 March. 'The view . . . may be expressed next Thursday,' he wrote, 'that a simpler, shorter and more popular statement of party policy should be produced.'[58]

Accounts of private meetings like that of the 1922 Committee are not often very reliable, but, if we are to believe newspaper reports the next day, the case for a restatement of party policy *was* made by a number of members ('not all Tory Reformers by any means') who argued that the lack of a clear statement of policy was a cause of the loss of the by-election. Churchill, who attended the meeting, was, according to one version, pressed to make a statement on Tory policy in which 'he is believed to have made it clear that the Conservatives [would] not try to outbid the Labour Party by offering a programme of more extensive reform'.[59] No specific promise of a policy restatement seems to have been extracted.

A controversy was also carried on vigorously in the correspondence columns of the 'opinion-leading press'. On 3 March, 1949, A. R. Harvie started the ball rolling in *The Times* with a long and constructively critical consideration of Conservative policy.[60] Before the argument finally died out at the end of March, Robert Boothby and Richard Law had staged a running battle (which most other writers found 'academic') on the subject of multilateral trade versus empire preference; Alex Spearman had jumped in to support Law; Sir Herbert Williams had come to the defence of the Baldwin–Chamberlain economic policy of the thirties; Lord Hinchingbrooke, Lord Salisbury, and L. S. Amery had got in their thrusts; and Quintin Hogg had thoroughly worried Fitzroy Maclean (and perhaps others too) with his reference to Conservative commitment to 'the creation and maintenance of a Social Democratic State'.[61] The 'debate' in *The Times* was echoed by other Conservative M.P.s, prospective candidates, and party members in the *Yorkshire Post*, *Scotsman*, and *Daily Telegraph*.

All this 'sound and fury' T. E. Utley found distressing. The correspondence in *The Times* was a mistake, he held, for it 'allowed the Opposition to be misrepresented as a horde of back-biting time-servers' preoccupied with the next general election.[62] But, mistake or not, it provided a fitting background to the discussion of party policy scheduled for the meeting of the Central Council which followed two weeks after the 1922 Committee's 'inquest'. The meeting was to be held in two stages with a short morning session on 17 March and an afternoon session on 18 March. The debate on party policy was to take place on the second day on a resolution submitted by Ian Harvey on behalf of the Harrow East Conservative Association stating that: 'the policy of the Conservative Party must be clearly stated without further delay, and must be clearly formulated in terms which can be readily understood and assimilated by the whole electorate'.[63] Since it had been known for some time that Churchill would not be attending the proceedings, the summing up of the meeting would be left to Lord Woolton. Butler was to reply to the debate on policy.

With the party in hot pursuit of an immediate statement of policy and Churchill still appearing to drag his feet on the issue, the position in which Butler and Woolton found themselves was hardly an enviable one. Butler's sympathies towards a policy restatement were well known. The report of the Advisory Committee on Policy and Political Education which was submitted to the Central Council meeting stated that: 'The Research Department has a great deal of material in readiness for the general election with a view to producing a general statement of policy directly this is required by Mr Churchill.'[64] Lord Woolton's commitment to policy restatement was, on the other hand, less certain. He was often represented in the press as being antagonistic to the attempt by Butler and Macmillan to bring the party around to a more progressive posture. Certainly the party chairman spent more of his time in public speeches advocating the removal of restrictive controls than in boosting the charters,[65] but the 'division between the two camps' was probably neither as real[66] nor as important as it was sometimes made out to be, and may be taken as a further example of the tendency on the part of political correspondents and editorial writers to exploit the space-filling advantages of the dialectic technique and their disposition to overplay Lord Woolton's importance in policy-making circles.

The situation was greatly relieved by Churchill's remarks at a private dinner meeting with prospective Conservative candidates on the eve of the policy debate. According to reports the Leader of the party promised to issue a personal statement of policy in May at the first big meeting he would be addressing after his return from the United States. This statement of policy would, Churchill apparently said, give 'no details', but would rather be a précis of the existing charters. Whether Churchill's promise was widely known by the delegates we do not know for certain – *The Times*, for example, carried only a brief notice that the meeting had taken place – but it was likely that most learned of it from the prospective candidate-delegates (like Ian Harvey himself). The fact that the meeting could be persuaded to adopt unanimously an amended resolution on party policy – one which took the urgency out of the original motion and settled instead for the milder affirmation that the party 'would welcome the restatement of . . . policy in simple clear-cut terms'[67] – suggests that most were aware of the Leader's remarks of the previous evening. Butler, who had borne much of the responsibility for encouraging the mass party to take a keen interest in policy formulation, was left with the pleasant task of commending the amended resolution to the gathering, affirming his belief that 'a restatement of Conservative policy should be published as soon as possible',[68] and suggesting that the party leaders could be left to determine best the date of publication. Lord Woolton, in his summing-up speech, welcomed what he chose to call the 'very dangerous' discussion on policy,[69] but he stressed the necessity for strategic decisions about publication of party policy to rest with the leadership:

> The party should not be too impetuous about a policy [he said]. We really know what we are doing. It is no use coming out now with a policy and saying to the Socialists 'This is the line we are going to the electors with – now you can tear it to pieces.' Let us employ our strategy with some sense. We shall win the next general election if we are determined to win it.[70]

The fright and disappointment of the Hammersmith by-election brought support for the idea of an immediate restatement of party policy to its peak. But party hopes, raised considerably by the success of Conservative candidates in the London County Council elections, became positively buoyant after further victories in the borough council elections on 13 May. With this the great anxiety for a new statement faded. Those who had not favoured an early policy statement now argued that party progress was satisfactory enough without a programme. Nor were these same people persuaded from their view by the publication on 11 April[71] of Labour's programme *Labour Believes in Britain*. 'Some opponents of the early publication of the Conservative programme have been arguing,' the

Financial Times' political correspondent reported, 'that it has now become altogether superfluous for the Conservatives to announce a detailed programme of their own because opposition to the Socialist programme would in itself be sufficient to secure adequate support to Conservative candidates.'[72] The 'let-them-hang-themselves view' of party strategy against which Butler and others had argued since 1945 still possessed a hold!

Behind the scenes, however, the formulation of a publishable document proceeded. Throughout May and June correspondents wrote of drafting and redrafting by the 'Central Policy Committee' – the sub-committee of the shadow cabinet. Then, in mid-June, it was announced that Churchill was to speak at Wolverhampton at the end of July and that his speech would coincide with the publication of the long-awaited restatement. According to a report in the *Observer* on 17 June, 1949, 'Tories Reject Call to Delay Programme', 'There was a suggestion in certain Tory circles last week . . . that the party's restatement of policy due next Saturday should be postponed.' 'The reason . . . was the economic crisis. It was thought that the party would show greater realism if it brought out a short statement on the economic situation.' The report added: 'The suggestion appears to have been discussed by the Conservative shadow cabinet last week but to have got very little support.' Labour's programme had been published, its party conference completed; the time seemed right for a strong Conservative effort to capture the initiative and drive home the advantage which local government elections suggested it was now the party's good fortune to possess.

The Right Road for Britain was the final product of many minds both in the parliamentary party and in the Research Department,[73] but its tone and structure bore the marks of Butler's general editorship, although Lord Woolton, at the party conference in 1949, stated that Brigadier Head was 'largely responsible . . . for having produced at any rate the outline of the statements which are made in *The Right Road for Britain*'. Churchill too played his part in the policy-process – 'I have myself spent many hours of thought and revision upon it', he told his audience at Wolverhampton[74] – although his influence appears to have been more on the language of the document than on the policy recommended.[75] Pendennis, who claimed to have seen 'the draft which was sent for final revision to Mr Churchill' testified to the Leader's having gone through it 'assiduously'. 'There are some sections,' he noted, 'with hardly any changes, but Mr Churchill has heavily sub-edited other chapters, notably those on the social services and on defence. Like all good sub-editors, he has simplified the English.'

In the event, publication of the policy statement preceded Churchill's speech by a day, and the appearance of extensive reports and editorials on *The Right Road* in the Saturday morning papers, followed by equal coverage of the speech in the evening and week-end papers, assured the Conservatives of a temporary monopoly of the public spotlight for their policy statement. Anthony Eden also made a party political broadcast in the same evening, Saturday, 23 July, 1949. In addition to attempting to impress the public with the appropriateness of its recommendations, there were two important sub-themes to exploit.

The document was presented as the final proof if proof were needed that Labour's charge that the Tories lacked a policy was totally unfounded. The Conservatives *had* a policy and, moreover – the joint presentation of the document to the press by Butler and Woolton was to be taken as a symbol of it – all sections of the party were united behind it. It is interesting though that Tom Driberg noted Lord Woolton's self-conscious attempt at the press conference to anticipate the suggestion that Churchill was perhaps not in full agreement with the new statement of party policy.[76]

At the special Central Council meeting on 15 July, 1949, Butler had described the party as a democratic one 'which appeals straight to the individual',[77] and, as evidence of this, had invited 'all Conservatives . . . to discuss the details of Mr Churchill's statement of policy at Wolverhampton and even to suggest amendments'.[78] Lord Woolton developed this theme further at the press conference on 22 July with his observation that the document they were publishing was not a programme: it would only be a programme, he said, 'after the party conference had had a chance to accept or reject it'.[79] Even Churchill, in his speech at Wolverhampton, extolled the virtues of a democratic policy-process within the Conservative Party: 'We shall seek approval of this declaration from our party at the next annual meeting in October . . . [he said]. We shall seek it not only by discussion, but, contrary to the recent practice of our opponents, we shall seek it by a free vote.'[80] In an article the same day ('Policy Making by the Whole Party) the *Birmingham Post*, always a keen upholder of Conservative Party democracy, stated that: 'The statement of policy is not to be imposed in the "Take it or leave it" manner of the Labour Party leaders; it will be submitted to the Conservative Party's annual conference in October, and the conference invited to put forward resolutions on any aspect of the policy. Conference decisions will be accepted by the Leader.'

H. G. Nicholas, noting that '[t]he aspect of the Conservative document which struck most readers without strong partisan leanings was the overlap between it and its Labour forerunner . . .',[81] added that '[t]his overlap was most marked in the section in which it welcomed the Welfare State, endorsed full employment and admitted even the possibility of retaining temporarily such controls as rationing and price regulation'. But it must be acknowledged that this 'overlap' was not the result of a sudden left-ward shift in Conservative policy. Indeed, the main feature of *The Right Road* is the extent to which Conservative policy-makers merely *recapitulated* the policy statements of the previous few years without adding very much that was new, while at the same time, by re-emphasis more than addition, giving the document a tone somewhat to the right of *The Industrial Charter*. The hot white light of free enterprise was present in *The Industrial Charter*, but it was blurred by a reddish filter – a filter which balanced support for free enterprise with the determination to apply strong central guidance over the operation of the economy. In *The Right Road* the white light burned as before, but, to extend the analogy, the reddish filter was replaced with one of a fainter hue.

The differences between the two documents are subtle but none the less real. The latter, like the industrial policy statement, affirmed the party's intention to use the powers of the state in a variety of ways;[82] but some of the urgency had gone. In place of specific references to a 'plan', control of monopolies, and a system of priorities for basic industries there was vagueness. The notion of a plan was not mentioned at all; anti-monopoly measures, so prominent in the charter, were mentioned only in passing. There was also no reference here to 'wage-fixing machinery' although the notion of Government–management–labour co-operation was reiterated. And though the references to denationalization are similar in both documents, *The Industrial Charter* had emphasized the point that denationalized industries would not be replaced by private monopolies;

The Right Road, characteristically, made no specific reference to anti-monopoly efforts on the part of a Conservative Government. The 'free enterprise can do it' theme was allowed the foreground.[83]

These differences apart, the main points of the preceding statements of party policy were duly repeated in the sections dealing with management and labour, agriculture, and the British Empire and Commonwealth. The spirit of the section dealing with nationalization in *The Industrial Charter* was copied in the new documents – i.e. the party accepted the necessity of leaving some industries nationalized – although they were able to provide a few more details of their threat (or promise) to reorganize their existing structures.[84]

The Right Road also rounded out party policy in a few subjects on which the party had not hitherto published statements of policy: on housing; the social services; local government; constitutional questions; foreign policy; and defence. But the details did not go much beyond repeating the party's intentions as already outlined either in speeches by leading party officials or in party propaganda. Conservatives promised to increase home-owning as part of their plan to create a property-owning democracy: widening the scope for the private builder and lowering costs would, they were confident, achieve this aim. They would amend the Town and Country Planning Act. Rent control would be continued 'until it could be shown that there is no housing shortage at any given rent level'.[85] As for the social services the Conservatives sought to make absolutely clear their commitment to maintaining the existing services; and in doing so they accepted the universalist implications of the *status quo*. 'The Social Services are no longer even in theory a form of poor relief. They are a co-operative system of mutual aid and self-help provided by the whole nation and designed to give all the basic minimum of security, or housing, of opportunity, of employment and of living conditions below which our duty to one another forbids us to permit anyone to fall.'[86] So committed were they, indeed, to the present arrangements that they claimed the credit for much which Labour had legislated.[87] The party pledged itself to the improvement of educational facilities; but they also forecast a stunting of the development of 'unwieldy multilateral schools'. On the constitutional questions the document's main proposals were for the calling of an all-party conference for the reform of the House of Lords[88] and for the restoration of the university constituencies.[89] On the House of Lords the Conservatives would put the following proposals before the conference: That '(*a*) The present right to attend and vote based solely on heredity should not by itself constitute a qualification to a reformed House; (*b*) a reformed House of Lords should have powers appropriate to its constitution but not exceeding those conferred by the Act of 1911.'

In emphasizing the extent of the 'overlap' between Conservative and Labour policy (qualified by the recognition of the extent to which *The Right Road* showed a movement away from the position taken up by *The Industrial Charter*), no mention has yet been made of those features of the document most likely to appeal to Conservative voters. On the one hand the Conservatives held out the 'safety-net' – the maintenance of the social services and essential controls which they would take over from Labour. On the other hand the party held out 'opportunity'. 'The final justification of Government,' the document held, 'is that it makes possible the fullest development of personality . . .'.[90] The full development of the personality was seen to occur when, as *The Right Road* put it, 'people find satisfaction and stability in the ownership of property . . .'.[91]

Wider home ownership was not only desirable but possible if only governments would release 'enterprise and initiative in the economic field', and encourage private thrift and home ownership. This the Conservatives proposed to do. They would curb government expenditure (wherein, they argued, there was at the time great extravagance and waste), decentralize production (and therefore increase it), and through general administrative saving make possible the crucial reduction of direct taxation and (later) purchase taxes. The reduction of direct taxation would provide the necessary stimulant and incentive to increase national production and, hence, to achieve prosperity.

The Conservative Party, according to *The Right Road*, then, was committed both to the maintenance (and even improvement) of the social services *and* the reduction of taxation – a commitment which the party's critics found ingenuous to say the least. Yet many people in the mass party, and for a while at least in the parliamentary party too, honestly believed that with 'greater production' and 'careful saving' the circle could be squared.

Press reaction to the publication followed very much the same lines taken with the earlier policy statements. Nearly all the large national dailies found the document to their liking. Only the *Manchester Guardian* and the *Daily Express* among the non-Labour press were critical, and neither was completely hostile. The former found the Conservative policy better written than Labour's but 'just as woolly' and differing little from it.[92] The *Express* admitted certain improvements in the Tory plan as compared to the Labour Party's but thought them 'improvements on a basically Socialist theme'.[93] The reaction of the Sunday papers was mixed. The *Sunday Chronicle* and the *Sunday Empire News* supported the new statement of policy, but both the *Sunday Times* and the *Observer* were critical (the former slightly more so). The *Sunday Express* gave more support to Churchill's speech which it called 'gin and ginger' than to the policy document which was 'milk and water'.[94] *Truth* was again the most hostile of the extreme right-wing journals, but the *Recorder* gave its half-hearted support for the document on the grounds that the Tories were the only hope of defeating Labour. The *Spectator* was not at all impressed by the new statement and doubted whether its publication had brought victory any nearer.[95] The *Economist* was extremely critical:

> Mr Churchill has, until recently, maintained that it is a weakness for a party in opposition to have a definite policy. Perusal of the Conservative Party's policy document . . . should be enough to convince most people that his earlier view was the right one.[96]

Faced with the problem of being either vague or insincere the Tories, the *Economist* claimed, had chosen vagueness.

At all events the policy statement, so long requested by many members of the party, had been published, and was on the whole well received by Conservative back-benchers. 'Even though individual Tory M.P.s [had] their own ideas about what ought to have been included and what ought to have been omitted,' the *Financial Times* reported, 'the pamphlet [was] regarded as a fair "common denominator" of the various views held by the majority.'[97]

II

Like the Two-Way Movements which had come into operation in connection with the *Industrial* and *Agricultural Charters*, the Movement dealing with *The Right Road* came into effect *after* the party had published its statement and in time to allow for the distribution of C.P.C. material supporting the policy statement before consideration by the party conference. Phase six of the movement – from October to December 1949 – was centred on only two topics: *The Right Road* and education. The *What Do You Think?* pamphlets for the guidance of group discussion were published in September. The overwhelming importance of the outward flow of the Two-Way Movement was demonstrated again.

But if the sixth phase of the Movement came too late to influence the content of *The Right Road*, might not the document have been influenced by earlier phases of the Movement and the expression of mass party opinion in general? Even though most of the earlier policy statements had been little affected by the ideas put forward by the discussion groups (because their consideration by the groups nearly always followed formulation) could it not be argued that, since the policy statement published in July 1949 was to a considerable extent a recapitulation of earlier statements, the discussion groups had still plenty of opportunity to make their impact on it? But it has been shown that discussion groups which operated before the publication of a policy statement produced few original ideas suitable for inclusion. Groups which discussed party policy after it was published also failed to produce many worthy modifications of the already published policy. The organizers of the Movement at the C.P.C. recognized this fact too, and their changing attitudes were revealed by the way in which they chose to describe the main purposes of the Movement and by the tasks which they set.

In the first two phases of the Movement five topics were each time suggested for study. In phase three only two new subjects were put forward; three topics on *The Industrial Charter* from the previous phase were carried over. The report on phase two conceded that in the majority of cases the reports were merely confirming published policy. The report on phase three underlined this fact by pointing to the difficulty which most groups found in dealing with the technical subjects of coal and economic recovery.[98] The brief 'reports' on these topics added little to the pamphlet sent out by the C.P.C., but it was considered that the Movement was nevertheless valuable:

If . . . the study of these subjects [coal and economic recovery] has not produced much in the way of concrete proposals, it has made us realize the difficulties with which domestic statesmanship is faced.

The purpose of the 'Two-Way Movement of Ideas' has always been two-fold: not only is it intended to provide a channel [for reaching] those . . . who are responsible for formulating national policy, but it is also intended to spread a knowledge and a clearer understanding of the problems with which our leaders are faced.[99]

In the fourth phase of the Movement discussion groups dealt with only two subjects – *The Agricultural Charter* and 'property-owning democracy'.[100] On both of these topics the 'reports' once again reproduced the gist of either the discussion pamphlet or the published statement of policy. The pattern was repeated in phase five when groups discussed bureaucracy, steel, and Western Union.[101]

Fundamentally, then, mass party influence on the content of *The Right Road* was slight. But a few specific cases in which the attitudes of the mass party were reflected in the published policy may be suggested. It has been pointed out that *The Right Road* chose to highlight the contribution to recovery that could be made by a more vigorous freeing of private enterprise at the expense of the collectivist notions – such as a national 'plan' and strict monopoly control – of the earlier *Industrial Charter*. This decision undoubtedly reflected the estimate by the policy-making *élite* of the situational factors, but it is a fact that it was in line with the expressed wishes of the mass party as revealed through the Two-Way Movement of Ideas. The report of the second phase of the Two-Way Movement had called attention to the rejection by a small minority of the participants of the word 'plan',[102] to the dissatisfaction of some with the machinery proposed by the charter for dealing with monopolies,[103] and to the feeling on the part of many that '*The Industrial Charter* [did] not lay sufficient emphasis on the importance of enterprise'.[104] The report of the third phase of the Movement revealed that 'the group opinions reached . . . in the third phase were almost identical with those of six months before'.[105] There remained at least a small core of party activists dissatisfied with this aspect of the party's policy. The removal of 'the reddish filter' may well have been a partial concession to these feelings.

One further influence of the Two-Way Movement can be detected.

It may be recalled that *Imperial Policy* had referred very briefly and in general terms to the party's support for the notion of Western Union. That subject had been discussed in the fifth phase of the Movement, but, as we have suggested, it was unlikely that the opinions of the reporting groups had been forwarded to the policy-making core. It is more likely, however, that the considerable confusion and division of opinion among the participants was made known to the formulators of *The Right Road*, and it is possible that the total absence of any reference to Western Union in the policy statement may be attributed to this fact.

These two influences were negative. Did the mass party have any positive effect on the content of *The Right Road*? Criticism of *The Agricultural Charter* in the debate at the 1948 party conference has already been seen to have influenced the wording of references to the same subject in *The Right Road*. But was there anything else?

In 1947 and particularly in 1948 Conservative party conferences had expressed support for a great variety of policies: for consideration of the 'great hardship to the lower salaried and fixed income groups'; for greater use of private house builders; for reform of the House of Lords; for reduced direct taxation as an incentive; for amendment of the Town and Country Planning Act; for decentralization of the nationalized industries; for a review of bulk buying; and for amendment of the Representation of the People Act[106] – all of which became embodied in one form or another in the policy statement published in July 1949. But there is nothing very noteworthy or surprising in this. Resolutions chosen for discussion at party conferences are carefully vetted by the General Purposes Sub-committee and in the main reflect support for aspects of party policy already intimated by the party leadership either in Parliament or in public speeches. In any case conference resolutions are not tightly binding. For example, a conference resolution calling for amendment of the Representation of the People Act had endorsed 'the declarations of the leaders of the party that the representation of the Universities and of the City of London will be restored when the party is returned to power'. By July 1949 the leaders had presumably changed their minds on the question of restoring representation to the City of London, for no promise to this effect was made in *The Right Road*.[107]

* * *

Debate on a resolution 'wholeheartedly' welcoming *The Right Road for Britain* took place on the morning of the last day of the 1948 conference after Clement Attlee, the Prime Minister, had announced, to the obvious disappointment of the Conservative Party, that an immediate election was not in the offing. As in the case of the debate on *The Industrial Charter* no constructive amendments to the policy statement were moved and seconded; as in the case of the debate on *The Agricultural Charter* many speakers suggested modifications in the course of remarks in which they generally supported the document. More speakers were openly critical of the policy statement than on either of these earlier occasions, but in the end Sir Waldron Smithers' amendment – calling for reference back to the policy committee on the grounds that changing economic conditions since publication had made it irrelevant[108] – was rejected, and the resolution was carried with only eight dissentient votes. Lord Woolton, summing up the week's proceedings, put his final (characteristic) stamp on the policy-process for the policy statement:

> You had an opportunity [he said] had you so desired today to reject that pamphlet in spite of the fact that it had appeared in print. That is the democratic way in which this party puts an alternative.[109]

POLICY FOR THE ELECTIONS

The task of studying policy formulation in opposition has certain advantages. The process is more open; conference resolutions and debates are available for scrutiny; policy statements are produced; party discussion-documents are distributed and reports circulated. The pace of innovation is gradual. But as the opposition party enters the election battle, these factors wane. Security is tighter; decisions revolve around in increasingly smaller circles; events – and the requisite policy response to them – change rapidly. At a time when the policy-output may increase sharply the policy-process becomes less susceptible to observation.[110] The content of party policies for the 1950 and 1951 general elections has already been studied in great detail and there is no need to repeat here the work of the Nuffield studies. It will be sufficient to grasp hold of a few main themes of the period up to the publication of *The Right Road* and follow these through the two elections to the return to power of the Conservative Party in October 1951.

I

Churchill was on holiday at Madeira when the dissolution was announced on 10 January 1950, but he was back on the job by the evening of 12 January. On 18 January the Labour Party issued its election manifesto, *Let Us Win Through Together*. A draft of the Conservative election policy statement was prepared under Butler's direction at the Research Department, edited by Churchill, and approved by the shadow cabinet. On 23 January Butler gave a preview of the party programme to a meeting of Conservative candidates at Church House, Westminster. The next day he introduced the party's manifesto (again with Lord Woolton's assistance) to the press. *This is the Road* was published the following day.

After the devaluation crisis some Conservatives had considered *The Right Road* no longer applicable to the new circumstances.[111] Many at the party conference in October had called for greater emphasis on retrenchment. Lord Woolton, in anticipation of the criticism that the policy statement's suggestion of increased expenditure in some areas of the social services was incompatible with reduced taxation, had availed himself of the columns of *Tory Challenge* to present the party's official line (which was repeated at the conference) that such action was possible because of the great savings which a Conservative administration could make. Even so Woolton had suggested that a 'needs test' for state aid might have to be imposed.[112]

The policy statement which the party produced for the election reflected to some extent this earlier criticism by emphasizing, even more than *The Right Road* had done, the 'substantial savings' which a 'complete change in the spirit of administration' would bring.[113] But there was no reference to – indeed there was scrupulous avoidance of – any suggestion of retrenchment in the quality of the social services or of the imposition of needs tests. *This is the Road* was, in fact, as H. G. Nicholas has put it, 'for the most part, a tauter, more pungent condensation of the earlier document'.[114] But there were also, as he noted, 'a few differences of substance':

> The treatment of food subsidies was more precise – no reduction without compensating increases to those most affected. The proposal in the earlier programme to supply health service drugs free

to private patients was dropped, as was the promise to continue university grants on their present scale. The dollar gap was given a high priority amongst the commitments of a new Conservative Government.[115]

The party manifesto also included details of the recently published party policy for Scotland and a strengthening of the earlier promise to amend the Town and Country Planning Act – now, so the manifesto said, the party would 'drastically change' the 1947 Act.[116] Perhaps more important than these variations in detail, however, was the slight difference in tone. Although in the manifesto there was even more reliance on the 'free enterprise can do it' theme than had appeared in any post-war policy statement, there was at the same time a little more emphasis on the Conservative Party's determination to deal with monopolies – whether private or public – than had appeared in the previous statement.

Press reaction to the Conservative manifesto broke predictably along party lines. Only the *Manchester Guardian* and *Observer* among the non-Labour critics of *The Right Road* failed to fall in enthusiastically behind its later counterpart.[117] The *Evening Standard* which had previously been luke-warm called it 'a winning policy';[118] the *Express* even discovered in the document 'a positive vigour which was lacking in some of the earlier party statements'.[119] The Conservatives, so Butler said at Enfield on 27 January, were well pleased with the reception of their manifesto.[120]

However, the electoral victory which Lord Woolton had expected was narrowly missed. Labour was returned to power with 315 seats; the Conservatives held 298 seats, the Liberals nine, and the Irish Nationalists two. With the Labour Party's absolute majority in the House of Commons cut to six it was inevitable that the campaign atmosphere would dominate proceedings there until a further election was called.

II

Despite the weakness of its parliamentary position the Labour Party clung tenaciously to power.[121] Weakened by illness in high places and lacking an agreed legislative programme, the party fought a holding operation. The Conservatives, frustrated by the closeness of the electoral result and aggravated by their inability to shake

Labour's grip, tried frontal assaults in the House and needling in the country, but Labour's unimpressive legislative programme gave little scope for manoeuvre.

Labour's new line of moderation pursued especially by Herbert Morrison in the hope of wooing Liberal opinion to the party caused Butler to think in the summer of 1950 that it was time to review party policy in the light of changing circumstances. But there was nothing much the party could do in that respect. It was generally felt by leading party officials that there was little need for a 'rethink': the ideas of the older charters were considered fresh, and they did not want to make it seem that these were now being discarded. Nevertheless, the Research Department began to consider a possible restatement of party policy.[122]

By the autumn of 1950 party members in the country were, to judge from the 'careful and cautious' resolutions submitted for debate at the party conference,[123] as incapable of originality as their leaders. Two bright moments alone relieved the *ennui* of the conference.[124] One was Churchill's rousing call, in his speech to the mass meeting at the conclusion of the conference, for 'one more heave' to oust the Labour Government. The other was the 'rebellion' during the housing debate:

> The conference [as R. T. McKenzie has related] was discussing a rather colourless resolution condemning the Labour Government's housing record and demanding (without mentioning a specific figure) an increased housing programme. In the course of the debate one delegate mentioned the figure '300,000' as a desirable annual goal for a Conservative housing programme. Other speakers picked up the figure amidst mounting enthusiasm and Lord Woolton . . . finally accepted on behalf of the party leaders the goal of 300,000 houses per year.[125]

McKenzie noted the embarrassment which the resolution, calling indeed for a *minimum* figure of 300,000 houses, caused the leadership and the advantage which might have fallen to the Labour Party had the Conservatives subsequently failed to reach their goal;[126] but he did not refer to the qualifications which were immediately placed on the resolution by the party Leader. In his speech to the mass meeting, Churchill accepted the 'target' of 300,000 houses as the party's first priority '*in time of peace*'.[127] Thereafter the figure of 300,000 houses was never referred to by official party spokesmen as a *minimum* target, and it was always qualified – quite sensibly – by the ultimate priority of defence expenditure.[128]

Meanwhile the Two-Way Movement of Ideas was continuing. Phase six, centred on *The Right Road* and education, ended in January 1950. The general election intervened, and no further phase was begun again until 1 September, when groups were invited to discuss housing, social reform, and the trade unions. C.P.C. pamphlets assisting group discussions were again prepared, but the possibility of an immediate election clearly overshadowed the concern of the Research Department and the C.P.C. for the working of the Movement. No date for the completion of the phase was indicated in the 'policy paper' distribution in the autumn of 1950, and the C.P.C. could only promise that 'if practicable, a summary of the reports received [would] be published'.[129]

As a matter of fact no further reports of the Movement were published, and it is therefore impossible to assess the impact – if any – of the Two-Way Movement on policy formulation after the phase which ended in May 1949 (phase five). The C.P.C. nevertheless continued to organize discussion topics. Phase eight which occurred during the spring of 1951 dealt with two topics – social reform and the trade unions brought forward from the earlier period – and three new subjects, 'The Workers' Charter', town and country planning, and the use of marginal land.[130]

Then, in the autumn of 1951, with the prospect of an election (and the clear possibility of a return to power), the arrangements for the Two-Way Movement which had operated since 1946 were sharply modified. At about the same time as the discussion topics were distributed for phase nine (a phase which was to last eight months and thereby cover the whole period previously divided into autumn and spring phases)[131] a special policy paper entitled *The Future Work of the Political Education Movement* was sent out for the guidance of Areas and constituencies. Instead of admitting forthrightly that techniques of consulting mass party opinion when a party is in opposition were no longer desirable or practicable when the party was returned to power, the memorandum chose to cloud the issue with double-talk. 'With victory at the next election in sight,' it said, 'we need to plan even farther ahead for political education purposes': the party must 'improve long-term training arrangements, while still preparing for the coming election campaign'.[132]

> On quite contemporary issues [it continued] we want to focus attention upon a special annual theme. . . . This kind of approach was hardly feasible in the midst of a period of opposition, but the political initiative is passing to the Conservative Party, and we shall soon, for instance, have to adapt our Two-Way Movement of Ideas to suit the rather different requirements of a period of office in which the choice of political ground falls to the majority party.[133]

The inward movement of mass party opinion from the discussion groups, never as important as Butler and some of its faithful participants had suggested, had outlived its usefulness. Political education, pure and simple, was henceforth to be the key to the C.P.C.'s activities.

III

As the summer of 1951 drew on Butler gave serious thought to preparing a statement of party policy in time for distribution before the party conference scheduled to begin at Scarborough on 11 October. Conservative M.P.s apparently expected that some type of statement would be issued before Parliament dispersed for the summer recess, but it did not come. There had been the same arguments over timing that had preceded the publication of *The Right Road for Britain*: Should the Conservatives take the initiative or wait until Labour had committed itself to print? But there was also delay because of the rejection of a few drafts of a proposed statement by the Advisory Committee on Policy on the grounds that the suggested document failed to capture the right mood. Butler immediately began to reword the drafts' proposals with the assistance of the Research Department and three colleagues – Selwyn Lloyd, Anthony Nutting, and Anthony Head. Selwyn Lloyd's special responsibility, in addition to assisting in the formulation of policy, was to perform the 'right-hand man' function of integrating the parliamentary party with the policy-process as Oliver Poole had done for the production of *The Right Road*. Together the small policy-making core 'sweated it out' at the Research Department to produce a satisfactory draft of a policy statement.[134] This was sent on to

Churchill on holiday and approved by an informal meeting of the shadow cabinet before the end of the first week of September. However, events were moving quickly, and before the document could be published[135] Attlee had announced the date for the coming election. Attention immediately shifted to the production of a party manifesto.

Attlee's announcement came on 19 September. The next day Churchill held a preliminary discussion with a few leading members of his shadow cabinet to discuss tactics and policy. On 21 September a full-scale meeting of the shadow cabinet was held at Churchill's London home at which an outline of the party manifesto was developed and left for the Leader's final touches before a final meeting early the next week.

According to an account in the London *Star*[136] the Conservatives did not intend to publish the manifesto as soon as they did. The *Financial Times*,[137] indeed, had reported on 25 September that the Conservative Party would wait until Labour's had appeared before publishing. But news of the document's proposal to introduce an excess profits tax (during the period of rearmament) was broken in the 'City Notes' of the *Star* on the afternoon of 27 September and repeated the next morning in the *Daily Express*. After hurried consultation between Woolton and Churchill the manifesto (apparently originally intended for publication on Sunday) was issued to the press on Friday, 28 September.

This is the Road, the comparable Conservative document in the 1950 election campaign, had been introduced by a short note from Winston Churchill. The party's *Manifesto* for the 1951 general election was in the form of a personal statement from the Leader of the Conservative Party – exactly similar to Churchill's *Declaration of Policy to the Electors* in 1945. 'Even if it had not been signed,' David Butler has commented, 'the imprint of the author's style would have been recognized in almost every sentence.'[138]

Only two specific details were added to the content of the 1950 statement – the excess profits tax proposal and the promise to aim at a target of 300,000 houses a year[139] (giving, of course, a first priority to national defence). Nothing of any importance in the earlier statement was omitted. And, except for an obtuse reference to facing up to 'our difficulties and dangers . . . as we did in 1940',[140] the manifesto paid rather less attention to the question of national security than did the more elaborate statement of policy, *Britain Strong and Free*, which followed. Everything else had been said before, and only the manner of saying it – raising the mountains of free enterprise and deepening the gorges of Socialism – distinguished this from the earlier election programme.

How much the document published on 3 October as *Britain Strong and Free* differed from the original drafted for distribution before the party conference (i.e. before the election forced the conference's cancellation) we do not know. Hugh Massingham reported on 23 September that 'the long statement of principles' prepared by Butler some weeks before had been cancelled as being unsuitable for election purposes.[141] But even if the particular format of that document had been regarded as unsatisfactory it is certain that its ideas were transferred to the revised document. Butler played an important rôle in the formulation of the extended policy statement, *Britain Strong and Free*, as he would inevitably have done in the formulation of the manifesto. It is entirely possible – evidence from correspondents' sneak previews of the original long statement earlier suggest it[142] – that the finally published document did not differ greatly from the one originally prepared for the party conference.

More important than the possible differences between the two extended policy statements prepared in 1951 is the striking similarity between the documents – both manifestos and policy statements – prepared by the party for the 1950 and 1951 general elections. The manifesto and *Britain Strong and Free* went little beyond the general shape of things as set out nearly 18 months before. Constructive critics of the 1951 manifesto[143] waited for an elaboration of how its proposals would be implemented: the direction promised by the manifesto, the *Observer* held, was promising enough 'but the road to be followed [was] not yet clearly mapped'.[144] But these critics waited in vain. The Conservatives, as Churchill put it, were content 'to proclaim a theme rather than write a prospectus',[145] and the theme they proclaimed was the theme of all party spokesmen during the last year and a half: national security depended on strength, and strength could only be achieved through freedom – Conservative freedom in which government waste and extravagance was eliminated, and the spirit of enterprise and initiative was encouraged by lessening controls and reducing taxation. With this simple message the Conservative Party fought the 1951 general election campaign.

BUTLER AND THE 'NEW CONSERVATISM'

Any figure who strides the political stage in so prominent a position and for as long as R. A. Butler must inevitably be observed in a variety of masks and poses: appeaser; opponent of Churchill over Indian constitutional advance; architect of Britain's educational system; intellectual powerhouse of the party's electoral recovery after 1945; pink-socialist in the Gaitskell manner; 'ideologist of inequality';[146] manipulator of an explosive situation in Africa. Versatility it would appear beyond even an Olivier's scope! How much of it has been real and how much has his audience been deceived by the floodlights and the critic's jeers? The present aim is limited: only the central act and his six-year rôle as a formulator of party policy are the real concern here; and yet some clues to a fuller appreciation of the man and his performances may be revealed.

I

While it is easy to exaggerate the importance of Conservative policy reformulation in opposition as a factor leading to the party's recovery, Butler's key position in that reformulation can hardly be overstated. Francis Boyd, who believes that the colourful picture of Butler and his back-room boys has been over-elaborated, has nevertheless admitted that 'there is a good deal of truth in it'. However, for him:

> The story is an over-simplification of the facts which conceals not only the real nature of the control exercised over Conservative policy, both before and after the Second World War, but also Mr Butler's relations with the controllers and the extent of his share in shaping policy.[147]

Boyd's assertion is intriguing, but nowhere does he specify what he calls 'the real nature of the control exercised over Conservative policy', nor, except for the observation that policy-making by Butler and the Research Department was shared with leading members of the party, does he elaborate his other 'over-simplifications'. Of course Butler was not solely responsible for policy reformulation.

At every stage in the process he was assisted by other leading members of the shadow cabinet, representatives of the back-benches, and from time to time by interested members of the National Union. Ultimately the Leader's opinions influenced the final product. But his was the crucial and *continuous* guiding hand. Experienced by virtue of his chairmanship of the Post-war Problems Reconstruction Committee, admirably positioned by virtue of his triple-headed control of the Research Department, C.P.C., and policy advisory committee, and committed by temperament and political philosophy to the need for Conservatism to adapt to changing economic, social and political conditions, Butler exerted an influence on Conservative policy reformulation in opposition unmatched by any of his colleagues. Not only was he important as an innovator; he also saw things through to the last detail, even to the point of presenting party policy to the press. 'Without Mr Butler,' one member of his Research Department ventured to say, 'there would have been no policy development at all.'

Accepting, then, Butler's prime importance in the process of policy-reformulation, his contribution to the content of party policy and the nature of the reformulated policy in general must be considered next.

The first point that must be made is that, comparing official party policy in 1951 with official *and* unofficial Conservative policy in 1945, *no revolution in party doctrine or policy took place in the six years of opposition.* Radical change was not only uncharacteristic of the Conservative Party; it was unnecessary. The gap which separated the position of the most progressive of the Conservatives in 1945 and the moderates in the Labour Party at the same time was not as wide as has sometimes been imagined. Nevertheless, for those who considered policy reformulation necessary three main tasks were set: to retrieve the Conservative Party from the image, which the 1945 election campaign had helped to foster, of a party relatively indifferent to social reform; to rationalize its response to Labour's innovations; and, by establishing the limits beyond which Conservative acquiescence would not go, to delineate the distinctively Conservative manner in which the party proposed to take over, administer, and improve upon the newly developed social and economic structure of society.

Two remarks by Butler – their sentiments, however, are by no means his copyright – help to define the spirit with which Conservative policy reformulation would be informed.

> Our attitude to politics [he told the Central Council in 1941] by which I mean the art of governing a nation is based upon principles which experience over many generations has proved to be of permanent validity. We believe that progress in human affairs is best achieved by modification and adaption of existing institutions that have proved their worth. . . .[148]

And, to a mass meeting of Yorkshire Conservatives in March 1945, he said:

> We believe in encouragement of individual initiative, devotion to the ideals of social service and self-help, loyalty to our well-tried institutions, our constitutional monarchy, our Imperial family of nations, our free Parliament, our incorruptible courts, our liberty to worship and think as we believe right.[149]

These quotations reveal Butler solidly within the *Tory* tradition. The extent to which his name has been connected with 'Butskellism' and 'pink-socialism' is a measure of his awareness that for Conservatism to survive it must adapt itself to prevailing pressures. And adaptability is the essence of the achievement of Conservative policy reformulation in opposition. Peel's empiricism provided the model;[150] the message came from many party traditions. From the social reformers of party history – from Shaftesbury to Neville Chamberlain – the party drew witness of its dedication to the social services. From the Tory Reformers came a rejection of *laissez-faire* and an argument for the complementary rôle of government guidance in a private enterprise economy. And from the neo-Liberals[151] came the notion of 'the opportunity state'. The first two strands of thought helped to provide the rationale for *The Industrial Charter*. Thus grounded at the most leftward extreme to which it was thought Conservative acquiescence could or should be brought, the policy could edge its way back with the help of the third strand 'towards freedom' – towards greater and greater emphasis on the advantages of freer enterprise and away from central control – as rapidly as the party considered changing economic and political conditions warranted.

II

It was suggested earlier that the period from 1945–51 is of considerable importance because 'it represented the first flowering of what is now called the "New Conservatism" '. In order to examine what is meant by this it is necessary to digress slightly for a moment to consider a crucial distinction between what might be called 'New Conservatism – Style One' (i.e. the official party policy as developed up to and including the 1951 general election) and the 'New Conservatism – Style Two' (a development of certain features of the previous period largely by individuals within the party but increasingly an aspect of official party policy and programme).

The essential feature of the New Conservatism – Style Two, is, as Saloma has put it, 'a distinctive Conservative interpretation of, and an implicit – although more recently, increasingly explicit – set of long-term goals for the welfare state'.[152] At first the brain-child of the One Nation group of Conservative M.P.s, three of whose original members, Iain Macleod, Enoch Powell, and Edward Heath, came from the Research Department, the general notions of the New Conservatism have been developed on a number of fronts – especially by the Bow Group – and are now flourishing at the Conservative Research Department. The One Nation group has tended to the 'moderate-progressive' position on the question; the Bow Group towards the right and the emphasis solely on self-provision. The Research Department has come increasingly under the spell of the self-provision school.

'There is,' to quote Saloma again, 'a range of opinion within the party between optimal state provision of certain essential services (notably health and education) and a virtually complete dismantling of state services in favour of self-provision,'[153] but in general the following assumptions are held in common:

1. The state does not exist to equalize the fruits of individual effort; its purpose ought to be the encouragement of opportunity – 'to see', as Iain Macleod once put it, 'that men had an equal chance to make themselves unequal'.[154] 'Equality,' wrote Mr Macleod, 'is an idea that finds little echo on the Tory side of the House. . . . Toryism is about opportunity.'

2. The state has the obligation to provide a minimum level of security below which none shall fall. Provision for the 'weak' (determined on a means test basis) out of the taxation of the 'strong' is an acceptable means of dealing with that small sector of society not participating as fully as the rest of the country in the increasing prosperity. But for the vast majority – and increasingly is this seen to be true as affluence develops – it is no purpose of the state to assume responsibilities (in the social services, education, housing, and general insurance) which can be left to the individual to provide for himself, either through contributions which meet the cost of the services provided *or* outside the state system altogether. Now that prosperity is generally enjoyed it is possible for most to achieve what was formerly the prerogative of only a tiny middle and upper class – what one Research Department officer called 'self-respect through personal responsibility'.

3. With welfare provided increasingly on an individual basis the vertical redistribution of income (resulting from payment for the services out of taxation) can be steadily reduced, net income equalization – the enemy of incentive upon which the productivity of a nation is presumed to rest – can be sharply reduced, and the state, able to divest itself of its 'current responsibilities' (health and welfare), might then 'concentrate its rôle on the "long-term capital area" ' (the provision of better environmental services: mental hospitals, roads, etc.).

This new Conservative thought has not been fully understood by commentators of the left and centre-right. The New Conservatism is not 'a reversion to the unrepentent Tory individualism of the 19th century',[155] nor is it a reversion simply to *laissez-faire*. The new thought represents a considerable advance for the neo-Liberal emphasis on self-help, but it is still presented in a basically Tory–Conservative framework in which rights and duties are given their due, the notion of a minimum standard of welfare is maintained, and the state assumes increasing responsibility for the provision of community services (now, however, redefined and narrower in scope). The new social order – Conservative style – does not in any way imply a complete vacation of state responsibility in the domestic sphere. Indeed the fundamental postulate on which the detail of 'the opportunity state' depends is the notion that national prosperity can be progressively increased. And to achieve this, state intervention will be required to encourage increases in national productivity, to maintain employment, and to stabilize prices and costs of production.

* * *

How far has all this moved from R. A. Butler and the New Conservatism – Style One? Some way, indeed, but not so far that regress is impossible. It ought to be clear that there exists a clear link between the official Conservative policy which has been discussed in this and the preceding chapter and the ideas of the New Conservatism – Style Two. But having acknowledged the link, it is important to recognize also the extent to which the two styles of Conservatism are different. Clear roots of the present strain of New Conservatism were apparent in the opposition period, but the notions were by no means fully developed.

The three key aspects of the official Conservative policy for the 1950 and 1951 general elections were: the notion of a 'property-owning democracy'; the dedication to the preservation and improvement of the social services; and the encouragement of initiative through the reduction of direct taxation. Although in currency (once again) after the party conference in 1946 – and despite David Eccles's efforts to elaborate its significance in a C.P.C. publication in June 1949, *What Do You Think About Property Owning Democracy?* – the property-owning democracy idea never developed much beyond the expression of the belief that the development of the human personality required the possession of individual property for its full development[156] and that the diffusion of property was an effective safeguard against the abuse of central political power.[157] The crucial importance of property in the development of the personality was an essential feature of L. S. Amery's thought before 1945, but unlike him, and unlike the neo-Liberals today the party chose (during the opposition years) not to stress the whole of his argument: namely that for property to be a real source of status it must be unequally distributed.[158] This is not to say that, in other connections, official party policy avoided altogether any suggestion of being anti-egalitarian;[159] but it did underplay this implication of its policy.

The other striking difference between official party policy in opposition and the New Conservatism today is their positions with regard to the social services. Especially in 1950, but still in 1951, Conservative policy stressed the savings that could be made in the administration of the welfare services and the increases in the national productivity that would have to be forthcoming if the services were to be maintained intact; but there was no *official* indication that the party intended to depart radically from the principle of universality which they shared with the Labour Party at this time.

We have emphasized the *official* policy of the party because, especially with regard to the social services, ideas were developing within the party which did not share the assumptions or the aims of the official line. As early as the 1949 party conference Norman St John-Stevas had argued that 'a property-owning democracy and a welfare state are mutually incompatible' and that the party should 'revolutionize the whole concept of the social services . . . [redesigning them] so as to give effect to the voluntary principle . . .'.[160] It is interesting to note that Butler, who replied very fully to nearly all the other points of criticism of *The Right Road* in the debate in which Norman St John-Stevas made these remarks, made no reference whatever to this particular point. In October 1950 the One Nation group produced its first publication in which the calm assumption that expenditure on the social services could be contained by administrative savings was dismissed, and the recommendation was made that 'in order to save the social services' low priority services should be omitted altogether, and charges should be applied for such items as hospital board, appliances, and prescriptions.[161] These notions of voluntary welfare followed logically from the general concept of the 'opportunity state' which official Conservative policy was developing, but the specific implications of the general idea did not find very full expression in the official policy statements at the time.

Thus, like official party policy for the general election of 1945, policy in 1951 did not reflect the entire spectrum of opinion within the party's ranks. In 1945 it was the Tory Reform opinion which failed to obtain full satisfaction in the official policy; in 1951 it was the neo-Liberal. By 1951 Conservative policy had redefined the party's attitude towards the rôle of the state in the direction of a fundamentally free enterprise economy and had absorbed completely the older radicalism of the Tory left. Now fused with the two notions of the 'opportunity state' and a 'property-owning democracy'

Conservatives stood poised once again to shape and adapt through gradual change the social and economic structure of Britain.

It might be thought that the party's absorption of neo-Liberal thought in the more than ten years of power has been slower than the adoption of Tory Reform notions during the shorter period of opposition. But Tories like Butler (who may still have a considerable influence in policy-making circles today) mix their dogmas with empiricism, and it may well be that it has been the failure of the Government's monetary and fiscal policy to achieve anything like the *assured* and steady development of national prosperity (on which the New Conservatism depends) which has kept the party from pushing further than it already has with the implementation of the 'opportunity state' in all its ramifications.

REFERENCES

[1] *Conference Report, 1947*, p. 28.

[2] *Conference Report, 1947*, p. 27.

[3] *Conference Report, 1947*, p. 30.

[4] *A True Balance* . . . (C.C.O., February, 1949).

[5] *Scottish Control of Scottish Affairs* (Scottish Unionist Association, November 1949).

[6] See below, pp. 176–7.

[7] *Conference Report, 1948*, p. 52. Butler also mentioned the advice received from R. S. Hudson and Walter Elliot.

[8] 'Press Release . . . Agricultural Charter', Conservative Central Office, 25 June, 1948, p. 2. See also *Conference Report, 1948*, p. 52.

[9] *Daily Express* (London), 'Opinion', 26 June, 1948; *Manchester Guardian*, 'Tories Agricultural Policy', 26 June, 1948; and *Economist*, 'All Carrots, No Sticks', 3 July, 1948.

[10] 'Memo on Agricultural Charter' [Conservative Central Office files 1948]. This report also noted: 'Of articles from 17 provincial papers only one from the *Salisbury Journal* (written by Mr Izzard of the *Daily Mail*) was not very favourable. Eight contained impartial summaries without comment; one was critical, and the remainder made a few favourable comments.'

[11] *Truth*, 'Tory Agriculture', 2 July, 1948. Cf. Norman Mackenzie, *New Republic*, 'British Farms and Food', 2 January, 1950, pp. 12–13.

[12] *The Agricultural Charter*, p. 17.

[13] *The Agricultural Charter*, p. 12.

[14] *The Agricultural Charter*, p. 35.

[15] *The Agricultural Charter*, p. 36.

[16] *The Agricultural Charter*, p. 37.

[17] The details of the so-called Agricultural Workers' Charter, are not gone

into here although some of the above-mentioned proposals are, in fact, included therein. While most of the suggestions are harmless enough – the provision of one telephone box in each hamlet; the hope for a contract of service, etc. – they had even less likelihood of being fulfilled without government action than did the Industrial Workers' Charter. See pp. 22–8.

[18] *The Agricultural Charter*, p. 21.

[19] *Birmingham Post*, 'Farm Charter for Conservatives', 26 June, 1948.

[20] *Conference Report, 1948*, p. 53. The resolution was passed with only one dissentient.

[21] *Policy Paper 5*, p. 4.

[22] *Observer* 'Social Services and Housing Untouched', 26 September, 1948.

[23] Mr Butler did, however, use the pages of *Tory Challenge* again to publicize *The Agricultural Charter*. See R. A. Butler, 'The Agricultural Charter', *Tory Challenge*, July 1948.

[24] *Conference Report, 1948*, pp. 46–52.

[25] This suggestion had been made already by the Two-Way Movement in the report of the first phase of the discussion on the agricultural subject. See *The Two-Way Movement of Ideas, The First Phase* (C.P.C., July 1947), p. 10.

[26] *Conference Report, 1948*, p. 52.

[27] *Conference Report.*, pp. 47 and 48, and *Right Road for Britain* (Conservative Central Office, July 1949), pp. 31–3.

[28] *Tory Challenge*, 'The Agricultural Charter: The Man Who Voted Against'. January 1949, p. 11.

[29] See Enoch Powell, '1951–59: Labour in Opposition', *Political Quarterly*, XXX (Oct.–Dec. 1959), p. 342, for an expression of this opinion.

[30] *The Conservative Policy for Wales and Monmouthshire* (Conservative Central Office, February 1949).

[31] *Conference Report, 1948*, pp. 71–4.

[32] *Conference Report, 1948*, p. 74. For the resolution on which Butler's presumptuous decision was based see p. 71.

[33] *A True Balance*, p. 31; *Birmingham Post*, 'Conservative Charter for Women', 10 March, 1949; and *Glasgow Herald*, 16 March, 1949.

[34] *Yorkshire Post*, 'The Women's Charter', 30 August, 1948.

[35] *Conference Report, 1948*, p. 108.

[36] *Conference Report, 1948*, pp. 110, 112 and 113.

[37] *Conference Report, 1948*, p. 113.

[38] *Conference Report, 1949*, p. 18.

[39] *Conference Report, 1948*, p. 114. There was a Two-Way Movement of Ideas discussion topic on the subject, however, in phase 6. See *Policy Paper 9*, p. 3. No reports of this phase were published.

[40] *Conference Report, 1949*, p. 70.

[41] *Yorkshire Post*, 'Imperial Policy Authors', 25 June, 1949.

[42] *Imperial Policy* (A Statement of Conservative Policy for the British Empire and Commonwealth) (Conservative Central Office, June 1949), p. 29.

[43] *Imperial Policy*, pp. 10 and 20. Cf. criticism of this aspect of the policy statement in *News Chronicle*, 'Red, White and Blue', 25 June, 1949; *Observer*, 'Comment', 26 June, 1949; *Economist*, 'Conservative Imperial Policy', 2 July,

1949. The *Manchester Guardian* found 'insight and imagination' in the suggestion for a new Commonwealth Tribunal, and concluded that it was probably Churchill's idea. *Manchester Guardian*, 'Tories and the Commonwealth', 25 June, 1949.

[44] *News Chronicle*, 25 June.

[45] *Imperial Policy*, p. 53.

[46] *Two-Way Movement* (Report on Phase 1), pp. 7–9.

[47] *What We Think* (Report on Phase 5), pp. 7–9.

[48] *Imperial Policy*, pp. 7–8.

[49] 'Principles of Policy'.

[50] Letter to Winston Churchill from Arnold B. Gridley, 27 February, 1949.

[51] 'Nine Points of Conservative Policy', n.d. [1949].

[52] For earlier criticism of party policy see, for example: Robert Boothby, *Scotsman* 'By-election Lessons for Conservatives', 29 November, 1947; and an anonymous Young Conservative in the *Yorkshire Post*, 'Way to Conservative Victories', 1 December, 1947. See also Norman Tiftaft, *Birmingham Post*, 'Lessons of Batley Election', 21 February, 1949.

[53] To this may be added the point that 'the highly publicized secrecy' and general interest surrounding the creation of Labour's policy statement at Shanklin added fuel to the flames. Nicholas, pp. 66–7.

[54] *Scotsman*, 26 February, 1949.

[55] *Sunday Times*, 'The Test of Results', 27 February, 1949.

[56] *Daily Telegraph*, 26 February, 1949.

[57] *Observer*, 'Tories to Recast Election Policy', 27 February, 1949.

[58] *Daily Telegraph*, 'Hammersmith Causes Conservative Unrest', 26 February, 1949.

[59] *News Chronicle*, 'Churchill States Tory Policy', 4 March, 1949. *The Times*, 'The Lessons of Hammersmith', 4 March, 1949. Cf. *Daily Express*, 4 March, 1949. *Yorkshire Post*, 4 March, 1949, commented: 'What many Conservatives would like to see – the demand is made both at Westminster and the constituencies – is some more concise document which assembles in simple form the main features of the charters and the salient points of policy on matters not yet covered by these documents.'

[60] *The Times* (correspondence), 3 March, 1949. See also *The Times*' correspondence pages for March, 7, 9, 10, 11, 12, 14, 15, 16, 18, 19, 24, 26 and 30.

[61] Quintin Hogg, *The Times* (correspondence), 16 March, 1949. For Fitzroy Maclean's letter: 24 March, 1949; Hogg's reply: 26 March, 1949.

[62] T. E. Utley, 'Conservative Dilemma', *Spectator*, 25 March, 1949.

[63] *The Times*, 3 March, 1949.

[64] *Central Council Annual Meeting* [Agenda], 17 and 18 March, 1949, p. 12.

[65] Lord Woolton's description of the purpose of the charters on 10 May, 1949, was a most curious contrast to Butler's references to them as 'blueprints of party policy': 'They are designed [Lord Woolton said] to teach the teachers of party doctrine, to provide data for speakers.' *Yorkshire Post*, 'Lord Woolton Tells of Election Hopes', 11 May, 1949.

[66] *Observer*, 27 February, 1949.

[67] Council Minute Book, II, 17–18 March, 1949, p. 5.

[68] *Manchester Dispatch*, 'Woolton Flays Whispers', 19 March, 1949.

[69] *The Times*, 'Conservative Policy', 19 March, 1949.

[70] *Manchester Dispatch*, 19 March, Cf. *The Times*, 19 March, and *Liverpool Daily Post*, 'All Together', 19 March, 1949.

[71] *Labour Believes in Britain* was distributed in the constituencies on 23 March and released to the press on 11 April. Nicholas, p. 66.

[72] *Financial Times*, 'The Labour Programme', 21 April, 1949.

[73] *Conference Report, 1949*, p. 69.

[74] *The Right Road for Britain* [Speech by Churchill at Wolverhampton, 23 July, 1949], Conservative Central Office, 1949, p. 1.

[75] *Observer*, 'Table Talk', 24 July, 1949.

[76] *Reynolds News*, 'Wolf Beneath the Frills', 24 July, 1949.

[77] *Financial Times*, 'Conservative Policy', 16 July, 1949.

[78] *Birmingham Post*, 'Policy and Programme', 16 July, 1949.

[79] *Birmingham Post*, 23 July, 1949.

[80] *The Right Road for Britain* [Churchill's speech at Wolverhampton, 23 July, 1949], p. 1.

[81] Nicholas, pp. 67–8.

[82] *The Right Road for Britain*, pp. 16–17; p. 22. See also *What Do You Think of the Right Road for Britain* (C.P.C., September 1949), p. 3.

[83] *The Right Road*, p. 17.

[84] *The Right Road*, pp. 27–9.

[85] *The Right Road*, p. 39.

[86] *The Right Road*, p. 41.

[87] *The Right Road*, pp. 41–2, 66–8.

[88] *The Right Road*, p. 49.

[89] *The Right Road*, p. 50.

[90] *The Right Road*, p. 8.

[91] *The Right Road*, p. 9.

[92] *Manchester Guardian*, 'Tory Socialism', 23 July, 1949.

[93] *Daily Express* (London), 'Opinion', 23 July, 1949. *Evening Standard* ('On the Road', 23 July, 1949) was by no means as critical as the *Express*.

[94] *Sunday Express*, 24 July, 1949.

[95] *Spectator*, 'Right Road?', 29 July, 1949.

[96] *Economist*, 'The Tory Alternative', 30 July, 1949.

[97] *Financial Times*, 'Reaction to Tory Plan', 26 July, 1949.

[98] *What We Think* (Report of Phase 3), C.P.C., November, 1949, pp. 4, 5, and 10.

[99] *What We Think* (Phase 3), p. 4.

[100] *What We Think . . . About the Agricultural Charter* (A Report of Phase 4), C.P.C., June 1949, and *What We Think . . . About Property-Owning Democracy* (C.P.C., June 1949).

[101] *What We Think . . .* (Report on Phase 5), C.P.C., November 1949.

[102] *What We Think* (Phase 2), p. 6.

[103] *What We Think* (Phase 2), p. 7.

[104] *What We Think* (Phase 2), p. 7.

[105] *What We Think* (Phase 3), p. 4.

[106] *Conference Report, 1947*, pp. 28–9; *Conference Report, 1948*, pp. 24–8.

[107] *The Right Road*, p. 50.

[108] *Conference Report, 1949*, p. 89.

[109] *Conference Report, 1949*, p. 112.

[110] David Butler, *1951 General Election*, pp. 4–5, on the difficulties of studying decision-making in the party hierarchy in elections.

[111] See the article by Major Guy Lloyd, *Truth*, 'What Road for Britain?', 21 October, 1949, and *Truth*, 'Conservative Policy', 23 December, 1949.

[112] *Manchester Guardian*, 'Prescription for Saving', 8 October, 1949.

[113] Cf. *Right Road*, pp. 15–18, and *This is the Road*, pp. 5–7.

[114] Nicholas, p. 87

[115] Nicholas, p. 88.

[116] *This is the Road*, pp. 16 and 20.

[117] *Manchester Guardian*, 'Tory Policy', 25 January, 1950; and *Observer*, 'Tories', 29 January, 1950. *Truth* ('Mr Churchill's Lead', 27 January, 1950) gave vague general acceptance of the document; *Sunday Times* ('The Choice', 29 January, 1950) which had been quite critical of *The Right Road* now professed to believe that 'only the Conservatives have a solution'; *Spectator* ('The Conservative Case', 27 January, 1950), formerly equally critical now saw the manifesto as an 'honest', acceptable statement.

[118] *Evening Standard*, 'A Winning Policy', 25 January, 1950.

[119] *Daily Express*, 'Events of the "Tory Road"', 25 January, 1950.

[120] *Daily Telegraph*, 'No Issue Shirked', 27 January, 1950.

[121] David Butler, *1951 General Election*, Chapter I, pp. 12–21, for an excellent summary of the 19 months between elections.

[122] In the meantime the mass party continued to transmit to the party leadership its ideas on party policy. See *Scotsman*, 'Demand by Unionists', 19 May, 1950, for details of resolutions passed at the Scottish Unionist Association conference in May, and *Scotsman*, 'Unionist Women call for Health Service Inquiry', 7 June, 1950, for certain suggestions on policy from the Central Women's Advisory Council conference the following month.

[123] *Daily Mail*, 'Mild and Dull', 29 September, 1950. The *Daily Mail* was bitterly critical of the programme for the party conference and called for an agenda that was 'stimulating – even outrageous'.

[124] Nicholas, *Parliamentary Affairs*, p. 146, for Butler's explanation of why there was no policy statement submitted to this conference.

[125] McKenzie, p. 197. Miss Marjorie Maxse, a Vice-Chairman of the party organization, had referred earlier in the year to the possibility of producing 300,000 houses a year – in a 'brains trust' conducted by Hugh Massingham and reported in *Illustrated*, 'The Case Against Mr Attlee', 11 February, 1950.

[126] McKenzie, pp. 197–8. See also: Ivor Bulmer-Thomas, 'How Conservative Policy is Formed', *Political Quarterly*, XXIV (April–June 1953), p. 202 (for Lord Woolton's reaction); Harris, p. 112, and *Manchester Guardian*, '300,000 New Houses a Year as Tories' Target', 14 October, 1950 (for Butler's reaction). The Chairman of the Research Department was not pleased with the 'emo-

tional and mass feeling' his generalities about party democracy had released! See *Conference Report, 1950*, pp. 20 and 56–65, for the resolution and the debate on housing.

[127] *Conference Report, 1950*, p. 112.

[128] See the report on Eden's broadcast, in *Daily Herald*, 'Houses', 30 October, 1950, the report of Lyttelton's speech in *Daily Herald*, '300,000 Houses – Tory Retreat', 28 April, 1951, and *The Manifesto of the Conservative and Unionist Party* (C.C.O., 1951), p. 4.

[129] *Policy Paper 10* (C.P.C. [autumn 1950]), p. 2.

[130] *Policy Paper 11* (C.P.C. [spring 1951]).

[131] *Policy Paper 13* (C.P.C. [September 1951]), p. 1.

[132] *Policy Paper 12*, 'The Future Work of the Political Education Movement', C.P.C., p. 1.

[133] *Policy Paper 12*, 'The Future Work of the Political Education Movement', C.P.C., p. 2.

[134] See Saloma, p. 420, for a reference to the contribution towards party policy of an *ad hoc* Policy Committee on the Health Service composed of parliamentary party and Research Department membership.

[135] A report in the *Evening News* ('Churchill Prepares for Poll', 13 September, 1951), stated that: 'The document will most probably be published after the Labour Party conference ends on October 5 and before the Conservative conference opens at Scarborough . . .'. The *Observer's* political correspondent (*Observer*, 'Tory Shadow Cabinet Meets', 23 September, 1951), noted that the statement of policy had already been sent to the printers.

[136] *Star*, 1 October, 1951.

[137] *Financial Times*, 25 September, 1951.

[138] David Butler, *1951 General Election*, p. 44.

[139] *Manifesto* (1951), pp. 3–4.

[140] *Manifesto* (1951), p. 1.

[141] *Observer*, 'Tory Shadow Cabinet Meets', 23 September, 1951.

[142] See, for example, *Evening News*, 'Churchill Prepares for Poll', 13 September, 1951.

[143] *The Times*, 'Conservative Policy', 29 September, 1951; *Financial Times*, 'Conservative Manifesto', 29 September, 1951; *Observer*, 'Tory Road', 30 September, 1951. See also David Butler, *1951 General Election*, p. 51.

[144] *Observer*, 'Tory Road', 30 September, 1951.

[145] *Manifesto* (1951), p. 3.

[146] The phrase is R. H. S. Crossman's in 'Ideologist of Inequality', in Martin, *New Statesman Portraits*, *op. cit.*

[147] Boyd, p. 15. For Boyd's comments on Butler's importance in the policy-process see pp. 95–8.

[148] *Looking Ahead*, pp. 1–2.

[149] *The Times*, 'Mr Butler's Creed for Conservatives', 3 March, 1945.

[150] See Butler's introduction to *Conservatism, 1945–50* (C.P.C., October, 1950), pp. 1 and 3.

[151] 'Business Conservatism', Dr Saloma has written, ' . . . tended to see welfare

in physical terms. It favoured an open aristocracy of merit (open enough to allow their entrance), equality of opportunity, as a means to the positive goal of *material progress*. Enterprise was one of the factors making progress possible, and the profit motive instrumental in calling enterprise into being.'

[152] Saloma, p. 448. Dr Saloma's chapter 'A Conservative Theory for the Future of the Welfare State' (Chapter VI) is a brilliant exposition of the main features of the new Conservative thought and a welcome antidote to the present pre-occupation with the consensual aspects of British politics. My remarks are indebted – but not exclusively so – to his research.

[153] Saloma, p. 449.

[154] Iain Macleod, *Daily Herald*, 'The Kind of Britain I Want', 20 February, 1962.

[155] Peter Townsend, *New Statesman*, 'Freedom and Equality', LXI. 14 April, 1961, p. 573.

[156] David Eccles, *What Do You Think About Property Owning Democracy?* (C.P.C., June, 1949); see also *Right Road*, pp. 8–9.

[157] R. A. Butler, 'Conservative Policy', *Political Quarterly*, XX (October 1949), p. 322.

[158] L. S. Amery, *Framework of the Future* (Oxford, 1944), pp. 147–8 especially.

[159] See, for example, *Britain Strong and Free*, p. 5, in which the rejection of egalitarianism is made slightly vague by the qualification 'centrally planned'.

[160] *Conference Report, 1949*, p. 93.

[161] *One Nation* (C.P.C., October 1950), especially p. 93. Cf. Angus Maude, 'Priorities in Social Reform', *Six Oxford Lectures, 1951* (C.P.C., February 1952), especially pp. 47–8.

CHAPTER VII

Parliamentary Opposition

TO UNDERTAKE a successful examination of the Conservative Party's activities as a parliamentary Opposition presents a considerable problem. Some shape and focus could be given to an analysis of the Conservative Party in opposition by attempting to assess the efficiency or effectiveness of its parliamentary actions, but the difficulty is to decide what criteria to employ in the assessment. The 'proof of the pudding is in the eating' approach – one which uses ultimate success in a general election as the means for judging the effectiveness of the party while in opposition – merely begs the question. Moreover, not only does this argument grossly simplify the complexity of factors which go towards determining election results, it suggests an unwarranted predominance of the influence of the parliamentary struggle. Nor should one expect much from a consideration of the occasions on which it appears that the Opposition exerts a major influence on Government policy. In most situations short of parliamentary stalemate the opportunities for such influence are few. Besides, where there does appear to be a correspondence between Opposition suggestion and Government acceptance it is a too extreme simplication of the decision-making process in British politics to isolate such an occurrence from the interplay of power and influence quite outside the parliamentary arena. The concessions on 'C licences' and compensation under the Transport Bill are an interesting case in point. These owe at least as much to the efforts of the interest groups involved and to the differences within the Government which were exploited during Herbert Morrison's illness as to the fact that such measures were desired by the Opposition.[1]

The problem of constructing criteria of efficiency is increased by the difficulty which the 'outsider' experiences in attempting to comprehend fully 'the spirit of the place' in which the parliamentary struggle occurs. If, as Lord Chandos believes, the women members of the House of Commons never succeed in getting the mood of the House right because they do not go into the Smoke Room,[2] how much more difficult is it for the non-member to reconstruct the impact of tactics and arguments from the flat pages of *Hansard*. Many 'insiders' attest to the difficulty – some say the impossibility – of getting the Commons' mood right,[3] and I am inclined to agree; for the special atmosphere of that most honoured of clubs does not lend itself readily to appreciation by those who bring to the task the tools of judgement learned outside that rarefied condition.

The crux of the matter is that what may be regarded as effective or efficient opposition by those within the House of Commons may be lost entirely on people outside; and what is selected by the mass media and played up outside the House may be regarded as of no particular virtue within the Palace of Westminster. A brilliantly delivered harangue of the Government's policy by Winston Churchill might have – and often did have – the desired effect on the Press Gallery, but within the narrower parliamentary context, the speech might be regarded, even by some of his own party, as a wild, unreasonable, and perhaps embarrassing display, whose only contribution was to unite a divided government party. Total war, it seems, is not always effective opposition. On the other hand, a conciliatory approach adopted by the Opposition confronted with a piece of non-controversial legislation might lead to the acceptance by the Government of a number of valued amendments, but the effect of such a bi-partisan approach on the party's supporters in the constituencies might be to aggravate a feeling of dissatisfaction with the efforts of their parliamentary representatives.

A parliamentary Opposition's leadership will have four main aims: to attempt to influence Government policy; to keep up the enthusiastic support of the parliamentary party; to convince the activists in the mass organization that the Opposition is doing its job well and is worthy of the efforts being made in the country on its behalf; and to win support for the party's views among the electorate as a whole. It is not always possible to pursue successfully all the aims simultaneously; nor are the conditions necessary for success always within the control of the Opposition. The extent to which the first goal can be achieved depends very much on the balance of power within the House of Commons at any particular time; the extent to which the last aim can be fulfilled by the party's parliamentary efforts alone depends greatly on the attention given to the Opposition's case by the media of communication. Information is limited about the extent to which what happens in Parliament is appreciated by the general public, but there is little reason to believe that such knowledge is very widespread. This does not mean that the parliamentary battle is of no importance whatever – for it is in Parliament that the issues are generated from which spring the points of conflict between the parties in the country – but it does suggest that 'the efficiency of the Opposition' is not something which the average voter is likely to know about or care about very much.

This may be true for the general public, but it certainly does not hold for the Opposition's active supporters inside and outside Parliament, or for sympathetic sections of the press. All are very anxious to see their party conducting an efficient opposition. But all do not necessarily stress the same priorities in assessing the Opposition's record.

The active Opposition back-bencher, often frustrated by his ineffectiveness, takes the pleasure of his parliamentary career where he can get it: from the persistent team-harassment of a vulnerable minister at question time and on the daily adjournment debate;[4] from keeping the Government's supporters around the House late at night to counter an expected 'prayer',[5] and then withdrawing it at the last minute; from a particularly clever exchange of 'points of order' at an early hour in the morning which delays a bill still further.

Taken together over a period of time the successful use of such ploys will have some influence on any assessment made by the individual member about the effectiveness of the official Opposition, but it seems perfectly clear that factors like these belong to an essentially private world centred on Westminster – they are occasions for a quiet smile (or scowl) on the Friday train back to the constituency, and little more.

If M.P.s are impressed by the subtle tactics of party warfare, the party activists and most of the press react more favourably to the rougher, more explicit signs of political battle. For them effective opposition is quite often little more than the rigorous application of the old maxim that 'it is the duty of the Opposition to oppose'. The more vigorous the opposition the better.[6]

There is much to be said, indeed, for making 'vigorous opposition'

– the concerted attack on the principles, policy, and personnel of the Government – the crucial criterion in this present estimate of efficiency. In the first place it is regarded as important by parliamentarians and their active supporters outside Westminster. Parliamentarians may find certain other matters, such as the resourcefulness and attention to duty of the Opposition front bench and the minor harassing techniques, also relevant in their judgements, and they will probably be more aware of the limitations imposed by procedure on the possibilities of all-out opposition, but it is undeniable that they share with the Opposition's supporters in Fleet Street and in the constituencies a high regard for vigour of attack.

The 'vigorous opposition' notion is useful for a second reason: it is relatively easy to select actions by an Opposition which quality as *prima facie* evidence of attack upon the Government, even if it is difficult to determine how effective the attacks have been. We can judge, in other words, an Opposition's willingness to wound as a question separate from its success in doing so.

A fairly wide range of activities rests with an Opposition intent on attacking a Government. The fiercest weapon at their disposal – the more dangerous to itself, however, for being two-edged – is undoubtedly the censure. The elaborately mounted two-day censure debate followed by as full a muster as possible in the division lobby is certainly the most explicit indication of an Opposition's hostility to a Government. The most frequent type of censure is the formal motion censure, but an official Opposition amendment to the Speech from the Throne (the statement at the beginning of a session of Parliament of the main lines of Government policy) is tantamount to a censure. Also effective for a similar purpose is the use of the supply day for attacking specific ministers, employing as the symbol of the party's disapproval of the minister and his policies the motion to reduce the minister's salary.

Only slightly less spectacular is the Opposition's frontal assault backed by the willingness to divide the House on a Government bill at its second or third reading stages.[7] In opposing a bill at either reading the Opposition may: attack the entire notion of the bill by attempting to negative the motion 'That the bill be now read a second time'; move an amendment to the motion taking out 'now' and adding at the end 'upon this day three [or six] months'; or move a so-called 'reasoned amendment' seeking to remove all the words in the original motion after 'That' and substituting a statement setting forth the reasons why the Opposition proposes to vote against the bill. The effect of all these tactics is to attempt to reject the bill, but the Opposition may sometimes favour the indirectness of the second and third approaches – the second for its suggestion that the objection is to the timing of the bill, the third for the possibility which it offers of seeming to vote not against the principle of the bill but against the way in which the principle is carried out. In cases of real hostility to Government proposals the Opposition will formalize that hostility by producing as large a turnout as possible in the appropriate division lobby.

The tactics of opposition at the committee and report stages are perhaps not as dramatic as those employed at other times, and it is notable that these stages of the legislative process receive less publicity from the mass media than others; but the use of certain procedures (especially in concert) at these two stages[8] will give a general indication of whether the Opposition is vigorous or token. The attacking Opposition will have two main objects at this time: to heap scorn upon the Government's proposals and, most important (whether the Government's majority is large or small and whether the guillotine is applied or not), to delay the Government's timetable as much as possible. It might also be said that an Opposition's object at this stage would be to seek favourable amendments, but when delaying tactics are used at the same time the spirit of the House is usually totally hostile to the granting of any Government concessions. Numerous amendments will be put down for many clauses to be debated at great length; amendments and new clauses will be forced to division; points of order will arise at frequent intervals; time will be taken to debate, perhaps several times in an evening, the motion that the committee 'report progress'. One has only to contrast the progress that can be made at two periods of the same stage of the same bill to appreciate the delaying power of these Opposition tactics.[9]

It has been argued that a consideration of the vigour with which an Opposition uses a variety of tactics available to it takes us some way towards a reasonable judgement of its efficiency. It is, however, too narrow a view to concentrate solely on tactics without any regard to the quality of the arguments put up in support of the Opposition's case. The Opposition may threaten a division at the second reading backed up by a three-line whip, and may pour forth a steady stream of criticism, but if the attack seems fabricated, if the speakers continually reproduce the same brief, the rest of the House loses interest, the press may take less note of the proceedings, the parliamentary occasion may be lost. Nor is it certain that vigorous opposition is always effective opposition. Not only may it be that an all-out assault serves to unite the Government without compensatory gains to the Opposition; vigorous attack may also place the Opposition in a trap set for it by the Government.[10] It does appear, therefore, that, although the notion of 'vigorous opposition' provides a starting point for this analysis, any assessment of the efficiency of the Opposition must take account also of the *consistency* with which and *context* within which their case is presented. Inevitably the focus of attention will be the activities of the Opposition in the House of Commons, but because the importance of consistency and context has to be taken into account, events in the House of Lords and the country generally will also be considered.

PERIOD OF ADJUSTMENT

If a number of Labour back-benchers found difficult the business of learning to support rather than attack the Government of the day, Conservatives found the transition from Government to Opposition decidedly painful. The first five months of opposition were most unhappy for the Tory Party.

In the few days before the first meeting of the new Parliament on 1 August, 1945, the Conservative press had advised that the public could not expect an immediate assault on the Government: the Tories would allow ministers a decent period of adjustment. In the event, the first weeks from 1 to 24 August passed off much as predicted. The Allied victory over Japan gave a temporary unity to public affairs that was not broken by the many maiden speeches – on the King's Speech; by tradition is heard without interruption – or the first piece of minor Government legislation.[11] Winston Churchill's first speech from the Opposition front bench was a study in moderation: 'Here and there,' he said, 'there may be differences of emphasis or view, but in the main no Parliament ever assembled with such a mass of agreed legislation . . .'.[12] Even the nationalization of the Bank of England raised, for him, no issue of principle. R. A. Butler's approach was equally conciliatory. He professed to recognizing measures in the Throne Speech which had been framed in the Coalition, and promised that the Conservatives would do their best 'to carry them through in the interests of the country as a whole'.[13] Anthony Eden, taking the Foreign Secretary's general line of policy as very much in keeping with the previous administration's, established the ground for a bi-partisan approach to international affairs which was to hold throughout most of the Labour Government.[14] When the cancellation of Lend Lease was announced by Attlee on 24 August, Churchill played to the full the rôle of responsible statesman by accepting the Prime Minister's request that the question should not be made the subject of an adjournment debate and emphasizing that restraint in comment was necessary in the national interest.

Relations between the two parties during the first weeks were not always so congenial. Once – in Churchill's cutting remarks about the totalitarian implications of the Government's proposals to abolish time for private member's bills,[15] and again during Oliver Lyttelton's speech in which he reminded the Government that if it wanted aid from capitalist America it would have to be less hostile to capitalism in Britain – the sparks of party controversy flew for all to see. But on the whole proceedings in the House of Commons during the first weeks were quiet. The Opposition's temperate approach to the new situation could be justified because the rules of the game seemed to require that the Labour Government should be given some time to find its feet. The problem for the Conservative Party was its proper response after a conciliatory approach was no longer expected of it and after the Labour Party began to put forward the major items of its legislative programme in October.

A consistent Opposition line was made difficult by real differences of opinion within the parliamentary party over tactics. Some Conservatives were reluctant to indulge in open abuse of the Government for fear of diminishing its prestige abroad; others, thinking the Labour Government incapable of conducting affairs for long, advised doing nothing and allowing it to collapse through its own ineptitude. The situation was not aided during the early months at any rate by poor communication between front and back-benches and occasionally inconsistent – not to say non-existent – leadership. It was not surprising, then, that on many occasions the Opposition seemed to lack drive and purpose. Moreover, the malaise was not allowed to pass unnoticed, and attempts by the parliamentary party to satisfy criticism (usually by taking a tougher line with legislation at a later stage) often led to rather bewildering unevenness of treatment.

Perhaps the best example of the Conservatives at their most inconsistent is provided by their handling of the Bank of England Bill. Although Churchill had stated during the debate on the Address that the national ownership of the Bank of England raised no issue of principle with him, his little addendum – 'I give my opinion – anybody else may give his own'[16] – gave a better guide to the reaction of the parliamentary party at the second reading of the Nationalization Bill on 29 October, 1945. By then the Tories had decided to oppose the bill. Churchill's ostentatious absence from the front bench merely added to the embarrassment of Sir John Anderson and Oliver Stanley, the two front-bench spokesmen who laboured to set out the reasons why the Tories had decided to vote against its second reading. The essence of the Conservative case was: (1) that the Bank of England's special connection with the sterling area made public ownership inappropriate; (2) that nationalization was unnecessary and might lead to loss of confidence abroad.[17] The decision to oppose the bill undoubtedly had the support of the great majority of the parliamentary party, but the effectiveness of the stand against the bill was greatly diminished by the absence of Churchill and Butler along with a number of back-benchers from the division lobby, while Robert Boothby actually voted with the Government. The bill was given a second reading by 348 votes to 153 and then committed to a select committee, whence it was returned to the committee of the whole House. Although it had apparently been agreed that the financial resolution would go through without difficulty, a number of back-benchers made a little trouble over the wording of the resolution. After token resistance the resolution was put to a division and passed by 190 votes to 86.[18]

Thereafter the bill enjoyed a remarkably smooth passage without any substantial alteration. During the recommital stage on 17 December fewer than 100 Conservatives stayed around the House to support party amendments to the first few clauses of the bill (especially the clause giving the Treasury powers to issue directions to the banks) and many later clauses were allowed to pass unopposed. At the third reading two days later Capt Crookshank claimed that

Conservatives were 'completely opposed' to the bill, but the tale was unconvincing. The bill was given a third reading by 306 votes to 126 – a fitting anti-climax to a month of anti-climax.

During any session of Parliament there is a considerable body of minor legislation which goes unopposed. What was particularly embarrassing to the Conservative Opposition was that a great deal of minor legislation should come in the first few months at a time when the party was finding it difficult to put up serious opposition to the Government's more important bills. To the background controversy over party name and policy[19] was added criticism of the ineffectiveness of the parliamentary Opposition – all of which were related to the party's disappointing showing in by-elections and the November local government elections.[20] This criticism reached a peak in the few days following Herbert Morrison's announcement in the House on 19 November that the Government intended to nationalize electricity, gas, and transport within the lifetime of that Parliament. That it should be said that the Conservative leaders had prior notice of the Government's statement merely deepened the dissatisfaction of a great many of the party's supporters with the response from the Conservative front bench. When the announcement was made only Oliver Stanley and Oliver Lyttelton were in the Chamber. The latter sought an adjournment to debate the announcement, but received only the Speaker's rebuke for being entirely out of order. Morrison exploited the Opposition's distress with great skill: if the Opposition had wanted to debate the nationalization proposals in general, why then, he asked, had they not put down an amendment to the Address when they had the opportunity; if the Opposition did not discharge its functions then, it was not part of his business to help them do it now.[21]

Morrison's shaft struck its target. Anger and frustration with the absentee leadership of Eden and Churchill, with the Coalition manners of the front bench generally, and with the inept display in the House on 19 November in particular welled up from the wounded Tory Party – anger which was relieved only by an immediate meeting of the 1922 Committee addressed by Churchill and Eden at which promises were made that opposition would in future be more vigorous and that either Churchill or Eden would be present in the House for major debates. The censure motion put down by the Conservative shadow cabinet later that week and Churchill's extremist speech at the Central Council meeting on 28 November can be seen very clearly as attempts to prove the sincerity of the leadership's desire to fight the Labour Government. The speech was probably harmless; the censure motion, based as it was on the aim of uniting the Opposition more than attacking the Government, proved a remedy worse than the disease.

After a gentle rise in the heat of party controversy at the second reading of the Emergency Laws (Transitional Provisions) Bill,[22] and the committee stage of the Finance Bill, the Government faced its first motion of censure on 5 and 6 December. Speaking to a formal motion deploring the Government's preoccupation with long-term socialist schemes for nationalization when more urgent tasks such as housing, demobilization and the curtailment of national expenditure needed attention, Oliver Lyttelton blamed the Government for everything from falling coal production to an overworked civil service. However, Clement Davies' brilliant condemnation of the Conservatives' failure to plan for the peace and his warning that the Liberals would not support the motion because it was 'wrong in its assumption . . . bad in its timing . . . and mistaken in its conclusions'[23] seemed to take the steam from a Tory attack which got increasingly out of gear as the first day's debate drew on. Churchill tried to right the balance at the beginning of the second day by focusing criticism on two main points: the Government was, he claimed, exacerbating party strife and demobilizing too slowly – but the Conservative Leader merely succeeded in setting himself up for Attlee's magnificent *coup de grâce*. Rising brilliantly to the occasion, the Prime Minister delighted his supporters and demoralized the Opposition with a sober yet extremely forceful counter-attack. Churchill and his party had, Attlee argued, plenty of earlier opportunities which had not been taken to debate the subjects brought up in the censure motion. This motion was a mere 'party move' inspired by the pressure of criticism by Conservative back-benchers of the inefficiency of the party's front bench. Far from exacerbating party strife the Government was beginning to implement the policy on which his party had been returned, and it was Churchill who was deepening party hostilities by refusing to accept that democratic decision. As for the charge that demobilization was too slow, the Labour Government was merely following the precepts laid down by Churchill himself – that men should be released according to age and service.

The Opposition produced its best turnout in the division lobbies to date – 197 supporters entered the 'Ayes Lobby' – but there was no doubt in many observers' minds that the censure motion had, on balance, achieved more for the Government than the Opposition.[24] 'The fact was,' Harold Nicolson wrote, 'that the Government had not failed badly enough to justify a formal censure, and even if it had the Opposition had no constructive policy to put forward as an alternative.'[25] Moreover, the effectiveness of the Conservative argument was cut away by the unfortunate timing of three events: a few days before the censure debate the Chairman of the Federation of British Industries had declared 'the willingness of the leaders of industry to co-operate with the Government in its economic policy and to fit private enterprise into its scheme';[26] on the very day of the censure debate the names of a committee set up by the Coalition Government to consider the future of the gas industry were announced;[27] and immediately after the division on the censure motion (6 December) the Government announced the signing of the Loan Agreement with the United States.

The debate on the Loan Agreement on 12 and 13 December revealed the Conservatives more divided than at any time in their six years as an Opposition. Forced into the open by the Speaker's refusal to accept amendments to the Government's straightforward motion for approval of the loan,[28] the severe fissures within the Tory Party and Churchill's inability to unite them were starkly revealed. Even the front bench was divided. Churchill, refusing to accept responsibility for the Government's action (but in fact trying to offer an escape route to his divided party), counselled abstention. In the end the party went three separate ways. A number of Conservatives, following the Leader's advice, remained in their places, but 71 Conservatives joined 23 Labour back-benchers in voting against the motion; a further eight Conservatives voted with the Government. Later in the day (13 December) a number of Conservatives disregarded their Leader's advice again and voted at the second reading against the Bretton Woods Agreement. Thereafter the Bretton Woods Agreement Bill had a quick passage through the Commons. Since the bill was an enabling bill there was very little to discuss, and the bill passed through its remaining stages on 14 December. Although it was expected that the Lords might delay ratification (which had to be given before the loan could take effect), only seven Peers disregarded Lord Cranborne's advice to abstain.

* * *

The conjunction of the failure of the party's censure motion, the disunity resulting from the American Loan vote, and the weakening of the opposition to the nationalization of the Bank of England, brought dissatisfaction with the inefficiency of the Conservative Opposition to the highest point it was ever to reach during the years of Labour Government. There was, it must however be emphasized, no remarkable or immediate improvement in the quality of Conservative opposition after the Christmas recess – indeed, criticism of its inefficiency was to break out from party supporters in Parliament and in the country on several occasions throughout the following years – but a number of factors prevented the Conservatives from re-living the prolonged nightmare which had characterized their first months of opposition. By March 1946 the Conservative Party had organized 15 'functional' or party committees[29] (assisted by the newly created Parliamentary Secretariat) to develop policy and tactics in specialized areas. Winston Churchill had turned increasingly to foreign speech-making and history-writing so that parliamentary leadership became better co-ordinated under Anthony Eden and his moderate colleagues. The Labour Government had begun to introduce more controversial legislation on which both front and back benches could unite in deeply-felt opposition. And, finally, the deterioration of economic conditions offered the Conservatives a continuous theme for exploitation, although so long as the party lacked an alternative policy its criticism often lost a good deal of its effectiveness.

OPPOSITION, 1946–50

I

The quiet first days following the Christmas recess resulting from the consideration of mainly non-controversial legislation were broken dramatically in the next weeks by vigorous Conservative opposition to the Coal Industry Nationalization Bill and to the repeal of the Trades Disputes Act (1927). In 1943 Churchill had accepted the principle of coal nationalization, but recognized that compensation would be the outstanding problem.[30] The Conservatives, led by

Anthony Eden in the two-day debate[31] beginning on 29 January, 1946, sought to avoid the difficulties imposed by Churchill's earlier acceptance by recourse to a reasoned amendment which attacked the methods by which the purpose was being implemented. The Conservative amendment rejected the bill because it suggested no immediate action to arrest the decline in output and increase in the cost of production, because it offered no safeguards to the employee against being adversely affected by the change in ownership, and because it did not compensate fairly.[32] It was chiefly to the terms of compensation which the party objected.

The Conservatives used every opportunity available to them to oppose the bill. After the second reading amendment was defeated by 359 votes to 182, the Opposition forced a division in an unsuccessful attempt to commit the bill to the committee of the whole House instead of a standing committee. Then at the committee stage of the financial resolution taken later that evening it pressed a number of amendments to division and kept the House sitting until nearly 2 a.m. The next day at the report stage of the financial resolution opposition manoeuvres ran foul of the Speaker's ruling on relevance, and most of the time was taken up with points of order before the resolution was put to a division and passed by 209 votes to 87. With compensation settled already by financial resolution, the Opposition concentrated in the standing committee on trying to induce the minister, Emanuel Shinwell, to define his powers more sharply and to protect consumers more effectively, but he was unaccommodating. The report stage was taken from 13 to 15 May. On each of these days the Government introduced a motion to extend the sitting of the House so that more time might be given to the bill and each time – as the Opposition was to do on so many occasions thereafter – the procedural motion was forced to a division. The Government was in an unyielding mood and the Conservative Opposition was beginning to flag, but this did not prevent some of the Tory lawyers from drawing Shinwell into time-consuming digressions. Although there had been some concessions,[33] Harold Macmillan, in summing up the party's position at the bill's third reading, claimed that Conservatives were completely dissatisfied. If this was so the party made no special effort to prove it; for, although they divided against the third reading, there was a very poor attendance for the debate and the division was carried by 324 to 143 votes.

The passage of the bill to repeal the Trades Disputes Act (which was given its second reading on 12 and 13 February, 1946, by 369 votes to 194 and a third reading on 2 April by 349 votes to 182) was an occasion for the hottest exchanges to date between Government and Opposition although the Attorney-General suggested that it was not as bitter as the debate on the Act had been in 1926–27 and that the Conservatives did not really have their hearts in it.[34] It was also the first major attempt by the Conservative Party to transfer the party fight in Parliament to the country as a whole. Meetings were organized throughout the country by the Central Office; as soon as the details of the bill were first published propaganda material, aimed especially at counteracting the 'political levy', was produced with these titles: 'What Repeal Means'; 'Civil Servants and Politics'; 'It's Your Money They're After'; 'A Plain Man's Guide to the Political Levy'. Led by Eden – Churchill took no part at all in debates on the bill – the Conservatives aimed at deprecating the bill as a cheap party manoeuvre and delaying its progress as much as possible at the committee stage, which was taken in the whole House. Considering the brevity of the bill, the Conservatives, and especially the lawyers among them, showed considerable ingenuity in keeping the sitting which began on 1 April going all night. Except for the last division late in the morning the Opposition's turnout in divisions was well above one hundred; but the effect of this prolonged display of antagonism to the Government's policy must have been mitigated to some extent by the fact that the only really stiff opposition to the bill seemed to come from Quintin Hogg's virtuoso performance in defence of his father's Act.

The House of Commons does not manage to stay at fever pitch for very long, and things quitened down over the next months, between sporadic attacks on the Government – for not planning for the world food shortage (14 February); for its decision not to open the Liverpool Cotton Exchange (28 March); for deciding to withdraw all military forces from Egypt (7 May); for its plans to nationalize iron and steel (27–28 May); and for the 'administrative mismanagement' which necessitated bread rationing (3 July) – a good deal of legislation was passed which had the support of the Conservative Party. Churchill secured consent for an adjournment debate about the withdrawal of forces from Egypt at which the Opposition put up an all-out attack on the Government. The Labour Party was, however, fully united for the first time on a question of foreign policy and the Opposition's motion was defeated by 158 to 327. The Conservatives used their supply day on 24 May to debate the Treaty negotiations with Egypt. The Minister of Supply's announcement of the Government plans to nationalize iron and steel on 17 April gave rise to a very acrimonious exchange between Churchill (who claimed the plan 'pure political ramp') and who wanted an adjournment debate and the Speaker and Attlee who did not. The debate on 27 and 28 May took place on the Government's motion for approval.[35] And on 18 July Churchill moved the annulment of the order bringing bread-rationing into effect. Meanwhile, the Opposition made the most of the outcry in the country led by the National Association of Master Bakers by presenting petitions to the Commons.[36] However, a good deal of useful legislation was passed which had the support of the Conservative Party. Undoubtedly the most important was the National Insurance Bill which was given unopposed second and third readings. Referring to the passage of the bill Butler stated: 'We have deliberately hastened rather than delayed the passing of this Measure.'[37]

The most important piece of opposed legislation to come up in the first session of the 1945 Parliament was undoubtedly the National Health Service Bill. It might be thought that the Conservatives, finding themselves with definite objections to the plans for the administration of a scheme whose main principle – universality of application – they accepted, would work out very carefully their response to Labour's bill, especially since the measure was known to be so popular. Instead, poor leadership and the absence of a coherent alternative policy allowed the party to drift into a reactionary posture and become the mouthpiece for the vested interests lined up in opposition to the bill. Thanks to the extremism of the reasoned amendments which the party put up at the second and third readings of the bill,[38] and thanks also to the virulence of the party's personal attack on Aneurin Bevan, the Minister of Health, both inside and outside the House, the Conservative Party placed itself in the position of seeming to oppose the principle of the National Health Service – a position which they spent the next four years denying. The irony of the situation was that, judged from the point of view of parliamentary tactics, the opposition to the bill in the Commons was neither particularly vigorous nor effective.[39]

The bill which reached its third reading on 26 July was not

amended in any major respect as a result of its passage through the committee and report stages, although a number of small concessions were made. The Conservative Party divided against its third reading, again on an amendment which allowed it to avoid voting against the principle of a national health service. However, to a fair number of Conservatives this device must have seemed too little protection against the hostility of electors; a mere 113 Tories found their way to the division lobby in support of the party line.

Conservative opposition in the House of Commons during the period from January to August 1946[40] was often better conducted than over the National Health Service Bill, and, perhaps merely because of the pleasant contrast with the first five months, criticism of the effectiveness of the party's opposition by its press friends trailed off almost completely.[41] It did, nevertheless, become the subject of debate at the party conference in October, as a result of a motion proposed and seconded by two members of the Frome Constituency Association. After a brief discussion in which the relationship of Central Office to the constituency associations received most attention, the resolution expressing the conference's 'dissatisfaction with the lack of vigour and direction shown in attacking the Socialist administration in its first year of office' and calling for 'relentless parliamentary opposition'[42] was defeated by a 'large majority'.

II

Two events – one near the beginning, the other at the end, of the period between the opening of the second session of Parliament on 12 November, 1946, and the second reading of the Transport Bill on 16 December, 1946 – provided interesting, and divergent, examples of the Conservatives as 'responsible Opposition'. Although the Conservatives pressed their own amendment – a condemnation of the Government's nationalization policy – to a division,[43] the most striking feature of the debate on the King's Speech was the Tory Party's support of the Labour Government against amendments tabled by a group of Labour back-benchers. On both these matters – on the amendment calling for a socialist alternative in foreign policy and on the amendment rejecting conscription – the Conservatives not only did not vote against the Government, many of them chose to go into the lobby with the Government. It required no particular effort for the Conservative Party to support the Government against an abrupt modification in foreign policy (especially in a socialist direction), but the decision to support the Government on the conscription issue did reveal the party prepared to support, rather than exploit, unpopular measures if and when its reading of 'the national interest' coincided with the Government's. In 1947 the opposition supported the National Service Bill against criticism from the Labour back benches. Conservatives were angered, however, by the reduction from 18 months to one year in the term of service which was made in response to Labour back-bench discontent.

That the reading of 'the national interest' could often be different was revealed equally vividly by the line which the Conservatives chose to take over the difficulties in the Muslim–Indian negotiations. When Attlee announced the existence of certain difficulties in these negotiations to the Commons on 11 December, he hoped that there would not be a general debate at that stage which might seriously destroy the prospect of a settlement. The Prime Minister had the support of the Liberal Leader, but Churchill, claiming that the Opposition had already shown great restraint, pressed very hard for a two-day debate. Herbert Morrison granted his request, and a debate took place on 12 and 13 December on a Government motion expressing the hope that a settlement would be forthcoming. Churchill dissociated himself and his party from the Government's policy in India, but did not aggravate the situation more than had been done already by pressing the Opposition's differences to a division.[44]

The Transport Bill which was given a second reading on 17 December was not the first bill of that session which the Conservatives had chosen to oppose,[45] but it was opposed with a greater show of hostility than any piece of Government legislation hitherto presented to Parliament, except perhaps the repeal of the Trades Disputes Act. For some time the Conservative Party had been closely associated with the anti-nationalization campaign being conducted by the Road Haulage Association – Lord Woolton was, in fact, President of the National Road Transport Federation – and it was expected that opposition would be stiff, first because it was known that Conservatives objected strongly to the principle of the bill, and secondly because a delaying action might prevent the steel nationalization bill being taken that session.[46] In their fight against the bill at the second reading the Conservatives had the support of the Liberals and produced (with a total of 204 votes at the second reading) the largest anti-Government division of the Parliament to date. However, Conservative opposition was never quite as bitter as the party's link with the agitation in the country might suggest. At the committee stage, it is true, the Conservatives delayed the bill's progress sufficiently to provoke the Government into introducing – for the first time – the guillotine in standing committee. By 20 February, 1947, the committee had disposed of only three of 127 clauses. Alfred Barnes, the Minister of Transport, wanted the bill to reach the Lords by Easter. But the Labour Party never accused the Conservatives of deliberate obstruction; in the debate on the 'guillotine motion' the Labour spokesmen merely argued that progress in committee was too slow. (The Government may have been reluctant to give any consolation to the Conservative Party's supporters who would have derived pleasure from knowing that their opposition had been obstructive.) It was said that despite the guillotine 'all the parties . . . worked together harmoniously and efficiently in the committee upstairs where all the main issues [were] hammered out in a very thorough discussion'.[47]

The guillotine motion on the allocation of time not only fixed 2 April as the date for reporting the Transport Bill from committee, it also put a three-day limit on the report stage and a one-day limit on the third reading.[48] The Conservative tactic at the report stage was, therefore, to take time over each clause so as to ensure that a considerable number would be reported without debate, thus presumably, strengthening the argument for Lords' amendments. In fact, the Conservatives achieved their purpose quite well: debate at the report stage got as far as Clause 40, after which no fewer than 87 clauses and 13 schedules were given a peremptory passage.

This same guillotine motion also fixed 2 April as the end of the committee stage of the Town and Country Planning Bill. The bill, which the Conservatives had opposed at the second reading at the end of January 1947 by means of a reasoned amendment criticizing the 'arbitrary compensation' and the compulsory acquisition of land related to outdated money values,[49] was not subject to anything like the degree of agitation or delay in committee that the Transport Bill had experienced; but once the guillotine motion limited the report and third reading to three days and one day respectively, Conservative tactics followed those used with the other bill. The party's approach was to keep things moving fairly smoothly – there were only 12 divisions in the three-day report stage – and to take time over the least consequential amendments so that as much of the bill as possible would be left to be taken altogether when the report stage expired. If this was the Opposition's sole purpose it must be said it succeeded admirably: only 14 clauses (13 of 130 pages of amendments) were considered in the Commons. A number of changes were made in committee which by the Government's admission were concessions to Conservative ideas with Labour support,[50] perhaps the most important Opposition suggestion being that relating to the provision of grants to war-damaged local authorities; but the Conservatives were not satisfied with the brief consideration given to the bill or its contents and divided against its third reading. Again the vigour of the party's stand against the Government's major legislation was diminished by relatively weak support in the lobby: the bill was given its third reading by 297 votes to 126.[51]

Since Opposition tactics in the Commons seemed designed to justify considerable revision in the second chamber, it is necessary to examine briefly the rôle played by the House of Lords in respect to these two major bills and Government legislation generally up to this time. Labour had expected difficulties but, according to Attlee:

> . . . things had changed since the great fight over the Lords' veto on 1910. The Peers had in Lord Salisbury a wise leader and we had in Lord Addison a skilful and conciliatory spokesman. Thus, for our first three years we experienced no trouble. The House of Lords fulfilled a useful rôle as a debating forum and a revising chamber.[52]

'At the beginning of the first session,' Lord Swinton has written, 'Lord Salisbury . . . advised the House that it would be constitutionally wrong, when the country had so recently pronounced its view, for the House to oppose proposals which had been definitely put before the electorate.'[53] Accordingly the Government's nationalization and social welfare legislation was approached with fundamentally constructive intent. Such bills were not opposed on second reading and the committee and report stages were used as occasions on which a considerable number of Government-inspired amendments could be made and concessions to the Opposition – which had been resisted in the Commons – might be incorporated. Whether due to more conservative Labour leadership in the Lords or merely to the Government's desire to expedite social legislation whose general principles had been preserved, it is impossible to say, but the Conservative Opposition enjoyed considerable success in achieving a number of important concessions which, judging from Government resistance in the Commons, seemed very unlikely indeed.

Occasionally – more frequently by 1947 – the Government was defeated in divisions in the Lords on amendments which it was not prepared to accept. A few amendments of this type to the Coal Bill, the National Health Service Bill, and the Town and Country Planning Bill were rejected by the Commons and afterwards dropped by the Lords.[54] The Transport Bill, however, gave rise to no fewer than 42 separate amendments which the Minister considered merely embodied Conservative policy and which were all rejected by the Commons in a sitting lasting until 6.45 on the morning of 5 August, 1947. This time the Lords did not acquiesce graciously in the defeat, but carried three alternative amendments which the Government had to find time to reject once again in the Commons. Although the Opposition may have felt that resistance was repaid by the Government's ultimate acceptance of one of the alternative amendments, the stand taken by the Conservatives in the House of Lords with the Transport Bill must have strengthened the hand of those members of the Labour Government who argued that the Parliament Act of 1911 would have to be amended.

The Electricity Bill was also vigorously opposed in the Commons; Conservatives divided against both the second and third readings. The Statistics of Trade Bill which was given a second reading on 21 January was to have been treated by the Conservative front bench as fundamentally non-controversial, but 48 Conservative backbenchers, regarding it as 'bad socialist business which should be fought every inch of the way', rebelled against the leadership and divided against the second reading.[55] Although the Conservatives disliked the Minister's power under the bill to vary the size of a crop to be marketed, the Opposition allowed the second reading of the Agriculture Bill to go unopposed on 27 January, 1947. But the Transport Bill and Town and Country Planning Bill provided the focus of legislative attention in the 1946–47 session, although the period will probably be best remembered as the time of the country's most serious economic crisis. The fragile recovery of the first 18 months was struck a crucial blow by the severe economic dislocation of the worst winter in living memory. To a background of currency difficulties resulting from the rapid drain on the American and Canadian Loans were added the special problems of coal, electricity, steel, and grain shortages, and rising unemployment. The opportunities for attack by the Opposition were too good to be missed, and the Conservatives went to it with great gusto in the Commons, Lords and country. In two separate debates in mid-February on the fuel crisis the Minister of Fuel and Power, Emanuel Shinwell, bore the brunt of an all-out attack by the Opposition in the Commons for too little planning and too much optimism. There was a similar debate in the Lords in which Lord Salisbury called for the Minister's resignation. Even newspapers normally sympathetic to Labour found the contrast between Shinwell's optimism in October 1946 and the reality of the late winter difficult to condone.[56]

Criticism of the Government's fuel policy came to a head in the three-day debate on the Economic Survey for 1947 which began on 10 March and ended with a motion of censure moved by Churchill. The gist of the Conservative case was that the nation's economic difficulties were being aggravated by the Government's doctrinaire programmes of nationalization and that the Government's proposals for the future were either inadequate or injurious.[57] It was a speech which bore many of the characteristics of the censure speech in December 1946 and the party's amendment to the Speech from the Throne in November 1946, and Attlee was probably justified in disposing of it – as he did magnificently – with a speech substantially repetitive of his earlier reply to Churchill's censure.[58] The Conservative amendment, which had the support of the Liberals, was defeated by 371 votes to 204.

The relative calm which followed, owing to the improvement in the weather, and perhaps to Churchill's very frequent absences from the House, was transformed abruptly by the currency crisis in late July 1947 resulting from the implementation of the convertibility clause of the American Loan Agreement. The political temperature had already begun to warm up in late June and early July as the Conservatives began to make effective use of a number of supply days to attack Government policies and ministers by attempting to reduce Ministries' votes, and this was intensified by a special attack on the Government for the currency crisis. Here the Conservative case suffered from the dilemma in which the party found itself once it stopped criticizing and tried to make positive recommendations: the party wanted economies but not cuts; it recognized that further planning would be necessary to bridge the export gap but shrank from the full implications.

The session reached its climax on 6 and 7 August, 1947, with an adjournment debate on the state of the nation[59] in which Attlee presented the Government's proposals for dealing with the exports gap problem. Many back-benchers were disappointed with the lack of any real plan, but the Conservative Party's alternative – essentially a policy of deflation[60] – was not one calculated to draw the dissentients into the Opposition lobby, and the Government's measures were given formal endorsement by 318 votes to 170. On 13 August the Conservatives tried to shorten the summer adjournment by more than a month (because of the crisis situation) but the Government successfully warded off this manoeuvre and went into recess for a much needed respite.

* * *

The 1946–47 session was a long, difficult one for the Labour Government during which public disapproval of the party increased until by the summer recess a B.I.P.O. poll indicated that if a general election were held at that time more people would vote Conservative than Labour. The Conservatives drew level with the Government in March 1947, following the period of coal and electricity shortages, when both parties (according to a B.I.P.O. poll) had the support of 44 per cent of the electorate. At the beginning of August the Conservative position increased to 44 per cent and Labour's dropped to 41 per cent. Discontent with the Labour Party reached its peak for the 1945 Parliament in November 1947 when 50½ per cent of people interviewed stated that they would then vote Conservative; only 38 per cent said they would vote Labour. And yet this situation must also have been less than fully satisfying to the Conservatives. In their criticism of the Labour Government, especially with respect to the state of the economy, Conservatives had utilized every opportunity to attack, and when they enjoyed the support of the press in general (as in the fuel crisis) they were able to put their points with great effectiveness. On 29 October, 1947, Attlee stated in the House of Commons: '... I have never known a party leader who more consistently followed the good old maxim that it is the duty of the Opposition to oppose. During the last few years he has seized every opportunity to attack the Government. ...'[61] If the number of divisions in any one session can be taken as the measure of the vigour of opposition – and it can be only a very rough guide indeed – the period from 21 October, 1946, to 13 August, 1947, was the most active for the Conservative Opposition during that Parliament. In the first session (July 1945 to November 1946) there were 293 divisions; in the second session referred to above there were 383 divisions. The last session of the Labour Government (31 October, 1950, to 4 October, 1951) had 170 divisions. Despite this, however, the Labour Party continued to frustrate the Conservatives by not losing a single seat at a by-election.

During the period Conservative activity was sufficiently vigorous to dispel most criticism of its effectiveness,[62] but it was able to create this impression to a considerable extent by taking advantage of the extreme difficulties in which the Labour Government found itself. Even then Labour Ministers revealed themselves quite capable of counter-attack, particularly when they challenged the Opposition to state an alternative policy. Fortunately for the Labour Government economic conditions were to improve in the next 18 months, and the problem for the Conservatives – who had just done their best (or worst) at a time of Labour's deep distress and had found the Government unshaken – was to continue to satisfy their supporters with the strength of their criticism of the Government's legislative programme, opposition to which, on many earlier occasions at least, had not always been regarded as especially vigorous or effective.

III

It is not essential to the task of describing the general characteristics of the Conservative Party in opposition between 1945 and 1950 to pursue further the detailed, session-by-session exposition which has been developed thus far, more or less chronologically. Already the major features of the period have asserted themselves and it is quite remarkable how much the following two or more years can be described simply as 'more of the same'.

While the Opposition continued its symbolic resistance to the Government's legislative programme by dividing against extensions of the sittings of the House, it maintained its general support for the Government's foreign policy. Conservatives, who were satisfied with the spirit, if not necessarily the methods, of the Government's handling of East–West relations,[63] regarded it as their 'object as an Opposition' – as Butler put it in May 1948 – 'to see that the self-reliance of the Rt Hon. Gentleman (Ernest Bevin) [did] not degenerate into self-satisfaction and his imperturbability into a majestic calm'.[64] Accordingly, the Opposition respected the Government's request not to press for a debate on the international situation at the time of the Berlin blockade,[65] supported the Marshall Aid Programme, and backed the Government's National Service (Amendment) Bill which raised the period of national service to 18 months, but attacked the Government very strongly indeed for its Middle East (especially Palestine) policy on 26 January, 1949,[66] and was critical of Labour's hesitant approach to European Union.

As before, certain bills were treated in a generally non-controversial manner. Unopposed second and third readings were given to the Overseas Resources Development Bill, the Monopoly Bill, the Housing Bill, and the National Assistance Bill, the Opposition being content in each case to attempt to make a few minor improvements in committee. There were also a number of bills which the Opposition opposed with less than all-out determination. The Local Government Bill, for example, was opposed at second reading by means of a reasoned amendment.[67] When this failed the Conservatives tried unsuccessfully to commit the bill to the whole House and to have Part III considered by the Scottish Grand Committee.[68] Thereafter the bill enjoyed a relatively easy passage through the remaining stages, although the Opposition divided against its third reading.

The Representation of the People Bill was something of a special case as far as Opposition tactics were concerned. The Conservatives did not divide with the Liberals against the second reading of the bill on 17 February, 1948, but they did press for a number of amendments at the committee stage – especially for the retention of the university seats and the business premises vote. Although the Opposition was sufficiently discontented, once these amendments were rejected, to vote against the bill on its third reading, it did not make any strenuous effort to delay the bill's passage. During the one all-night sitting Conservatives wasted some time by the traditional means of debating the motion to report progress, but the late hour of the sitting reflected as much the Government's desire to cover as much ground as possible as the effectiveness of the Conservative tactics. In spite of a great many amendments from all parts of the House, the Government was able to complete the committee stage in the expected time of seven days without particularly frequent use of the closure. Indeed, progress was so smooth at one point that Eden was anxious to assert that no arrangement had been made with the Government to speed the bill through.

Four highly controversial pieces of legislation – the Parliament Bill, the Gas Bill, the Iron and Steel Bill, and the Licensing Bill – were considered during the last half of the 1945 Parliament, but the treatment they received at the hands of the Conservative Opposition in the Commons differed only in slight degree from that given to earlier (and perhaps less controversial) measures. As in the case of the National Health Service Bill, Conservative opposition to the Licensing Bill and the Iron and Steel Bill tried to take advantage of anti-Government campaigns organized by the interests concerned in the country. The Opposition had already gone to the brink, so to speak, in registering its disapproval of previous legislation. Given the Government's large resolute majority and the techniques available to it for countering dilatory actions by the Opposition, there was therefore little Conservative M.P.s could do to indicate more serious disagreement with, say, the steel nationalization bill (which was undoubtedly Labour's most hated legislation) than had already been shown to, say, the Town and Country Planning Bill. A guillotine motion limited the committee stage (in standing committee) of the steel bill to 35 sittings (85 hours) and the report stage to four days. The one way in which Conservatives did make their objections to the bill more evident than on any earlier occasion was in the very intensive fight the party put up at the Lords' amendments stage in July 1949. Conservatives put a good deal of front-bench material into a party fight which was described by Bromhead as 'carrying on the struggle with all the means at their disposal'.[69] The contrast with the House of Lords is important. Here the more or less constructive approach taken with all earlier Government legislation left the Opposition some room for manoeuvre: 'escalation' to outright rejection of the Parliament Bill where, after an unsuccessful conference on Lords reform broke down, the second reading of the bill was defeated in the Lords by 117 votes to 80, and to stubborn insistence on the 'vesting date amendment' to the Iron and Steel Bill was politically viable simply because it was not overworked. The Lords gave the bill an unopposed second reading but at the committee stage a large number of anti-Government amendments were added. The unacceptable Lords' amendments were rejected by the Commons, and on all but one the Lords then gave way. Insistence on their amendment postponing the date at which nationalization was to take effect led to a Government 'compromise amendment' in which, by inserting a new provision that 'no member of the Corporation was to be appointed before 1 October, 1950', the Government in fact accepted the Opposition's demand that nationalization should not take effect until after the general election. Opposition to the Parliament Bill was thwarted by its passage under the 1911 Act,[70] but the delaying of the vesting date of steel nationalization was undoubtedly the most important concession extracted from the Labour Government during its term of office.

It is generally true that Conservative tactics of opposition in the Commons during the second half of the 1945 Parliament may be characterized as either an extension or an intensification of those used in the earlier period, but it is necessary to make an exception of the Opposition's approach to the committee stage of the Gas Bill. In this case the familiar tactics of delay became exaggerated into something unique for that Parliament – obstruction. Although Alfred Robens assumed that the bill would be treated no differently than any of the earlier nationalization bills,[71] in fact it had a rougher passage through standing committee than any other. Owing largely to the efforts of Brendan Bracken, who talked and urged others to talk on even the accepted amendments, the bill spent 127 hours in committee as compared to 60 hours for the Electricity Bill (in all respects a comparable measure). The Committee stage set a record for an all-night sitting on 13 May, 1948. The Gas Bill committee spent an average of 23 minutes on every amendment discussed; in the Electricity Bill committee an average of only nine minutes was taken for the same purpose. There were 156 divisions in the Gas Bill committee, 35 in the Electricity Bill committee.[72] The Government did not apply the guillotine, and, as a result, amendments to the bill were given a very full consideration – in many cases, over-full: four columns of the record of the committee debate were devoted to whether 'nationalization' should be spelled with a 'z' or an 's'.[73]

It would be wrong to say that Conservative tactics in committee merely wasted time, for they were successful in getting no fewer than 76 amendments accepted by the Government, but their 'filibustering' on the Gas Bill provided the Labour Party with ample justification for imposing the guillotine on the later Iron and Steel Bill.[74] Moreover, the extreme vigour of their approach to the Gas Bill in committee when contrasted to a more 'normal' treatment of the report stage of the bill in the House exposed the party's behaviour upstairs for the disorganized protest that it was. Although Labour members were kept around the House by a three-line whip for the all-night sittings of 9 and 10 June, 1948, the Conservatives made no really concerted effort, and during the second night's sitting their numbers fell well below 50. The Opposition had been given a little more time at the report stage than the Government had originally planned, but agreement was reached between Government and Opposition that the debate would end on a set date. In fact the debate ended on 10 June and did not require the further day (16 June) for completion of the report stage. Conservatives voted against the third reading of the bill and produced a good turnout in the lobby. They did not, however, make any serious protest against the Government's rejection of the Lords' amendments. They divided only 6 times; 109 was their best turnout. They did not even bother to resist Labour's rejection of one Lords' amendment requiring the addition of one worker to the Gas Board. On 5 April, 1949, a number of Conservatives led by Boyd-Carpenter had tried to annul the Gas (Vesting Date) Order.[75]

The Conservative Opposition had some very good moments between November 1947 and the dissolution of Parliament in December 1949. Among its most spectacular efforts were the all-out fight against the Iron and Steel Bill especially at the second reading which produced the largest anti-Government vote to date – there were 211 votes in favour of the Opposition's negative amendment – and the attack on the Government in October 1949 for the inadequacy of its measures to deal with the crisis following upon devaluation. This gave rise to the largest anti-Government vote of the 1945 Parliament:

353 to 222. More subtle, but equally effective, were the attempts to exacerbate Labour back-benchers' discontent with the 1949 budget, by suggesting that the Government had adopted Conservative views, and Anthony Eden's persistent aggravation, by means of private notice questions, of the Government's unease in having to deal with the dock strike in July 1949.

The Conservatives had a number of bad moments as well. Throughout 1948 Conservative opposition to Labour's major legislation was vigorous enough to prevent serious outbreaks of criticism from its wellwishers, but there was a continuous undercurrent of dissatisfaction with the party's staff work in the House of Commons and frequent support for an arrangement (comparable to Labour's use of Herbert Morrison as Leader of the House) from which it was hoped Conservatives would derive steady front-bench leadership. Public dissatisfaction with the Labour Government, which – to judge from the results of public opinion polls – reached its peak in late 1947, declined as economic conditions improved slightly over the next year. Conservatives, still denied the satisfaction of defeating the Government in a by-election, had to content themselves with the encouragement that could be derived from an increase in the swing of votes away from Labour. The first months of 1949 brought a short period of relief from the earlier tensions of foreign and domestic crises, and with this Labour confidence was restored and Conservative unease deepened.[76]

The acute crisis over policy that came to a head following the Conservative Party's failure to win the Hammersmith South by-election was accompanied by a period in which criticism of the parliamentary Opposition approached the severity displayed in late November and December 1945. Three things contributed to this development. The first was Churchill's threat – and embarrassing retreat from the threat – to move a vote of censure against the supplementary estimates required by the Government to cover the extra costs of food subsidies and the National Health Service. After Morrison had indicated that the supplementary estimates would be taken on 17 February, Churchill demanded a three-day debate and stated that it might be necessary to put down a motion of censure.[77] A great many Conservative back-benchers were by no means happy with the position in which their Leader had placed them, for it seemed to many of them that opposition to the estimates would allow the

Labour Party to exploit the charge that the Tories were opposed to the Health Service as such. In the end the Conservatives decided not to divide against the estimates, and Churchill took no part in the debate. It was suggested by one commentator that he may have had no real intention of pressing the censure, but 'merely flourished the threat to draw attention to what he called the "Government's extravagance" '.[78] Seen this way his intervention may have served some useful purpose, but it was certainly outweighed by the despondency among his supporters which resulted from the merciless drubbing handed out by Aneurin Bevan in the Commons.

The second incident giving rise to criticism of the Opposition came less than two weeks later over the handling of a private notice question to the Prime Minister arising from a remark by Christopher Mayhew at the United Nations Economic and Social Council. Apparently the Conservative front bench had heard that Brigadier Fitzroy Maclean, a party back-bencher, had put down a private notice question, and it had left the matter at that without troubling to take it up officially. The Speaker held that the question had not reached him in time and refused to allow it on that day (28 February, 1949). The House was then treated to the spectacle of the Conservative front bench pretending that the question was one of very great importance, although it had not been sufficiently moved earlier to put the question from that source.[79] 'It is safe to say,' the *Manchester Guardian*'s correspondent wrote, 'that this contretemps would never have happened if the Opposition front bench had taken up the question instead of leaving it to a private member.'

> The hurried colloquing that went on between Mr Butler, Mr Stanley and Capt Crookshank after the Speaker's ruling proclaimed for all to see that someone had blundered. The health debate fiasco and now this blunder proved to demonstrate that the Tory Leadership has gone to pieces.[80]

As if to confirm the diagnosis, the Conservative leadership left itself open to two separate criticisms of its handling of the Government's Defence White Paper which was debated on 3 March, 1949. In the first place, some Conservative back-benchers were disappointed with what they called the 'sitting-on-the-fence amendment',[81] which the party put down to the Government's motion of approval. But more important – and this gave rise to a stiff rebuke from the *Daily Express*[82] – the party decided to hold its post-Hammersmith 'inquest' while the defence debate was proceeding. As a result, vigorous criticism of the Government's proposals was allowed to go by default to the Labour back-benchers, and the Government party was able to jibe at Tory absenteeism when the Prime Minister was summing up.

But Conservative Opposition did not remain for long in the tail-spin of confusion and indecision which it entered during February and early March 1949. Success in the local government elections of the spring of 1949, the acquisition of a policy which the bulk of the party found acceptable, the resumption of the parliamentary battle over the Lords' amendments to the Iron and Steel Bill, and, finally, the devaluation crisis of the summer of 1949 contributed to the recovery of party spirits. The crisis of confidence which shook the Conservative Party in the late winter of 1948–49 is, however, a useful reminder of the fact that, whatever may be regarded as the main causes of the party's recovery of political fortunes in the general election of 1950, consistently effective, united work as a parliamentary opposition was not one of them.

OPPOSITION, 1950–51

Throughout the 1945 Parliament, so long as the Labour Party remained united – as it always did when it mattered – the Conservative Opposition was incapable of affecting the course of government in any fundamental way. In the Parliament which lasted from March 1950 to October 1951 the situation was very different. The gap between willingness to wound and ability to wound was, thanks to Labour's meagre over-all majority of six, slight indeed. For several months, however, the Conservatives seemed frightened of using their new-gained power.

I

Before Parliament met there was a good deal of speculation over the line the Opposition would take. It was generally thought that the Government would not last long, but the unsettled question was whether the Conservative Party's immediate action should be 'total war or armed watchfulness'.[83] Something of this uncertainty was revealed by the two-faced approach which the Opposition took in the debate on the Speech from the Throne. Eden began by assuring the Government that national unity would take top priority: there would be 'no factious or fractious opposition';[84] they would not 'seek to deny the Government its essential requirements in supply'; and the bi-partisan foreign policy which had characterized the previous Parliament would be continued. But the Conservatives also put down two official amendments to the King's Speech,[85] which, since they amounted to motions of confidence, seemed on the face of it at any rate direct attempts to bring the Government down. It now appears certain that the Opposition was not in fact anxious to achieve this result at that time:

> For the King's guidance and information, Sir Alan Lascelles took careful sounding among the leaders of the Government and the Opposition and also in official circles. As a result of these he reached the conclusion that, despite appearances, the real imminence of a parliamentary crisis was not as great as it seemed. The majority of the Conservative front bench were not anxious to bring down the Government at the moment and the political manoeuvres then in progress were being conducted, as it were, with blank rounds rather than with live ammunition.[86]

The *Observer*'s political correspondent, guessing correctly that the Opposition would not force a crisis over the King's Speech, suggested two reasons why this approach might be adopted: 'One consideration . . . is that the party is not ready for an immediate election. Both sides need a little time to recover and especially to raise fresh funds. Nor would the Opposition care to force an election now with the prospect of having to present a budget immediately if the Conservatives were returned.'[87] During the debate on the King's Speech Churchill, having 1910 very much in mind, indicated also that he was not sure that another election would change things very much.[88]

At all events the Government survived the two divisions on the amendments – as it was to survive all further 'first class occasions' – with majorities of 14 and 25 respectively. The Liberals voted with the Opposition on the first amendment which regretted that no reference had been made to the future of steel nationalization in the King's Speech, but voted with the Government on the second amendment which regretted the lack of an adequate housing programme. In the division on the Conservative amendment to the Supplementary Civil Estimates, which deplored the Chancellor's overspending, taken on 14 March the Liberals abstained. This division the Government won by 308 votes to 289.

The Opposition had accepted the Labour Party's motion stating that only Government business would be taken until Easter, and the Commons settled into a fairly mild period in which a number of pieces of minor legislation were given unopposed second readings. On 29 March, 1950, the Labour Government suffered its first defeat when, during a debate on fuel and power on an adjournment motion, the Opposition orally converted a two-line whip into a three-line whip and defeated the Government in a snap division by 283 votes to 257.[89] Although the event served to emphasize the precariousness of Labour's parliamentary position, its only real effect was to adjourn the House without the normal half-hour adjournment debate. The next day Attlee, citing the precedents for his view, chose not to treat the matter as a challenge to the continuation of the Government.

After the Easter recess the Opposition continued the general approach adopted in the earlier period of allowing the Government's minor legislative programme to go through unopposed while selecting special occasions, especially supply days, for snap divisions against the Government. At this period they could certainly not be charged with obstructing the Government's legislative programme. On 25 May, Morrison appealed for the co-operation of the House in getting through the last stages (i.e. the committee stage and third reading) of the Foreign Compensation Bill, the Highways Bill and the Coal Mining Subsidies Bill and then to take the second reading of the Maintenance of Order [Lords] Bill. In fact the three bills completed their passage through the House by 7.50 p.m. and the Lords' Bill was given, thereafter, an unopposed second reading.[90] On 1 May, towards the end of a supply debate on road haulage, the Opposition moved the reduction of £1,000 in the salary of the Minister of Transport (and others associated with him) 'to show disgust at the treatment of road hauliers'.[91] The motion was pressed to a division as a result of which a deadlock of 278 votes to 278 had to be decided by the Chairman's vote cast for the Government. On 11 May a vote was taken on an Opposition attempt to reduce the minister's salary at the conclusion of the Scottish housing debate, and on

22 May another debate – on the building industry – led to an attempt to reduce Aneurin Bevan's salary. Although the Conservatives tried once again late in the session (18 July) to score a tactical victory by unexpectedly (but, as it turned out, unsuccessfully) challenging the Government with a vote over the failure of the groundnuts scheme, the Opposition did not persist with the tactic, partly perhaps because it was recognized as unpopular, and probably chiefly because its use frequently led to the suggestion that there was a split in the shadow cabinet between the 'hardliners' around Churchill and the 'softliners' associated with Eden. On 7 May Churchill found it necessary to issue the following press statement: 'In view of the various statements which have been circulated in the last few days about the policy of the Conservative Party in challenging the Government by division on several occasions during the session, it is desirable to state that there has been no difference of opinion among the leading members of the Opposition upon the course to be adopted. ... In particular, Mr Churchill and Mr Eden have been in the closest accord on every step that has been taken and are actively supported by the Conservative Party.'[92] In this connection, Col Walter Elliot's remarks to a conference of the Federation of University Conservative and Unionist Association on 27 March are interesting: 'It is not our intention to continue to throw in our forces to three-line whips,' he said. 'It would be bad for the party and from the nation's point of view, which, I think, does not want to see the Opposition clawing at the Government with the intention of pulling it down from its pedestal at the earliest possible moment.'[93]

The main business of the session was the budget, and some commentators expected that the committee stage of the Finance Bill might be the Government's Waterloo. It certainly did not prove so. The Government planned to complete the committee stage in five days; with the help of an all-night sitting on the first day and a session lasting until 5.15 a.m. on the fifth day, that timetable was adhered to. Although the 1950 Finance Bill was rather shorter than either of its two predecessors, there was still plenty of scope for delay by the Opposition had it so wished. Indeed, the first night's proceedings gave a warning of the type of heavy going that could occur when the House took until 2.20 a.m. to pass the first clause dealing with the petrol tax. Thereafter, however, the Conservatives resorted only once to the device of debating the motion to report progress, and despite the great number of Conservative amendments and new clauses the debate progressed with reasonable speed and smoothness. Throughout the five-day committee stage there were only 18 divisions on amendments and new clauses; there also were only five divisions on closure motions. At the report stage the Opposition made a further attempt to reduce a number of tax charges, but the two report days also progressed easily, and the bill was accorded an unopposed third reading on 10 July.

The only other major test of the Government's survival before the summer recess came on 27 and 28 June with the Opposition's motion – which Attlee treated as a motion of censure – requesting the Government to take part in the discussion on the Schuman Plan for the unification of the coal and steel industries in Europe.[94] The Government's position, which Attlee put very succinctly in the debate, was that it did not propose to give control over these vital matters to an undemocratic supra-national authority. For a time it had been known that some Conservative back-benchers – especially certain members of the party's Foreign Affairs Committee – were concerned over the official party line,[95] but just before the debate it was believed that there would be no falling off of full support for the censure motion. With the votes of the Liberals who had welcomed the Schuman Plan from the beginning, the Opposition clearly expected to put the Government in a very difficult position. When the division was taken, however, six Conservatives and one Liberal abstained, and the Opposition motion was defeated by 309 votes to 289 – a Government majority of 20.[96]

* * *

The outbreak of hostilities on Korea in June 1950 put defence policy at the very centre of national politics. A major debate was held formally under the second and third readings of the Consolidated Fund Bill on 26 and 27 July immediately before the House rose for the summer, in which Churchill, although critical of the Government's preparations for war, pledged his party's support for anything they did to aid national survival.[97] The summer recess was to have continued until 17 October, but the Government found it necessary to recall Parliament on 12 September to get approval for its defence proposals and to secure the passage of the National Service Bill.[98] Although there were rumours that Churchill wanted to censure the Government defence proposals,[99] the debate passed off without incident. Indeed the short interruption to the summer recess might have meant nothing more than an annoying break in back-benchers' holidays had Churchill not decided to make the Minister of Supply's announcement of the membership of the Iron and Steel Corporation (on 14 September) the occasion for a further all-out challenge to the Government over steel nationalization. The debate took place on the following motion: 'This House regrets the decision of His Majesty's Government to bring the Steel Nationalization Act into immediate operation during this period of tension and danger thus needlessly dividing the nation on party political issues and disturbing the smooth and efficient working of an industry vital to our defence programme.'[100]

In selecting the issue of steel nationalization as a test of the confidence of the Government Churchill 'staked high', as the *New Statesman and Nation* put it: had the Conservatives won in the division lobbies on 19 September the election which would have had to follow 'would have taken place on a ground of his own choosing, and the Labour Government, accused by practically the whole national press of furthering its partisan Socialist schemes, would have been forced on the defensive'.[101] Despite some Liberal support for the Conservative motion, however, the Government's forces were sufficient to win the day, and the motion was negatived by 306 votes to 300.

II

The second session of the 1950 Parliament – soon to turn into the toughest struggle between Government and Opposition – began without exceptional heat of party controversy. The Opposition did not divide against the Government's motion taking precedence for its own bills until further notice, and allowed the rapid passage of the Expiring Laws Continuance Bill and the Restoration of Pre-war Trading Practices Bill which the Government said had to be passed by 10 December. The debate on the Speech from the Throne, as usual, gave rise to an Opposition amendment[102] – this time one regretting 'that the Gracious Speech show[ed] no resolve to ensure a steady increase in the rate of house building up to at least 300,000 houses a year'[103] – but the Conservative case was somewhat weakened by the unscientific origin of the minimum target figure, and in any case the Government's majority held sufficiently to defeat the amendment by 300 votes to 288. Thereafter the Commons settled down to give unopposed second readings to a number of non-controversial bills. Only the passage in the Lords, against the Government's will, of a bill to amend the Transport Act (on 21 November), an altercation during discussion of the business of the House arising over the Government's sale of arms to Egypt (on 23 November), and a threat of committee divisions against the Leasehold Property Bill (on 6 December)[104] disrupted the prevailing coalition-like atmosphere.

Quite suddenly, however, in the second week of December, party conflict flared up again. While Attlee and Hilary Marquand were in the United States for discussions with President Truman on the Korean War, the Conservatives put down a motion of censure on the coal situation. The two ministers returned in time to participate in the division, but their presence was not really required: the Conservative motion, lacking Liberal support, was defeated easily by 298 votes to 284. Then on 14 December, towards the end of a fairly mild speech in a debate on the international situation, Churchill attacked the Government viciously for continuing with steel nationalization, which, he claimed, would interfere with the war effort. The yelps of indignation from the Government benches following the revival in this particular context of that by now well-worn theme, drew from Churchill a new charge of exceptional bitterness: '. . . we cannot in these circumstances,' he said, 'feel confidence in the loyalty of the Government to the people of this country.'[105] The debate did not end in a division; there was therefore no fresh direct challenge to the Government's position before the Christmas recess. But Churchill said later (on 7 February, 1951) that it was the first time he had seen anyone booed in the House of Commons during his long parliamentary career,[106] and the angry scene which followed his verbal assault was a grim prologue to the extension of the parliamentary battle when the House met again in January.

Throughout 1950, despite sporadic efforts to defeat the Government through snap divisions and the occasional vote of censure, the Conservative Opposition had refrained from using the full potential of its imposing parliamentary position to try to topple the Labour Government from power. The decision to reverse this policy and to try to upset the Government by every means within its power in the first three months of 1951 was influenced by two factors. The first was that Conservatives were deeply incensed at the Government's determination to press ahead so soon with the nationalization of steel: the vesting date could occur any time within the year, but by persisting in an early date the Government showed, according to Conservatives, that it preferred the support of its own left wing, which was doubtful on rearmament, to responsible behaviour in the national interest.[107] The second and more important reason was that for the first time in nearly a year public opinion polls indicated a sharp fall in the Government's popularity. From the election on 23 February, 1950, until November that year B.I.P.O. polls revealed a continuous – if nevertheless small – preference for the Labour Party over the Conservatives. At the beginning of December, however, the Conservative Party went into the lead, and by the beginning of February a poll indicated that no less than 51·5 per cent were prepared to vote then for the Tory Party. United in hostility against nationalization and inspired by the improved political circumstances, the Conservative Party set out to attack the Labour Government on every subject on which – given an abstention or two through illness or intention – the Labour Party might be brought down.

In the first eight days of February the Opposition, using each of its three available supply days, put down three motions of censure. On 1 February the Conservatives attacked the coal shortage; on 7 February the decision to give immediate effect to the nationalization of the iron and steel industry was assailed once more; on the following day the 'confidence in the capacity of His Majesty's Government to deal with the meat problem' was at stake. Each time the Government's majority held and in the steel nationalization division the Government vote increased by four over that achieved in September 1950. Meanwhile the Opposition slowed down – but did not obstruct – the passage of the Leasehold Property Bill through its committee stage in the whole House. The committee took all of the first day and until 4.10 p.m. on the second day to debate the first clause. Thereafter the Conservatives apparently agreed to allow a smoother passage provided that the Government did not extend the normal sitting of the House. Government and Opposition agreed to an hour's extension of the sitting on 5 February (the date on which the

Government expected to complete the committee stage), but consideration of the bill was not completed by that time. The committee stage had, therefore, to be carried over for completion on 22 February.

The debate on the approval of the Government's Defence White Paper on 14 and 15 February led to a further motion of censure. The Opposition's decision to take this extreme step – for 'even the anti-Labour press,' according to Tom Williams, 'professed dismay that . . . the Tories were prepared to make National Defence a gallows for the Government'[108] – was undoubtedly encouraged by the hope that internal differences within the Labour Party over rearmament would be sufficiently aggravated to allow the Conservatives to win the day, but it failed utterly to achieve its main objective and the Conservative censure amendment was defeated by 308 votes to 287. 'The wherefores,' the *Christian Science Monitor*'s correspondent wrote, 'are not hard to discern':

> They lie in the form which the proposal for a vote of censure took, in the manner in which Churchill debated it, and in the fact that rearmament is just too serious a business in the eyes of middle-roaders to be used as a political football.
>
> The Conservatives did not challenge the Government rearmament programme, but called for a vote of no confidence in the ability of the Attlee régime to carry out that programme. They thus failed to exploit the real differences in the Labour Party. These are divisions over policy rather than over leadership.

'The entire manoeuvre by Mr Churchill and his followers,' the same correspondent continued, 'seems to have postponed rather than hastened the day whan Labour will be called to account for itself in a general election.'[109]

Undaunted by this conspicuous failure, the Opposition diversified its attack. In the Lords it pressed hard for Ernest Bevin's resignation as Foreign Secretary; in the Commons it used a reasoned amendment on the second reading of the Overseas Resources Bill on 20 February to replay its criticisms of the failure of the groundnuts scheme and a further supply day (27 February) to attempt to reduce the vote of the Board of Trade. The Government survived the implicit censure of the reasoned amendment calling for an 'impartial inquiry' into the failure of the groundnuts scheme before granting more money to the authority by 302 votes to 295. The Opposition allowed the committee stage of the bill to go through smoothly and the bill was given an unopposed third reading.

The Conservative Party's treatment of the Reserve and Auxiliary Forces Bill (the so-called 'Z' Bill) during the committee stage on 1 March offered a further interesting example of the party's version of 'responsible opposition' in the midst of a heated parliamentary battle. Although it had attempted to shake the Government over its ability to carry out the defence programme, it nevertheless supported the essential features of that programme. Accordingly, in committee it did not attempt to exploit the revolt by a number of Labour back-benchers which followed the Government's refusal to satisfy their demands on the treatment of conscientious objectors: in the division on Clause 2 which caused 34 Labour back-benchers to vote against the Government and a number of others to abstain, Conservatives voted heavily with the Government supporters. But the Opposition was not above trying to utilize the latent back-bench dissatisfaction to embarrass the Government over a less essential matter in the same bill. At 2 a.m. the Conservatives proposed to vote against Clause 12 which provided for the continuation of the bill for three years. They clearly hoped to gain through abstentions or defections sufficient resources to defeat the Government on this point. The tactic failed, however, when just enough disgruntled back-benchers put loyalty above conscience to support the official position in the lobby.[110] The division which ended in a result of 82 votes to 82 was resolved in the Government's favour by the chairman's vote.

A good deal of excitement was caused by the near defeat of the Government in committee during the early hours of 2 March and its clear defeat on a Private Member's motion later the same day. The motion regretting that the Government had not built up stocks of raw materials was approved by 167 votes to 163, but the Government chose again not to take the matter seriously: an adverse division on a Private Member's motion was not, Morrison argued, the same thing as a vote of censure. But subsequently relations between the two parties entered a short period of tranquillity following the failure of the Opposition's attempt to reduce the Board of Trade's vote on 27 February. The respite proved a mere calm before the storm – the fiercest political storm of Labour's six-year rule.

On 7 March Winston Churchill returned to the Commons after a short illness. Promptly the Conservatives adopted a tactic of opposition which they had not resorted to in this Parliament: they divided against the Government's motion to extend the sitting of the House. It may be recalled that the Conservatives had often done this in the previous Parliament. Then, however, the move could be regarded as little more than token resistance to the Government. Under the new conditions in which the Government's majority was so slight the tactic might be more effective. It required a full muster of Government supporters each time the Government intended to prolong the sitting; otherwise the Opposition might defeat the motion and throw the Government's legislative timetable into disarray. The *Daily Telegraph*, the following day, explained the move as part of the Opposition's plan to increase the pressure on the Government.[111] In fact, however, the Conservative Party thereafter put no special reliance on this easily counterable tactic; instead it found that by putting down a number of 'prayers' (motions to annul ministerial orders) for the same evening it could harry the Government much more effectively by forcing it to keep its forces up to full account late into the night.

On 8 March – a day which began in great controversy over the Government's decision to increase its representation on standing committees[112] – no fewer than seven Conservative motions to annul ministerial orders appeared on the order paper. The House sat until 2.10 a.m. dealing with army estimates; it continued sitting until 5.40 a.m. to complete the last prayer. That Conservatives were indulging in a tactic designed to wear out the Government supporters was fully revealed by the fact that no Conservative was prepared to support the annulment of the orders being prayed against. Geoffrey Bing (joined by Desmond Donnelly) forced a debate on each prayer by repeating his tactic of adding his name to Conservative motions. In this way he was able to force a division on the motion to annul the order to permit an increase in the prices of 'women's overalls and aprons' which was defeated by 182 votes to nil. (Bing and Donnelly acted as tellers for the Ayes.)

There was nothing revolutionary in the use of the prayer. Prayers had been moved on very many occasions during the 1945 Parliament. Earlier in the 1950 Parliament several Conservative back-benchers – especially members of the Conservative Active Back-benchers group

– had experimented with the harassing possibilities of putting down a few prayers (thereby forcing the Government supporters to stay around after ten o'clock) and then, having achieved the desired effect, not pressing the motions to a division. What made the use of this tactic in March 1951 so important was the context within which it occurred.

Throughout February 1951 the Opposition had assailed the Government on every occasion on which it was possible that a fall of the Labour Party could result. On 7 March it had adopted a new technique hailed as the beginning of a still fiercer campaign to bring pressure on the Government. Then, on 8 March, the praying tactic was revived with a vengeance and repeated on three occasions the following week. Coming when it did – during a week of censure on the Government[113] and open attack upon the Speaker[114] – and enjoying as it did the support of the Leader of the Opposition, this further manoeuvre had to be regarded as much more than a playful game by back-benchers. Churchill and the rest of the leadership of the party were not credited with the original idea of using the prayers as a means of harrying the Government. It is probably quite true that the plan to use the tactic intensively grew spontaneously among back-benchers who observed the Government's anger at being kept up so late on 8 March. Once the manoeuvre was well under way, however, and certain criticism of it had come, especially from the Liberals, Churchill supported his party's tactics in a party political broadcast on 17 March as one of the 'legitimate Parliamentary and political means' the Conservatives were proposing to use to force an early election.[115] Given the additional burden on Attlee's Government resulting from the virtual loss through ill-health of Ernest Bevin and the death of Stafford Cripps and the continuous strain imposed by the Opposition's persistent censures, it was hardly surprising that Robert Boothby's much-reported statement that it was the Tories' intention 'to make the Government sit up night and day and grind away until they get absolutely hysterical'[116] was taken seriously. This speech did not come as David Butler suggests, 'after a week or two of this policy' but during a speech on the second night of the 'campaign' (12 March). Although Robert Boothby has lent his name to the journalists' catch-phrase for the praying manoeuvres – 'The Boothby Harriers' – he did not, in fact, play a prominent rôle in the parliamentary debates.[117]

Yet, it is necessary to keep the matter in perspective. Time has added certain embellishments to the events of March 1951 with the result that the strenuous Opposition efforts of a few days have been exaggerated into a norm for the whole of the session, or even for the entire six-year period of Conservative Opposition. The truth is that the special effort to harass the Government by the heavily concentrated use of the nullifying prayer lasted effectively for only four sitting days. As soon as the House began to consider the first prayer on the order paper on Monday, 19 March, Chuter Ede rose to move the adjournment of the debate. His suggestion that Government and Opposition should get together to discuss how in future the business of the House could be more seriously conducted was presented in such reasonable terms that Capt Crookshank – Churchill was not present – felt constrained to accept the adjournment motion without a division and to promise to consult his shadow cabinet colleagues about Chuter Ede's proposals. Two nights later the Government moved the adjournment of the House at ten o'clock, thereby preventing the consideration of the prayers on the order paper for that evening. The next day the House rose for the Easter recess and a much-needed rest for all concerned.

When the parties returned to Westminster on 3 April no agreement had been reached (indeed no meeting had been held) over the arrangement of prayers. The Conservatives had put down three prayers for the first night, but owing to the early completion of the committee stage of a non-controversial bill and the withdrawal of one of the prayers, the House was able to rise at a normal time. The next day Chuter Ede wrote to Winston Churchill in an attempt to remove the major stumbling block to discussion between Government and Opposition over the future treatment of prayers. Harold Wilson, President of the Board of Trade, had been insisting that talks between the two parties should be begun *before* he and his department began negotiations with trade associations to increase controlled prices. Wilson's position was understandable, since the result of such negotiations would be the issuing of further ministerial orders (which in turn would – or could – provide the Conservatives with yet another opportunity to harass the Government by means of prayers to annul the orders). The Opposition, on the other hand, objected to Wilson's blackmailing efforts, and insisted that discussion between Government and Opposition could only begin after the

President of the Board of Trade had begun his negotiations. Ede's letter to the Leader of the Opposition accepted substantially the Conservative Party's position. No firm agreement seems to have been reached in the ensuing discussion between Government and Opposition, but never again during the 1950 Parliament were prayers used as part of a concerted effort to harry the Government from office (although prayers continued to be put down at intervals). On 9 April a prayer against the order reducing the cheese ration was considered at the end of business (9.07 p.m.) and led to a division in which the order was annulled by 237 votes to 219. It is notable that after the 'prayer campaign' the Conservatives were more selective in choosing the orders for annulment and often pushed their motions to divisions.

The session between the Easter recess and the Whitsun recess on 11 May was a remarkably calm one altogether. Although the *New Statesman*[118] and the *Evening Standard*[119] were agreed that the budget might lead to more vigorous opposition than had yet been seen in the post-war House of Commons, both seem to have over-estimated the possibilities which modern procedure now allows for obstruction in this matter. For, as Geoffrey Bing pointed out in a very interesting article:

> . . . changes in the Standing Orders made in the last Parliament have destroyed many opportunities which used to exist for obstruction during financial business. Today, immediately after the Budget Speech is concluded, all the Budget resolutions, except for a purely formal one which declares that changes in the law are expedient, have to be put to the vote without debate.
>
> When the budget resolutions are 'reported' to the House they are, it is true, 'exempted': they therefore, in the past, gave many occasions for all-night sittings. But, under the present Standing Orders, although the resolutions continue to be exempted, no debate is allowed upon them nor is any amendment permissible. . . .[120]

In any case Hugh Gaitskell's budget was a popular one – except for the imposition of charges for spectacles and dentures with which the Conservatives had no real quarrel.

During these five weeks several uncontroversial bills were considered, including the National Insurance Bill and the National

Health Service (Amendment) Bill. At the committee stage of the latter bill a number of Labour back-benchers, boggling at the implementation of the controversial clause in the bill which imposed charges for teeth and spectacles, defied a three-line whip and either voted against the clause or abstained. The Conservative Party did not try to defeat the Government on this point; some Conservatives even voted with the Government.

But the Opposition did not withdraw from the ring altogether. On 19 April it utilized a supply day to attack the Government over the question of having an American as North Atlantic Supreme Commander, and very nearly succeeded later the same day in annulling an order to increase postal charges. The attempt early the next month to exploit differences in the Labour Party over the costs of rearmament (brought to a head by the resignation of Aneurin Bevan, Harold Wilson, and John Freeman) misfired rather badly. Using their fourteenth supply day, the Opposition put down a motion expressing the anxiety of the House that the rearmament programme was based on estimates which were not accepted by the ministers concerned.[121] Eden, who opened for the Opposition, then proceeded to devote his attention to the disagreements between ministers regarding the budget, about which the motion said nothing. As a result of the imprecise wording of the motion the debate wandered widely without succeeding in driving a wedge between the dissidents and the Government. In the end, with Bevan, Freeman, and Wilson supporting their party, the Government's majority of 13 was better than it had been for quite some time.

Undoubtedly the most important matters occupying the attention of the Commons during the final months of the Labour Government were the Finance Bill and the question of Britain's proper response to the Persian threat to nationalize the Anglo-Iranian Oil Company. Interestingly, they are both matters on which the Opposition gave the Government less trouble than might have been expected.

Although the opportunities for obstruction are slight in the early stages of the financial business derived from the budget, the committee stage of the Finance Bill – being exempted business – provides an excellent occasion for delay. In 1950 the Opposition had allowed the Finance Bill through the committee stage without much difficulty within the planned five-day timetable. In 1951 the

Government provided for one more day in committee and hoped that the House would complete that stage on 13 June. This time the Opposition was not so yielding. It was not that the debates were particularly fiery – Churchill's praise of the 'singular calm, composure, and great patience on the part of ministers'[122] could have been applied to his own front-bench speakers as well. It was simply that the Opposition made the Government work very hard and very long to complete the task. Some measure of the intensity of the committee proceedings can be seen from the fact that there were two all-night sittings (one a continuous sitting for 31 hours), and no fewer than 45 divisions on amendments or new clauses and 17 divisions on motions of closure in the committee stage alone. Throughout, both sides kept their forces at nearly full strength – in a division at 7.30 a.m. on 8 June the Government won by 287 votes to 279!

The Opposition would not agree to a timetable, and before long it was clear that Labour's schedule had been thrown out. Even so the delay derived almost entirely from straightforward debate on amendments and was not caused – with one exception attributable to Churchill – by the deliberately dilatory tactic of debating at great length the motion to report progress. On 14 June, to the great delight of the Tory press, the Government was forced to announce the extension of the committee stage by two days. It seems likely that some bargain was struck through the usual channels: in any case the Government felt confident enough not to extend the sitting on the first extra day. The Opposition kept up the pressure on the Government until 11.30 p.m. on the final 'allotted' day when Churchill's attempt to report progress was defeated. The Government was determined to finish, and by this time the Conservatives had had enough. At 1.19 a.m. their total in the division fell to 53; at 3.43 a.m. the endurance trial was over. After a two-day report stage during which the Opposition concentrated on reducing the petrol tax, the bill – which had not been changed in any major respect as a result of the long debate – was given an unopposed third reading on 3 July.

Once the committee stage tactics had failed to secure a more substantial prize than the two-day delay, the resulting anti-climax, coupled with the frustration of being so near power for so long without actually achieving it, began to have its effect on the unity of the Tory Party. The first sign of difficulty – the *Yorkshire Post* took it to be only a 'problem of liaison' between front and back benches[123] – occurred when 15 Conservative back-benchers abstained in a division on the Liberal amendment (which had Opposition front-bench support) deploring the continued banishment of Tshekedi Khama. This action allowed the Government one of its largest majorities for several months. Much more serious, however, was the feeling among a number of back-benchers – which was given forthright expression by Lord Salisbury – that the Opposition was not pressing the Government hard enough to take positive action over the Persian oil dispute. On 27 June Churchill asked for and was granted private talks with the Government over the Middle East question; no agreement was reached during these discussions, according to his account,[124] but it was nevertheless clear that, thereafter, the Opposition line in the House of Commons was a good deal less aggressive than that of Conservatives outside the House.

A further all-out attack on the Government might have appeased the dissident units in the Tory Party – Churchill may have been trying to have it both ways in the debate on the Middle East on 30 July when he made strong personal attacks on Bevin and Morrison while at the same time accepting the withdrawal of personnel from the oil fields to Abadan[125] – but so long as he and his front-bench colleagues were not prepared to take an extremist position over events in Persia it was hard to imagine the issue on which the Opposition would make its stand. Besides, leading Conservatives were fully aware that a full-scale attack on the Government united the Labour Party as much as their own. At a time when the public opinion polls revealed a slight improvement in the position of the Labour Party, undoubtedly the wisest course was the course chosen: namely, to slacken the pace and allow the Bevanite dissentients, the rising cost of living, the threat of further austerity, and the Government's loss of nerve to take their toll.

On 4 October, Parliament was recalled and promptly dissolved. The way was clear for the general election which during the last 18 months Conservatives had both longed for and feared.

WINSTON CHURCHILL AND THE CONSERVATIVE OPPOSITION

Perhaps because it is easier to point with certainty to occasions on which parliamentary opposition was inefficient than to those when it was efficient, this survey may have presented a too negative view of the quality of Conservative opposition between 1945 and 1951. If so, it is a useful antidote to the view (influenced largely by what has been considered the poor record of Labour opposition since 1951) that Conservative opposition during these years was some classic illustration of the fine art. Certainly this critical assessment bears more resemblance to contemporary estimates.

It is, of course, necessary to distinguish between the quality of opposition during the long 1945 Parliament (in which the huge Labour majority made the task extremely difficult) and the shorter 1950 Parliament (in which merely a full Opposition turnout in a division posed a serious threat to the Government). The list of 'elements of inefficiency' in the Conservative performance between 1945 and 1950 has not been drawn up in order to criticize the Conservatives for failing to achieve the impossible: some right-wing critics were dismayed by the Opposition's failure to force the Government from office. I am not concerned with that. Rather, I have concentrated on those occasions on which opposition was either erratic or badly timed. It has been shown that Conservative opposition in the House of Lords, while generally less vigorous, was rather more effective in achieving concessions from the Government. The Conservative record in the Commons was undoubtedly much better in the last years of the Labour Government, but even then the really vigorous attack was concentrated in a relatively short period. During much of the second Parliament, it is true, the Opposition was not very anxious to take over the reins of government, but on at least two occasions – the two censures over the Government's rearmament programme (in February and again in April) – when there could have been no other purpose than to unseat the Government, the Conservative Party's tactics were very badly directed towards achieving the desired effect.

Several general explanations can be given for the inefficient features of the Conservative Opposition. Right-wing critics objected to the 'weakness' of the party's resistance to social welfare legislation; but the Opposition (rightly) felt obligated and restrained by the commitments undertaken in coalition. Had it gone back on these, the ensuing split in the party would undoubtedly have been much more serious than the lingering right-wing criticism. One Central Office official pointed to the party's inexperience as an Opposition and to the tendency for the party leadership, especially, to continue to think like office holders, directing their attention too much to the administrative details of Government policies. This same official also noted a tendency for the front bench to be 'too gentlemanly' among themselves: if a particular item came within the scope of one shadow minister nobody else tried to move into 'his area' to comment on it. If the 'responsible' shadow minister did nothing, more often than not no comment from the Conservative Party was forthcoming. Related to this point was the criticism which recurred frequently, especially during the 1945 Parliament, that talented back-benchers were not given sufficient opportunities on important occasions: it was frustrating for back-benchers to have to sit and watch Churchill's former Coalition colleagues – a few of whom were not even members of the Conservative Party – carrying on as the official spokesmen when younger men might be given a chance.

The main reason for the difficulties must be traced to Churchill's leadership. The *Daily Telegraph*, in August 1945, had high hopes for Churchill: 'With experience of nine government departments,' it wrote, 'Mr Churchill promises to be the most formidable Leader of the Opposition the Commons has known for many years.'[126] Churchill was formidable enough: his prowess as a debater assured that; but the qualities of mind and temperament which made a war leader did not suit the less heroic rôle of Opposition Leader. Unlike Stanley Baldwin – whom many Conservatives today regard as a model for the part – Churchill spent little time in the House; consequently he had little feeling for the mood of the Commons in general or for his own party's views in particular.

It was not that Churchill was consistently more reactionary than his supporters – although his 'splendidly anachronistic High Toryism'[127] was occasionally embarrassing; sometimes – as with the American Loan Agreement and especially the Anglo-Persian relations in 1951 – he was more progressive than many of his followers. He was essentially an individualist, speaking from the Conservative front bench almost incidentally as a party Leader, self-cast as the Nation's Protector and determined 'to prevent the great position we won in the war from being cast away by folly and worse than folly on the morrow of our victory'.[128] Despite his qualities as a parliamentarian, he lacked the ability to carry his party along with him in this enterprise. Sporadic appearances in the House, indifference to the consolidation of a *party* effort, and occasionally outright disregard for the views of his shadow cabinet colleagues imposed strains upon the Conservative Party which from time to time seriously affected the quality of opposition. Had it not been for Oliver Stanley's greater tactical sense[129] there is no telling how many times Churchill would have led the Conservative Party into difficulties; but even with his colleague's restraining hand, Churchill's passion for parliamentary battle for the sake of battle often isolated him from his cohorts following on – sometimes reluctantly – behind.

Finally, it may be worth noting (since the question has been brought up in connection with the proper rôle of a Labour Opposition[130]) that the Conservative Opposition between 1945 and 1951 did not conform to either extreme theory of opposition – the simple 'oppose the Government on every issue' view or the so-called 'alternative responsible opposition' view. Conservatives did not shirk from attacking and attempting to embarrass the Government on crucial issues (issues on which from the Government's point of view they were acting irresponsibly) such as rearmament, relations with the Egyptian Government, and the transfer of power in India and Burma. Nor was the Conservative Opposition averse to attempting to undermine the support of the Labour Party by attributing all the post-war economic difficulties – many of which were beyond the control of any British Government – to the inefficiency of Socialism. But the Conservative Party did not, on the other hand, set out to oppose every Government measure: it recognized – as surely all Oppositions are forced to recognize – that, despite differences over administrative details, the principles of many items of a Government's legislative programme will be entirely acceptable. The notion that it is the proper duty of the Opposition simply to oppose is, as it was between 1945 and 1951, not so much a prescription for parliamentary tactics as a battle cry in an intra-party struggle over policy. It is essentially a plea (which can be readily accepted) that the Opposition ought not to be a mere carbon copy of the government.

REFERENCES

[1] Morrison, *Memoirs*, p. 259, and *Annual Register, 1947*, p. 16.

[2] Chandos, *Memoirs*, pp. 337–8.

[3] See 'Phineas', 'Reflections in Recess', *New Statesman and Nation* (5 January, 1946), p. 4, and for a slight variation of this idea: Enoch Powell, '1951–59: Labour in Opposition', *Political Quarterly*, XXX (December, 1949), p. 336.

[4] See Peter G. Richards, *Honourable Members* (London, 1959), pp. 117–25, for details of the M.P.'s rôle in the control of policy and administration at question time and in the adjournment debate.

[5] A 'prayer' is a motion to annul rules or regulations made by a minister ('Statutory Instruments') in order to complete the detailed purposes of an Act. Prayer debates begin after the end of the main business of the day and may end in a division. Although a Sessional Order now terminates prayer debates at 11.30 p.m., the standing orders during the years of the Labour Government permitted debate to continue so long as there were prayers on the order paper.

[6] See Hugh Dalton, *High Tide and After* (London, 1962), p. 46, for a suggestion that Government supporters may also be happiest when the Opposition is fighting hard.

[7] See *Hansard* 461, col. 1460, for Bevan's remarks on the significance of a division against a bill's third reading as an indication of root-and-branch hostility.

[8] The Financial Resolution stage is often passed easily and is therefore not singled out here. Because there is often so little that can be said at this stage (because of the Government's wording of the resolution) the most frequent Opposition tactic is to waste as much time as possible with points of order about what can be discussed. See, for example, the debate on the financial resolution of the National Health Service Bill, *Hansard* 422, col. 418 ff.

[9] See below pp. 253–4, for a reference to this tactic during the committee stage of the 1950 Finance Bill.

[10] See Dalton, p. 65, for the following diary entry: 'I have had great fun, with a Tory amendment to prevent me from increasing the surtax. They fell completely into our hands and were fools enough to take their amendment to a division. I, indeed, had worked very hard, by provoking them, to secure this, but up to the last moment had not hoped to succeed. This vote will stand on the record and we shall make full use of it.'

[11] The Local Elections (Service Abroad) Bill was given a rushed, unopposed passage through the House during the first three weeks.

[12] *Hansard* 413, col. 95.

[13] *Hansard* 413, col. 94.

[14] *Hansard* 413, cols. 312–13: See also Lord Avon, *The Memoirs of Sir Anthony Eden* (London, 1960), I, 5–7, and Harold Macmillan, *The Conservative Approach to Modern Politics*, p. 2.

[15] *Hansard* 413, cols. 172–4. This gave rise to the first division of the Parliament in which the Government's motion passed by 329 votes to 142.

[16] *Hansard* 413, col. 94. See Dalton, *op. cit.*, p. 35, for his explanation of Churchill's absence.

[17] *Hansard* 415, cols. 57, 145 and 147–8.

[18] *Hansard* 415, cols. 248 and 539.

[19] See above, pp. 137–8.

[20] See, for example, David Farrar, 'Fame Beckons 69 M.P.s', *Evening Standard*, 9 October, 1945, and 'Here is a Lead for the Tories', *Evening Standard*, 3, November, 1945. Farrar, Lord Beaverbrook's personal secretary at the time, was especially critical of the Opposition's weak handling of the Supplies and Services Bill and the Bank of England Bill.

[21] Morrison continued his taunt of the Tories ineptitude in an interview contained in the *Labour Press Service*. 'Were it not for the fact that I might be misunderstood,' he said, 'I am very tempted to offer His Majesty's opposition a private lesson in a House of Commons' committee room to give them good counsel and guidance in the execution of their duties.' *The Times*, 30 November, 1945.

[22] *Hansard* 416, cols. 259, 264, 279, and 281–2.

[23] *Hansard* 416, cols. 2352–3.

[24] *Annual Register, 1945*, p. 100; *Spectator*, 'The Opposition's Attack'. 7 December, 1945, p. 531; *The Economist*, 'Vote of Censure?', 8 December, 1945, p. 817.

[25] *Spectator*, 'Spectator's Notebook', 14 December, 1945.

[26] *Annual Register, 1945*, p. 100.

[27] *Spectator*, 'Opposition Attack'.

[28] *Hansard* 417, col. 422.

[29] The party committees were as follows: Defence (with three sub-committees); Demobilization and Labour; Social Services and Education; Housing and Health, Home Office and Welfare; Town and Country Planning; Finance; Trade and Industry (with a Transport sub-committee); Fuel and Power; Agriculture; Foreign Affairs; Imperial Affairs; India; Civil Aviation; Scottish Affairs. Conservative Party Committees, 1946–51 (Conservative Research Department), pp. 1–2. The work of these committees was co-ordinated by the chairman of each committee meeting as a Business Committee under the shadow cabinet. See Quintin Hogg, 'Political Grouping', *London Forum*, winter 1946, p. 20, for a criticism of the leadership of these committees.

[30] *Hansard* 418, col. 701.

[31] The Conservatives had tried to get a three-day second reading debate. *Hansard* 418, cols. 36–7 and 307.

[32] *Hansard* 418, cols. 905–6.

[33] *Hansard* 423, cols. 129–30.

[34] *Hansard* 421, cols. 1151 ff., 1203.

[35] *Hansard* 421, col. 2709.

[36] *Hansard* 424, col. 2133

[37] *Hansard* 423, col. 1381.

[38] *Hansard* 426, col. 398, for the reasoned amendment to the third reading. Dr Saloma has written: 'When contrasted with the postions taken in the White Paper and the subsequent negotiations, the reasoned amendments

sounded as though the party were reverting to 1911–1912.' Saloma, p. 418.

[39] The Opposition made a much greater impact on the bill in the Lords. See P. A. Bromhead, *The House of Lords and Contemporary Politics* (London, 1958), pp. 162–3, for a consideration of the treatment of the bill in the Lords. See also Saloma, p. 416, for a list of the concessions made by the Government at one time or another.

[40] The first session resumed after the summer recess for a further period from 8 October to 6 November, 1946, but, except for a brisk debate (which did not however lead to a division) over the Government's amendment of the Fair Wages Clause to be inserted in government contracts relations, between Government and Opposition, passed off quite quietly.

[41] But see the criticism of the inefficiency of parliamentary opposition by two Conservative M.P.s: W. W. Astor, 'The Conservative Party in Opposition', p. 348, and Christopher Hollis, 'Personalities in Parliament', *New English Review*, XII (June 1946), pp. 567–8.

[42] Conference Minutes, 1946, p. 9.

[43] The Conservatives also supported the Liberal amendment against the principle of the 'closed shop'.

[44] *Hansard* 431, cols. 1359–73.

[45] The Opposition divided against the second readings of the Exchange Control Bill (26 November), the Civic Restaurants Bill (28 November), and the Cotton Bill (2 December), but at no stage in the passage of these bills was the Opposition particularly determined. In the case of the first two bills the Conservative vote at the second reading division was only 125 and 116 respectively. 144 Conservatives voted against the Cotton Bill at the second reading, but only 72 Conservatives supported the party's vote against the bill's third reading on 18 April, 1947.

[46] *Tribune*, 20 December, 1946.

[47] 'Phineas', 'Parliament: The Guillotine Falls', *New Statesman and Nation*, XXXIII (3 May, 1947), p. 307.

[48] During the debate on the allocation of time motion Eden rejected Ede's offer of a fourth 'report day'.

[49] *Hansard* 432, col. 1129. The Opposition also tried, again unsuccessfully, to have the bill taken on the floor of the House.

[50] *Hansard* 437, col. 2191.

[51] Bromhead notes the lack of Opposition enthusiasm for W. S. Morrison's attempted amendment to the Lords' amendment which was designed to shorten still further the period within which designated land must be taken over by public authorities. See pp. 164–5.

[52] Attlee, p. 167.

[53] Viscount Swinton, 'The House of Lords', *New English Review*, I (November 1948), p. 155.

[54] Bromhead, pp. 60–7.

[55] *Star*, 22 January, 1947.

[56] *Daily Herald*, 8 February, 1947.

[57] *Hansard* 434, col. 1333 ff.

[58] *Hansard* 434, cols. 1429 and 1435 ff.

[59] The Conservatives allowed the Consolidated Fund Bill to go unopposed through *all* stages in order to allow more time for the state of the nation debate.

[60] See especially Sir John Anderson's speech *Hansard* 441, col. 1689 ff.

[61] *Hansard* 443, col. 984–5.

[62] But see the criticism of the weakness of Conservative Party opposition by Sir Arthur Page, 'Awaiting the Crash', *National Review*, CXXVIII (March 1947), 188, and by 'Crossbencher', *Sunday Express*, 29 December, 1946. Aubrey Jones, however, thought that Conservatives may have opposed some issues too vigorously. See Jones, 'Conservatives in Conference', p. 219.

[63] See Churchill's remarks on this point, *Hansard* 460, col. 647.

[64] *Hansard* 450, col. 1121.

[65] See Morrison's tribute to the efficiency of the usual channels on this occasion: *Hansard* 454, col. 1342.

[66] There was a small amount of cross-voting and a number of abstentions in the division. The vote which was taken on the motion to adjourn the House was defeated by 283 votes to 193.

[67] *Hansard* 444, col. 1161. The bill was given a second reading by 286 votes to 138.

[68] *Hansard* 444, cols. 1227–38.

[69] Bromhead, pp. 167–70.

[70] Passage of the bill in the Commons the second and third times – in September 1948 and November 1949 – was made speedy by a procedural motion which limited debate to the third reading. But even the passage of the bill the first time was remarkably smooth – considerably quicker, for example, than the repeal of the Trades Disputes Act in 1946.

[71] *Hansard* 452, col. 435.

[72] *Hansard* 452, col. 436.

[73] *Hansard* 452, col. 436.

[74] The Labour Party would undoubtedly have imposed the guillotine on the Steel Bill in any case, but the argument was made easier by the previous experience in the Gas Bill committee. For references to this experience as justification of the 'allocation of time motion' for the steel bill see *Hansard* 458, col. 1431 ff.

[75] *Hansard* 463, col. 1993 ff.

[76] In April 1949 a B.I.P.O. poll indicated that Labour, for the first time since March 1947, would receive more votes than the Conservative Party in a general election held at that time – 44 per cent as compared to 42 per cent.

[77] *Hansard* 461, cols. 536–7.

[78] *Observer*, 'Opposition's Second Thoughts on Censure Vote', 13 February, 1949.

[79] *Hansard* 46, cols. 37–40.

[80] *Manchester Guardian*, 'Someone has Blundered', 1 March, 1949.

[81] For the amendment see *Hansard* 462, col. 564.

[82] *Daily Express*, 'Inept Tories', 5 March, 1949.

[83] *Evening Standard*, 'A Hot or Cold War?', 28 February, 1950.

[84] *Hansard* 472, col. 50.

[85] Attlee claimed (*Hansard* 472, col. 590) that two official amendments to the Address had never before been put down by an Opposition.

[86] Wheeler-Bennett, *George VI*, p. 773.

[87] *Observer*, 'Tories Discuss Early Challenge to Cabinet', 26 February, 1950.

[88] *Hansard* 472, col. 144.

[89] On 23 March the Opposition tried to defeat the Government in another snap division, but this was defeated by 288 votes to 240. The poor showing by the Opposition on a ground of its own choosing gave rise to very critical comment from the *Evening Standard*. See 'What Will Become of the Tories Now?', 27 March, 1950. The defeat of the Government on 29 March in the other snap division led the *Economist* to call for 'a halt to these manoeuvres at least until after the Budget'. See *Economist*, 'Which Policy for the Tories?', 1 April, 1950.

[90] *Hansard*, 475, col. 2245.

[91] *Hansard* 474, col. 1527.

[92] *Western Mail*, 'Tories are United on Division Policy – Churchill', 8 May, 1950.

[93] *Manchester Guardian*, 'Tories "Choosing their Moments" ', 28 March, 1950.

[94] *Hansard* 476, col. 2104.

[95] See *Observer*, 'Conservatives' Views of Schuman Plan', 25 June, 1950.

[96] The Government's amendment to the motion approving the Government's action in staying out of the talks was carried by 309 votes to 296 – a majority of 13 votes.

[97] *Hansard* 478, col. 714

[98] The bill was given an unamended passage through both Commons and Lords by 18 September.

[99] *Daily Herald*, 'Churchill Opposed', 7 September, 1950; *Yorkshire Post*, 'Conservative Shadow Cabinet Meets', 8 September, 1950; *The Times*, 'Conservatives and Defence', 11 September, 1950.

[100] *Hansard* 478, col. 1719.

[101] *New Statesman and Nation*, 'The Two Hundred Firms', XL (23 September, 1950), p. 285.

[102] There was also a Liberal amendment on the cost of living and Thorneycroft's amendment critical of Government controls. These were defeated by majorities of 13 and 10 respectively.

[103] *Hansard* 480, col. 605.

[104] The bill was given an unopposed second reading.

[105] *Hansard* 482, col. 1371.

[106] *Hansard* 483, col. 1746.

[107] See Sir David Maxwell Fyfe's explanation of the Conservative Party's continued attack on the Iron and Steel Act: *Liverpool Daily Post*, 'Why Tories are Fighting the Steel Act to the End', 5 February, 1951.

[108] Tom Williams, 'Parliament: Guns and Groundnuts', *New Statesman and Nation*, XLI (24 February, 1951), p. 207.

[109] *Christian Science Monitor*, 17 February, 1951. A few days before the defence debate Donald Wade, the Liberal M.P., had said: 'The tactical advantage of introducing votes of censure once or twice a week under the present conditions is doubtful. Its effect is to strengthen the blind loyalty of Labour supporters to

the Government.' *Liberal News*, 'A Limit to Party Warfare', 16 February, 1951.

[110] The Opposition tried once again at the report stage to remove Clause 12, but it was retained by 244 votes to 217.

[111] *Daily Telegraph*, 'Opposition to Increase Pressure', 8 March, 1951.

[112] *Hansard* 485, cols. 668–75. On 23 February, 1951, the Opposition had succeeded in passing through second reading a Private Member's Bill (John R. Bevins's, then Conservative M.P. for Toxteth, Liverpool), the purpose of which was to extend the radius of road hauliers under the Transport Act from 25 to 60 miles. Having had the anomaly brought to its attention because of the defeat by two votes in standing committee on the Sea Fish Industry Bill, the Government proposed to adjust the mistake in representation on standing committees – and thereby make possible the defeat in committee of Bevins's bill – so that the Government would have its rightful majority of one over all other parties. To the great consternation of the Opposition, the Speaker deemed the adjustment proper.

Bevins's bill was killed in Standing Committee B on 5 April, 1951, and especially on 10 April, when all the major clauses were defeated by 25 votes to 23. See *Standing Committees Session 1950–51* (London, 1951), pp. 742–878.

[113] On 12 March, 1951, the Opposition used its eighth allotted supply day to bring a motion of censure on the Government for the financial losses caused by the collapse of the Gambia poultry scheme. The Government survived with a majority of eight.

[114] See Tom Williams' 'Parliament: Targets and Tactics', *New Statesman and Nation*, XLI (24 March, 1951), p. 331, for a good summary of the hectic events of the week beginning on Monday, 11 March.

[115] *The Times*, 'Parties in Parliament', 19 March, 1951.

[116] *Hansard* 485, col. 1546.

[117] David Butler, *General Election 1951*, p. 13.

[118] *New Statesman and Nation*, 'Mr Churchill to the Rescue', XLI (24 March, 1951), p. 329.

[119] *Evening Standard*, 'Boothby is Right', 3 April, 1951.

[120] Geoffrey Bing, 'Obstruction', *New Statesman and Nation*, XLI (7 April, 1951), p. 386. See *Hansard* 448, col. 1439, for details of the changes in the Standing Orders.

[121] *Hansard* 487, col. 1015.

[122] *Hansard* 489, col. 401.

[123] *Yorkshire Post*, 'Problem of Liaison', 7 July, 1951.

[124] *Hansard* 491, col. 992.

[125] *Hansard* 491, col. 994. Churchill stated, however, that the Opposition would oppose and censure by every means in its power the total evacuation of Abadan.

[126] *Daily Telegraph*, 18 August, 1945.

[127] John Wheeler-Bennett, *John Anderson, Viscount Waverley* (London, 1962), pp. 340–1.

[128] Cited in Lewis Broad, *Winston Churchill* (London, 1952), p. 560.

[129] See Oliver Lyttelton's praise of the rôle performed by Col. Stanley in opposition: 'He had a great eye for parliamentary weather and kept us, and Winston

in particular, out of much trouble. Our leader sometimes plunged into a fight just because it was a fight and he liked fighting. When in this mood the only man to restrain him was Oliver. His wit was devastating, and he was prepared to use it on his leader.' Lyttelton, p. 336.

[130] See R. H. S. Crossman, *Labour in the Affluent Society*, and Bernard Crick, 'Two Theories of Opposition', *New Statesman*, LX (18 June, 1960), pp. 882–3.

CHAPTER VIII

Conclusion

THE three most important aspects of the history of the Conservative Party in opposition have been considered in some detail in the preceding chapters: the party's reconstruction of its organization, its formulation of policy, and its actions as a parliamentary Opposition. A further question now poses itself. To what extent is it reasonable to assume that these activities assisted the recovery of political power? It may be best to take a fresh look at the investigation from this viewpoint.

Since there is unlikely to be a simple first cause of a complex political event, it is not surprising that no single action by the Conservative Party during its six years of opposition springs to mind as *the* crucial explanation of its recovery. What, perhaps, comes out clearly from this analysis is the recognition that certain actions thought to be crucial explanations have not stood up to closer observation.

The difficulty of establishing satisfactory criteria for judging the effectiveness of parliamentary opposition has already been discussed and the question gone into as to whether 'efficiency of parliamentary opposition' is a viable factor at any time contributing to a party's success (or failure) in a general election. But assuming that a record of efficiency as a parliamentary Opposition does help a party to recover political power, there is room for considerable doubt whether the Conservative experience justified its inclusion in the list of relevant factors. The four and a half years preceding the general election of 1950 – the election in which the bulk of the 'Tory Revival' was achieved[1] – were not notable for consistently vigorous, to say nothing of efficient, opposition.

Certain aspects of the party reconstruction have proved themselves of considerable importance. The so-called 'democratization' of the Conservative Party did not result in the transfer of effective decision-making, but the expansion of the membership of the party and the elaboration of a number of organs of the National Union – the development of the Young Conservative movement and the creation of advisory committees at the national, Area, and constituency level, for example – brought many more people into partisan politics, thereby expanding the number of activists working for the return of a Conservative Government. The Conservative Political Centre's Two-Way Movement of Ideas enjoyed a very limited rôle in the actual creation of party policy, but the function which the Movement and the related activities of the Conservative Political Centre performed as agents of political education was useful in establishing a body of well-informed campaign workers. The party's entry on a large scale into the politics of local government after the war was also significant. Aided by the Advisory Committee on Local Government and the Local Government Department at Central Office, constituency associations played a part in the transformation of local government elections into trial runs for the general election campaign fought on a national scale.

The two major recommendations of the *Interim Report on the Party Organization* – the reduction of financial limitations on party candidature, and the creation of a central fund – were also of some importance. Even if the new regulations governing the candidates' constituency expenses did not have, within this period at least, any great effect on the type of candidate selected, some people may have thought that it did, and the image of a progressive, democratic, classless party may have been furthered. Even if this was not so, the effect of removing an easy source of income from the constituency associations resulted in an increase in the efficiency of their general operations. The 'quota system' to provide for the Central Fund was, indeed, a rather timid and over-elaborate invention, but it cannot be denied that its product – an additional £100,000 (and probably more) yearly at the disposal of Central Office – was a very useful contribution to the furtherance of the Conservative cause.

Nor can Lord Woolton's part in the 'Tory Revival' be ignored. Although his 'revolution' appears on closer examination to have been exaggerated, there is no doubting his great value to the Conservative Party as an inspiration to the party machine, as a fund-raiser, as a link with big business, and (perhaps most important) as a propagandist. Drawing on his earlier experience as Minister of Food and the very favourable image, it was said, he had with the housewife, Lord Woolton played a very useful rôle as critic of the Government's food and rationing policy. It was striking that Conservative candidates in their election addresses, particularly between 1945 and 1950, were much more prepared to draw on Lord Woolton's connection with the party than Winston Churchill's. His modernization of the techniques of party warfare in the country – especially his use of the public relations firm of Colman, Prentis, and Varley to assist the Central Office's 'pre-campaign' poster campaigns – brought a new level of sophistication to the fighting of general elections, the full significance of which has only recently been recognized.

Finally, the relevance of the contribution of R. A. Butler and the revitalized Research Department towards the reformulation of Conservative policy cannot be overlooked. No radical change in party policy was achieved or intended, but over the years the progressive features of pre-1945 Conservative thought were better exposed to public view, a distinctly Conservative rationale of the *status quo* was worked out, and the grounds were laid for the development of a new strain of Conservative policy which, drawing from the neo-Liberal inspiration, would accord conveniently with the increasing affluence of the fifties.

It may seem, however, that not only has no single, all-important, explanation of the recovery yet emerged, but that – taking all the factors set out together – no *sufficient* explanation has yet been presented. This should cause no surprise; when other possible explanations of the Conservative recovery are taken into account – the Government's loss of energy and momentum for radical reform; the effects of redistribution of parliamentary boundaries; the adverse turn in economic conditions; and the swing to Conservatism on the part of formerly Liberal voters unable to vote for Liberal candidates – it is clear that the most important factors lie outside the control of the Conservative Party itself. There is no way of knowing what the results of the two general elections would have been had the Conservatives not made the reforms in organization and policy: it is possible that Conservative indifference to these matters between 1945 and 1950 might have allowed the Labour Party to carry on after 1950 to reap the benefits of a general improvement in the economic situation and therefore continue for perhaps a further decade as the Government. All that can be said with some certainty is that despite everything the Conservative Party did for itself to improve its electoral viability, and despite all the external factors working in its favour, the recovery was a qualified – and, for many, rather disappointing – result. Despite the Maxwell Fyfe reforms, Lord Woolton, R. A. Butler and his back-room boys, *The Industrial Charter* and the Central Office propaganda machine, the best the Conservative Party was able to do against a physically and spiritually exhausted Government was to slip into power in 1951 with a slim majority of 17 on a total vote smaller than the Labour Party's.

REFERENCES

[1] H. G. Nicholas has written: 'A good case could be made out for the thesis that the election of 1951 was simply the second phase of the election of 1950.' The swing of 1·1 per cent, which was even throughout the country, represented a 'trifling deviation' from the 1950 result. See 'The British General Election of 1951', *American Political Science Review*, XLVI (June 1952), pp. 398 and 404.

Index

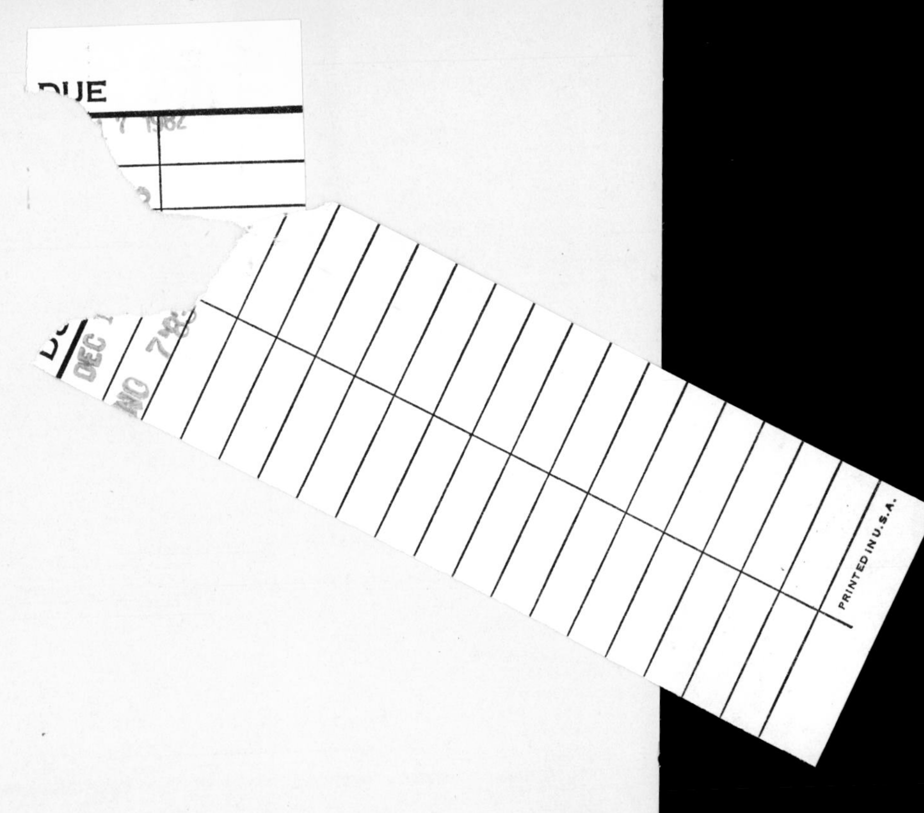